Women in Sports

Books in the **Contemporary World Issues** series address vital issues in today's society such as genetic engineering, pollution, and biodiversity. Written by professional writers, scholars, and nonacademic experts, these books are authoritative, clearly written, up-to-date, and objective. They provide a good starting point for research by high school and college students, scholars, and general readers as well as by legislators, businesspeople, activists, and others.

Each book, carefully organized and easy to use, contains an overview of the subject, a detailed chronology, biographical sketches, facts and data and/or documents and other primary source material, a forum of authoritative perspective essays, annotated lists of print and nonprint resources, and an index.

Readers of books in the Contemporary World Issues series will find the information they need in order to have a better understanding of the social, political, environmental, and economic issues facing the world today.

Women in Sports

A REFERENCE HANDBOOK

Maylon Hanold

ABC-CLIO™

An Imprint of ABC-CLIO, LLC
Santa Barbara, California • Denver, Colorado

Library of Congress Cataloging-in-Publication Data

Names: Hanold, Maylon, author.
Title: Women in sports : a reference handbook / Maylon Hanold.
Description: Santa Barbara, California : ABC-CLIO, LLC, [2018] | Series: Contemporary world issues | Includes bibliographical references and index.
Identifiers: LCCN 2017056229 (print) | LCCN 2017059263 (ebook) | ISBN 9781440853708 (ebook) | ISBN 9781440853692 (acid-free paper)
Subjects: LCSH: Sports for women—Juvenile literature. | Sex discrimination in sports—Juvenile literature. | Women athletes—Biography—Juvenile literature.
Classification: LCC GV709 (ebook) | LCC GV709 .H34 2018 (print) | DDC 796.0922 [B]—dc23
LC record available at https://lccn.loc.gov/2017056229

ISBN: 978-1-4408-5369-2 (print)
    978-1-4408-5370-8 (ebook)

22 21 20 19 18   1 2 3 4 5

This book is also available as an eBook.

ABC-CLIO
An Imprint of ABC-CLIO, LLC

ABC-CLIO, LLC
130 Cremona Drive, P.O. Box 1911
Santa Barbara, California 93116–1911
www.abc-clio.com

This book is printed on acid-free paper ∞

Manufactured in the United States of America

Much of sport history has traced the athletic achievements of men. From the ancient Olympics Games, records of who won specific events were kept, leaving a trail of men's achievements for civilizations that came afterward to follow. Not only were achievements recorded, but also the structure, rules, and regulations. In these histories of the organization of sport are many examples of how and why women were excluded from athletic events as well as under what conditions they could participate in competition and physical activity. At the Ancient Olympics, married women were not allowed to be an athlete or a spectator. However, just prior to the main Olympics, there was a festival in honor of the Greek goddess, Hera. This festival featured footraces and other activities in which unmarried girls could participate. Some sport historians believe that the purpose of the contests was to help make the young girls stronger so that they could bear children. Unmarried girls and women could also watch the main Olympics. Interestingly, the story of motherhood and the story of women's participation in sport have been intricately entwined since the records of participation in organized athletic events have been kept.

In modern times, women have a relatively short history of participating and competing in sport. Being physically active as a normal and enjoyable part of their lives is a very recent occurrence for girls and women. Early participation by women began during the late 19th century when the industrial revolution significantly changed the daily lives of Americans. Many Americans moved from working on farms to working in factories. As more families moved into the cities, there were many sentiments about keeping the working class physically active as a means to assimilate immigrants and other Americans into this new way of life. The upper classes also began to develop courting practices around leisure and sporting events. Thus, sport began to become woven into American society at all levels. As sport took on a stronger social and cultural significance, more and more women became interested in participating.

Yet, it was the growing cultural significance of sport that also was problematic for women. Through the visible display of physicality, sport symbolized fortitude, strength, and virility. All these attributes were associated with men, not women. Society's views of women's roles in society also made sport an activity that was in direct opposition to what women should do. Fears that sport and physical activity would jeopardize women's bodies and health for childbearing were pervasive. Fears that women who participated in sport would become manly were "logical" conclusions at the turn of the 20th century. Culturally, sport was for men.

Although these views about women seem incredulous in today's context, the idea that sport is a male domain and perhaps "not healthy" for women still has a hold in modern society's psyche. The forms in which these views manifest today are often more subtle than in the early 1900s. The fact that most sports are organized by gender is based on and, as a result, reinforces the view that fundamentally boys and men are superior physically to girls and women. Tensions around what constitutes female and femininity are accentuated in sport and physical activity due to the deeply held "sport as masculine" belief. These beliefs create issues and problems for nonheterosexual individuals and individuals who do not clearly fit into a biological male or female category. Sport media remains predominantly focused on men's sports, and female athletes are rarely depicted as athletes when they do make it into mainstream media coverage. Fear for women's health has few strongholds in today's society, but notable exceptions exist. It was not until 2014 that women's ski jumping was allowed to be an official sport in the winter Olympic Games. Reasons for the omission were stated as lack of interest as well as concern for women's bodies. Despite the fact that women's ski jumping had met the international requirements that confirmed interest and appropriate levels of organization, views that ski jumping could not be good for women's bodies prevailed until 2014.

The purpose of *Women in Sports* is to provide the reader with information, resources, and current views about experiences, challenges, policies, and possibilities for women in sport. The context and perspectives in this book are primarily focused on women's experiences in North America and the United States. The history and background chapter provides important context for understanding the current issues and problems women face as participants and leaders in sport. Chapter 2 presents those issues and problems thematically. Chapter 3 provides unique insights and opinions from a variety of women who have athletic backgrounds and now work in a sport context. The next chapter provides profiles of important individuals, organizations, or advocacy groups for women in sport. The remaining chapters present summary data showing participation trends, excerpts from key documents that highlight important policies, and lists of resources by media type. Finally, there is a chronology of important dates in the history of women in sport and a glossary of key terms, concepts, and theories that help frame the current problems and solutions.

Women in Sports

Introduction

While women have historically never participated in sport to the extent that men have, women have also not been utterly excluded from sport. Throughout the ages, women have found ways to be physically active or compete in sport. In many ways, the story of women in sport parallels the larger story of women's movements toward equality. In other words, despite what cultural norms have dictated, there has never been 100 percent compliance. That is, the history of women in sport is made up of all the times women have not been complacent, and insisted on sport and physical activity because they simply wanted to play, move, participate, and compete. That story is complex and nuanced as it has intertwined with society's views of gender—of female and male, of feminine and masculine and the behaviors and societal roles associated with each at any given historical moment. It has also depended as much on social class, race, and other identities. There were different sport opportunities for upper-class women compared to women of working class. White women enjoyed significantly greater and different opportunities in sport than women of color. These differences shaped which women pursued what kinds of sport. The early struggles and differences shaped the current landscape of sport for girls and women today.

American tennis player Helen Wills, a pioneer in women's sports, practices at the California Tennis Club in San Francisco on June 11, 1941. (Paul Popper/Popperfoto/Getty Images)

1

This chapter presents various perspectives, attitudes, and challenges women faced as they began to participate in sport and physical activity in greater numbers during the late 19th and early 20th centuries. Early attitudes toward women's sport participation were to question women's capacity for sport and physical activity due to the belief that their bodies were fragile. Larger social trends continually influenced the ways that women saw themselves as athletes or physically active. As women began attending colleges, light physical activity for girls and women was thought to be beneficial so that they could improve their strength for intellectual work. For decades, the debate between physical education philosophies of cooperation and moderation for the upper classes coexisted with more competitive forms of sport for working class and female athletes of color. The rapid rise of women in sport throughout the 20th century brought about practical challenges, such as what should women wear and what policies should govern their inclusion at the highest levels of sport such as the Olympics and professional teams. Key debates and issues around the above topics are taken up in this chapter.

Brief Overview of the Early History of Women in Sport

Sport on the Rise

Sport was not always the ever-so-popular activity as it is today. Prior to the late 1800s, sport and leisure activities were mostly reserved for the upper class, who had ample time and money. With the emergence of a new middle class in the late 1800s, people began to have more leisure time and more disposable income than they had in the past. As more men gained access to time and money, sport emerged as a primary activity for the middle class as well. As sport popularity was on the rise, women's interest in athletic participation also grew. Although women have participated in sports since the beginning of time, their journey toward athletic participation as a common activity for many women was slow. For the majority of the 1800s, women's physical activity was predominantly recreationally based. There were few opportunities for women to actually compete; instead they participated in informal, ruleless physical activities. During this era, people worried about women exerting too much energy, and thus opportunities for physical activity were limited.

At the turn of the century, women's place in society began to transform, and they became more educated, politically involved, and a part of the workforce. At the same time, the general idea of sport grew as a whole in the United States, which offered a platform for women to portray the new modern idea of womanhood. The increased inclusion of women in sport was not entirely taken in a positive manner. Many people were uncomfortable with women participating in a domain that was perceived as masculine, fearing that those female participants would become less womanly and were behaving in ways so contrary to feminine ideals that they were considered immoral. Similar to opinions of the late 1800s, society feared that excessive athletic participation would damage female reproductive capacity and confuse gender binaries. Thus, the notion of the female athlete came with both concern and celebration during this time period.

Flapper Era

The 1920s were a golden age of sport. American society was facing significant changes that increased the popularity of sport even further. Corporations began to utilize the commercialization of leisure to the middle class through selling of recreational equipment, sportswear, and entertainment. As the economy became primarily focused on mass-marketed consumer products and entertainment, people became more and more concerned with personal fulfillment through consumption and leisure. Many sports such as baseball, boxing, college football, and swimming, all thrived in the 1920s, with people of diverse backgrounds attending sporting events in record numbers.

The 1920s began to open the door for female heroics as well. Post World War I, the 1920s gave birth to the flapper era in which women were encouraged to explore new social behaviors, emphasizing sexuality and urban nightlife. Traditional views were put aside in certain contexts, and a new modern idea of female sexual desire was born. As views of female sexuality became more recognized, their acceptance in public leisure also increased. Thus, flapper women symbolized women's break from traditional gender roles and helped pave the way for women to challenge the idea that leisure, sport, and physical activity were only meant for men.

Female athletes were thought to have adventurous spirits and controversial sexual appeal similar to flappers. Women began to find many and varied opportunities to participate in athletic activities. As women gained more access to leisure and sport, their skill levels began to increase significantly. The public began to become enthralled in the successes of female athletes, yet anxiety still crept up from skeptics who feared that this new-found mindset would jeopardize the social order. Media began to express this unease in their reporting of successful female athletes. For example, Helen Wills was a remarkable female tennis player who won her first women's Wimbledon tournament in 1927. She continued on to become an icon after garnering eight more Wimbledon championships, and was often referred to as the "American girl" throughout her career. While her success had the public raving about the advancement of women as a whole, media began to portray the opinions of the uneasy traditionalists. As Wills continued to excel, her media attention turned from "charming American girl" to being criticized for being a disturbing and heartless fighter.

Despite these tensions and paradoxes, women's sports continued to grow rapidly throughout the decade. Female athletes eventually not only established their place in sport, but also shaped a new ideal of womanhood through their athleticism. Elite female athletes became celebrities, and the increased popularity caused sporting organizations to include female sports. Previously a male-only entity, the Association of American Universities (AAU) began to sponsor female national championships in swimming, track, and basketball throughout the 1920s. Although not as popular as their male counterparts, these events drew significant fan attraction and media attention.

Inclusion in the Modern Olympic Games

Success on the national level eventually paved the way for women's inclusion internationally. The Olympics, considered to be a pillar of international excellence and the dominant arena for athleticism, was slow to include women as part of the Games. The first modern Olympic Games took place in 1896 as an international competition where countries of the world competed across several sports. The ideals on which they were founded include fairness, tolerance, and equality in support of peace and goodwill throughout the world. However, when Pierre de Coubertin first proposed the modern Olympics in 1892, he did not view that these ideals applied to women. In fact, de Coubertin was adamantly opposed to women competing, as he deemed their participation would be "inappropriate." To him, the idea was unnatural. "Women have but one task," he said, "that of crowning the champions" (Chatziefstathiou, 2008, 101). As late as 1912 he wrote, "The Olympic Games . . . [are] the solemn and periodic examination of male athleticism with internationalism as a base, loyalty as a means, art for its setting, and female applause as reward" (Chatziefstathiou, 2008, 102). Not surprisingly, not a single woman participated in the first modern Olympics in 1896.

Although the Olympics were open to female athletes in 1900, their inclusion was ostensibly limited. Twelve women were allowed in the second Games in 1900 in de Coubertin's hometown of Paris. Those 12 came from Great Britain, France, Switzerland, Bohemia, and the United States. They competed in women's tennis, sailing, croquet, equestrian, and golf. A five-foot-eleven socialite from the Chicago Golf Club won the nine-hole golf tournament. Said to have received an Olympic gold medal, in reality she received a gold-trimmed porcelain bowl. Other than this gesture, the other female athletes received no kind of recognition. They were ignored. Four years later, eight women—all American archers—participated in the 1904 Games. Recognition came very slowly in large part due to the resistance to allowing spectators to watch female Olympians. As de Coubertin argued, "If some women want to play football or box, let them, provided that the event takes place without spectators, because the spectators who flock to such competitions are not there to watch a sport" (Chatziefstathiou, 2008, 100).

The International Swimming Federation (ISF) was the first main sporting federation to openly support the inclusion of women in the Olympics and voted to include women's swimming in the 1912 Olympics. As a result, other sporting federations slowly began to include women in their competitions. The United States sent its first female teams to the 1920 Olympic Games in swimming and skating. At these summer games (held in Antwerp, Belgium), a total of 288 athletes competed, of which 14 were women. Given that there were no separate winter and summer Olympic Games, sports such as ice hockey and figure skating took place in conjunction with other traditional summer sports. Theresa Weld from the United States medaled in figure skating, and the *New York Times* reported that her performance surpassed the best performances of male contestants. The U.S. women's swim team also outperformed the men's team relatively. Six female U.S. swimmers took home 7 medals, while 9 medals were won by 16 male swimmers. Despite these kinds of successes, female participation in the Olympics was constantly under scrutiny. Controversy sparked at the 1928 Olympics in Amsterdam when female runners collapsed at the finish line of the 800-meter race. This incident enabled skeptics to reiterate and exaggerate the fragility of women and their inability to participate in sports at such a high level. Even though many men collapsed in the 1904 Olympics during the same event, the women's 800-meter race was subsequently excluded from the Olympics until 1960.

Although women were excluded from specific events, women's overall participation steadily increased until 1960, when a total of 20 percent of the overall participants were women, as additional sports were added to accommodate female Olympic athletes. Thirty years later in 1991, the executive board issued a historic decision that any new sport seeking to be included on the Olympic program had to include women's events. From the first modern Olympic Games to the most recent 2016 Olympics, women have experienced over a century of transition. There are more opportunities than ever for women to participate in sport, and the Olympic Games stands as one of the most notable events in which that struggle has been viewed globally.

Women's Bodies, Health, and Movement

During the late 19th century, beliefs about women's bodies influenced perceptions about the appropriateness of physical activity and sport for women. Commonly held beliefs posited that women were born with a limited amount of "vital energy." A commonly held perception was that a significant amount of this energy was taken up by a woman's reproductive functions. The view that women's physical activity needed to be limited was framed as a medical concern. Medical professionals warned that a woman's "vital energy" was required for puberty, menstruation, and childbirth. In particular, women were warned to abstain from any type of physical exertion during menstruation. The idea that women should limit their physical activity was codified in medical texts. For instance, in 1874, Dr. Edward Clarke published *Sex in Education* and stated that "both muscular and brain labor must be reduced at the onset of menstruation" (102). Given that the prevailing thinking positioned motherhood as a woman's primary function, physical activity and sport were considered detrimental to women and women's health. Some historians suggest that such concerns extended from the public health concerns at the turn of the century. Living conditions were poor and access to good nutrition was essentially nonexistent. Deaths from disease and illnesses were commonplace. Thus, there was a hypersensitivity toward making sure women could bear children.

Attitudes about women's and men's roles in society contributed to this mindset. First, women who desired to exert themselves physically, as was the case for sports, were often viewed as having an illness. Doctors prescribed rest for these women. The cure consisted of confining women to rooms where they were to remain inactive to preserve their energy. Second, the "rest-cure" was also thought to have positive psychological effects. Given that the desire to be physically active was considered an illness, part of the thinking was that, by resting, women would be able to reflect on their true role in society, that of motherhood. Because motherhood was considered critical to femininity, women who did anything that might jeopardize their role as mothers were outliers. Being pregnant was a sign of femininity, as it was a visual display of the primary role that women were thought to serve. This thinking had other effects. One effect was that a pregnant woman also reinforced male dominance. That is, for a man to have a pregnant wife not only reinforced a narrow view of women, but also represented male physical strength. Ironically, women were not thought to possess strength through their capacity for childbirth. Childbirth was thought to take away their energy. In contrast, men were thought to be strong if they were fathers. That is, fathering contributed to their "strength." The implications of these mindsets on women's sport participation are significant. For women, sport represented a threat to their societal role. For men, sport continued to symbolize strength and reinforced men as strong.

Despite turn-of-the-century practices of keeping women from physical exertion, women enjoyed sport, played sport, and participated nonetheless. However, the underlying belief that women's bodies were weak and fragile shaped the way sport and physical activity were developed. There were two significant developments during the first half of the 20th century that shaped women's sport. First, the degree to which a sport had the potential to cause harm to women's bodies determined whether or not it was considered okay for women to participate. While there were sports deemed appropriate and played by both genders, history records show a strong tendency to list sports as either appropriate for girls and women or appropriate for boys and men. Although not aligned exactly with the way sports are gendered today, the "gendering" of specific sports becomes unquestioned and "normal" during the early 20th century. Women were consistently denied access to sports in which injuries or the threat of significant bodily harm was a possibility. Contact sports such as boxing and football were strictly for men while sports such as golf, tennis, and swimming were considered more appropriate for women. Second, when women were allowed to play, rules and regulations were developed to reduce the amount of physical exertion in order to keep women from expending their energy. Although women began playing basketball only a year after it was invented, special rules were developed to keep women from overexerting themselves. For instance, the basketball court was divided into sections, and players could not move outside of their section. The intent was to keep women from running around too much. Also, players could not run with the ball, and dribbling was limited to three dribbles. In addition, there were very strict rules forbidding aggressive play so that a woman's reproductive organs would not be harmed. However, these strict rules were mostly for white women. Basketball for black female players had different rules, and these women were allowed to run more and play more aggressively. This allowance highlighted vastly different social expectations and views of blacks rather than progress toward equality. Blacks were thought to be naturally more physical, and concern for reproduction was a white concern, not an American concern. Still, differences between basketball for black women and all men remained, and warnings about the dangers of sport for girls and women continued. In 1911, one doctor noted, "basket ball is injurious and should not be engaged by girls or women . . . the nature of women should keep them from this dangerous sport." This pattern of designing rules specifically for women persists to this day; that is, as women desired to play a sport or game that men played, women's versions of the game emerged in order to make the game less strenuous.

Fragility was not only considered part of a woman's physicality, but also was perceived as an integral part of femininity. Women were supposed to appear fragile, dainty, and subdued in order to adhere to the social constructions of female and femininity. With respect to physical activity and sport, women were simply not supposed to take up space. Common expectations about how women were to move within sport were that their movements should be limited because they were "unnatural" and "unladylike." For instance, it was believed that girls could not throw overhand in baseball because such movements were not natural for girls. Women were taught how to move conservatively, that is, not letting their bodies move around too much because it was not only considered strenuous, but also not feminine. These beliefs further "gendered" sports, as sports such as gymnastics, skating, and tennis were considered graceful and therefore in line with feminine ideals. The inverse was also thought to be true. That is, if women participated in sports, their femininity would be diminished. Perhaps the most compelling example of the thinking was when women started to ride bicycles. Medical personnel warned that women would develop "bicycle face," a medical condition that rendered a woman's appearance less feminine. In an 1885 news article in the *New York World*, there were over 40 things a woman should do when riding a bicycle in order to maintain her "dignity and decorum." One of the recommendations was that women should not strive to compete nor aim for "records" as that behavior is "too sporty" and unladylike.

While the fragility of women's bodies mostly warned of the "dangers" of sport participation for women, paradoxically this belief also gave way to promotion of women's sports in colleges. Women's fragility was not only associated with their bodies, but also their intellectual capabilities. Although women's colleges emerged at the turn of the century, popular opinion was skeptical of women's abilities to handle rigorous academic work. This public doubt about women going to college was also bolstered by the fear that such pursuits would take women away from their role in society (to bear children and become mothers) on two levels. First, education would be physically too hard for women. Second, the process of education would make women "manly, indelicate, and unsexed" (Sack and Staurowsky, 1998, 52). In other words, no "normal" woman could withstand the rigors of academic life, so those who did pursue such activities must surely have to develop "manly" traits in order to survive. Such beliefs placed pressure on administrators of female colleges to justify their existence.

In response to these beliefs, women in charge of these colleges looked for medical tenets that might support the value of physical activity for women. This impetus for physical activity as part of a women's college education was grounded in the idea that women would gain the physical strength needed to pursue academics through "physical education." Embedded in this view was also the idea that although women should participate in physical activity, they should be monitored closely to avoid all the undesired consequences. As a result, the physical education profession was born, and the practice of scrutinizing women's bodies by keeping track of their weight, eating habits, exercise, and female reproductive processes. Further, classes in parenting and socially acceptable ways to move and act like a lady were part of the curriculum. Thus, concurrent to women's desire to take up sport and physical activity were numerous practices that served to control the ways that women participated—all for the sake of protecting women's bodies from harm and "masculinization" so that they could fulfill their roles as mothers.

Early Organization of Women's Sports

Beginning in the 1920s, there was much debate about how women's sports should be organized. This debate was pronounced in higher education. During the late 19th century, colleges shifted from offering women calisthenics to organized sports. As women began to compete in interscholastic and intercollegiate competitions, there was a resurgence of resistance to women's participation in any form of organized sport that resembled men's sport. In 1923, the Women's Division of the governing body for intercollegiate athletics at the time decided to reform sport for girls and women. As sport became more prominent in schools and colleges, physical education departments developed across the United States. Because physical education was considered a teaching profession, women constituted that majority of physical education majors. Given that the emphasis in these departments was on physical activity and sport for all individuals, this group developed an anticompetitive stance. Ironically, it was the female physical education professionals who became the most vociferous opponents of interscholastic and collegiate sport for girls and women. As primary administrators of intercollegiate athletics for women, they worked hard to eliminate competitive sports for women in schools, colleges, and other organizations. As a result, organized sport for women in schools and colleges declined steadily until the 1950s. State championships for girls were discontinued in many high schools during this period, as was intercollegiate competition. Competitive teams were replaced with intramurals and activity days.

One reason for physical educators' de-emphasis on competition was due to their desires to protect women from the rigors of sport based on established ideas about sex differences. The ideology of the Women's Division focused on fair play, cooperative games, and the belief that everyone should play. These beliefs were the foundation upon which this group argued for the replacement of men with women for administrative and coaching positions. While such beliefs meant that more women moved into leadership positions for women's sport during the first half of the 20th century, such ideology reinforced the stereotypes that men and masculinity were associated with competitive sport and that women were associated with cooperative and inclusive sport. At this juncture in history, the effects of leadership on the course of women's collegiate and interscholastic sport were significant. These dominant views of leadership regarding women's sport participation won out for most of the 20th century despite conflicting desires of collegiate female athletes. For instance, in 1924 at Wellesley (a college for women), the undergraduates voted 237 votes to 33 votes in favor of intercollegiate athletics. This interest in competitive sport by women was representative of the way many female collegiate athletes felt at the time. However, by the 1950s, competitive interscholastic and intercollegiate sport experienced a significant decline and intramural sports became the norm for women in the educational context. Intercollegiate competitive sports for women remained marginalized until the 1960s, when the women's movement gained ground. In 1971, the Association for Intercollegiate Athletics for Women (AIAW) pushed for change in intercollegiate athletics, and competitive sport once again began to make significant progress within schools and colleges.

Other opportunities to participate in sport outside the educational system for women during the early 1900s included club sports. In response to closed doors for women in most sport clubs, women formed their own urban sport clubs such as outdoor clubs and archery clubs. However, they were the exception rather than the rule. Instead, women's sports for middle- and upper-class women were supported in summer resorts and country clubs. Sports such as croquet, tennis, golf, archery, and curling were played in these contexts. In these spheres, women were able to play in tournaments organized by the clubs and related associations. Notably, the descriptions of these female athletes as being strong, healthful, and skillful while graceful and physically attractive were the focus of commentary, rather than actual athletic achievements. Within the country clubs, women were highly encouraged to participate in sports such as tennis and golf. As cities became more crowded, the elite moved to the suburbs, and both men and women enjoyed sport in country clubs. The sports supported in this environment were those that required less contact and more perceived skill, and could be considered leisure as much as competition.

While there were very few opportunities and available time for working-class women to participate in sport, one notable exception provided opportunities for women who desired to compete in sport. During the mid-1900s, corporations decided to fund industrial sport programs. The sport programs were considered an effective way to keep the working class satisfied and indoctrinated into American ideals. Given that many women worked in manufacturing or larger industrial corporations, competitive sport opportunities for women were much more prevalent for working-class women than what was available to middle- and upper-class women. Higher education and country clubs were still very much a privilege. Industrial leagues sponsored many female athletes and teams. Winning reflected favorably on the corporations, so it was in their interest to support competitive play, often sending talented female athletes to national competitions en route to the Olympic Games. Other benefits included hosting tournaments in basketball and softball, charging admission so that the players as well as the corporation could benefit financially. These early industrial leagues paved the way for women's professional leagues. For instance, in 1943 during World War II, the All-American Girls Baseball League was formed in Chicago. With many men serving in the military, Chicago Cubs owner, Phillip Wrigley, founded the women's baseball league. Women were offered salaries and played games all over the Midwest. At the league's height, annual attendance reached over 1 million spectators. When Wrigley lost interest, the league folded. However, the relatively short-lived success inspired other women's leagues throughout the latter half of the 20th century. For instance, the Women's Basketball League was formed by William Bryne in 1978. While the league folded after four years, Guttman (1991) notes that this pattern of failed attempts at professional league play for women was very similar to the pattern of start-up and failure for men's sports leagues. Despite the fact that women's leagues were 100 years behind men's leagues, the argument that women's professional sport was not financially viable took hold and has held weight ever since.

Differences among Women's Sport Experiences

While the history of sport participation remains primarily a male history, there are even fewer accounts of female athletes from ethnic and racial minorities—namely, there is little recorded history of female athletes from ethnic or racial minorities. Part of the issue is sexism within each ethnic minority. Although men and masculinity were privileged in these cultures, the writers of history were primarily white men. Nevertheless, some history is available regarding sport experiences for women of color. It is important to consider that women of color are not merely "oppressed more" in sport, but that their experiences of sport differ qualitatively than white women. In this section, patterns of how race, ethnicity, and social class intersect with gender is illustrated with brief overviews of African American female athlete experiences and Canadian aboriginal sportswomen.

Early collegiate experiences of African American women differed from their white counterparts. Due to the civil rights movement, many black men advocated for female athletic participation in sport competition because they believed that the attention for sports achievements would bolster the civil rights movement. Thus, black men advocated for black female sports and supported efforts to expand, not reduce, competitions for black female athletes. Between 1920 and 1950, white women's collegiate sport experiences were being reformed to be in line with dominant gender ideology, while larger racial equality efforts gave many more opportunities for black women to play sport. For instance, the organization and rules for black female collegiate basketball players contrasted many white women's experiences. These teams often charged admission to their games, which allowed them to raise money to travel for tournaments. In many ways, the black community rallied around these aims because competent black female athletes were believed to send a larger social message about capabilities. Black colleges worked hard to situate black women in opposition to white women from "finishing" schools. Thus, academic rigor was the norm, and competitive sports teams were thought to enhance the black woman's position in society as someone who was strong and could endure. Administrators also believed that sport could help black women become solid examples of success for younger black women. Many black female collegiate athletes moved into teaching or coaching positions themselves in order to pass along black pride and notions of self-respect.

As a result, black female athletes were often supported alongside male black athletes. Many women's basketball teams played using the men's rules, and they were encouraged to play aggressively. Also, many women's basketball games were held in conjunction with the men's games. Black men coached most of the women's basketball teams, encouraging play and game strategies similar to the men. Some teams even scrimmaged against high school boys' teams to learn more techniques and styles of play.

While women's basketball was perhaps the most popular sport among black female college students, track and field athletic opportunities grew in a few Southern black colleges. For instance, during the 1930s and 1940s, Tuskegee and Tennessee State recruited and supported many female black track and field athletes, giving them opportunities few white women had at the collegiate level. Notably, there was fairly equal support for both female and male athletes. For instance, female track athletes trained with the men's team, following similar workouts and testing themselves against the men. Both colleges instituted year-round training, offered summer camps, provided funds for national meets, and helped athletes gain work-study jobs to help fund their education. However, black colleges were not immune to the pressures from the physical education proponents. There were some black colleges who worked to conform to middle-class sensibilities by adopting a similar stance toward athletics as white women's colleges.

The intersections of race and class produced different experiences for black female athletes during the mid-20th century. Working-class black women who gained access to athletics in college recount the joys of playing hard and having little to no tension between black female femininity and their athletic bodies. Sport scholars believe that rural black women's socioeconomic roles in the mid-20th century contributed to their different athletic experiences as female athletes, especially from the South. The fact that rural black women had always done hard manual labor throughout menstrual cycles, pregnancy, and motherhood served as counterevidence to the myth that women were fragile. For these women, fragility was not an option. These roles helped black female athleticism to be accepted more within the black community. Athleticism and strength did not disrupt black femininity. Instead, these displays of strength complemented the roles of rural black women in society, whose commitment to family was symbolized through active engagement. For example, the "Miss Tuskegee" award was frequently given to female athletes, proving that athleticism and beauty were not at odds in this context. Furthermore, some black female athletes were more drawn by the financial benefits of participating in sport, a motivation not viewed as un-womanly in African American views. For instance, in 1953, Mary Horton was described in *The Afro-American* as well educated and intending to become a college teacher, but "upon learning of the financial success of girl wrestlers, she changed her mind" (23). For upper- and middle-class black women, pursuit of competitive middle-class sports such as tennis was met with ambiguity in terms of black femininity. On the one hand, tennis participation served to minimize the racial divide. On the other hand, black female tennis players were subject to similar ideals of femininity as white women. These tensions continued

titles and three regional titles while the hockey teams won four regional titles. Perhaps the strongest women's teams were softball/fastball, who collectively won nine league titles and nine provincial titles, as well as had players who earned a few Most Valuable Player (MVP) awards. A few female athletes played for other teams outside the reserve, going on to play for Canada in fastball. Softball teams also had success in the all Indian leagues. Paraschak noted that softball was the only sport played at aboriginal cultural gatherings at longhouses. Four prominent Six Nations Reserve female athletes are Bev Beaver, Ruth Hill, Phyllis Bomberry, and Doris Henhawk. Bev Beaver competed in fastball, hockey, and bowling. She won the MVP eight times for fastball. She competed in the EuroAmerican sport leagues in hockey, winning five MVP awards during that time. Phyllis Bomberry was a catcher in fastball and played on the gold medal team at the Canada Games in 1969. Ruth Hill was a fastball pitcher who averaged over 13 strikeouts per game over a 20-year period. Doris Henhawk was a softball player who later went on to coach numerous young girls and winning teams.

Paraschak notes that the variety of sports in which aboriginal women participated is much more varied than prior historical accounts posited and that they were accomplished athletes. Yet, sport experiences for these young girls were not entirely homogeneous. During informal interviews during her study, she learned that aboriginal girls who came from Indian, longhouse traditions were encouraged to participate in sports. In contrast, she learned that Indian girls growing up in "Christianized" communities were discouraged from participating in sport. Further, there was the belief among some aboriginals that they were "naturals" at sport and did not need to learn the specific game strategies or drills commonly practiced in EuroAmerican sports. Such ideology set up tensions for young girls and women who tended to participate in both the EuroAmerican leagues as well as the all Indian leagues.

Early History of Women's Sportswear

In the period of time between the end of the American Civil War and the end of World War II, women's desires to participate in sport grew exponentially and brought about a whole new area of development: American sportswear. As powerful as the commanding puritanical views of modesty and propriety were for women in these years from 1865 to 1950, fashion and education eventually brought an end to those beloved but unreasonable crinolines, corsets, hats, and gloves. Despite the fact that there were growing numbers of women with increased leisure time on their hands and a growing interest to be more than spectators, the evolution of what to wear during physical activity and sport was relatively slow. Due to sports' close relationship to courting practices, women begrudgingly dropped one complicated layer of clothing after another. It took almost a century to make their way into the trousers, which had worked so simply and winningly for male athletes, but they did evolve. This period of time was arguably the greatest dress reform in history, with women's sportswear spawning significant developments in women's clothing in general.

The urbanization of America was the biggest factor for positive change affecting indoor women and outdoor men. Parks and green spaces created public places where the two might mix. Healthier exercise opportunities for middle-class women were available for the first time. Frederick Law Olmsted's New York Central Park was the design inspiration for many other notable parks around the country. The virtue of physical exercise for women, which had been nonexistent, was at last praised. Even staunch Victorian doctors joined in the demand for women to run, climb, swim, ride, and play games, especially in these newly developed green spaces.

The first two games girls played were the imported English activities croquet and skating. Women wore the most elegant dresses they had. It was understood by all that croquet and skating weren't really what was important. These rare public mixings of the sexes were all about courting. The women wore their finest to these sporting events in order to attract husbands in such social settings. The sporting events served primarily as social gatherings. Women hiked their skirts so numerous decorative petticoats would be on display. Tiny feet and ankles became the body's erotic zone. Thanks to the vulcanization of rubber, the first kind of sneaker—the first shoe designed specifically for sport—became popular as a "croquet sandal." Dressing appropriately took a distant second place to dressing attractively. At this period in genteel mixed company, no other sportswear alternatives had yet evolved.

Skating was decidedly unladylike and cold. But women eventually warmed to it as they had to croquet and for the same social reasons. Because skating was inexpensive, even more women could play out of doors. It was more democratic and less upper class than croquet was and lawn tennis would be. Dresses for all women were very decorative while being heavy and large. Horsehair crinolines supported wide, bell-shaped skirts. Due to their size, stories of gusty winds lifting the bell-shaped skirts high and revealing feet, shoes, boots, legs, stockings—and even pantalettes and petticoats!—are early evidence of the sexualization of women's bodies within the sporting realm. At this point in time, men's sportswear was crafted with purpose in mind, and revealing bodies was not at all considered erotic. Each feminine item became a new article of fashion interest, adding to the overall decorative effect. One sensible modification was made to dresses to prevent tripping on skates. Skirts were at last permitted to be inches shorter. That was a breakthrough. Newly visible ankles were soon displayed in colorful knit stockings tucked into new sturdier skating shoes. Fashion continued to rule, but a Turkish costume known as the bloomer earned distinction as the standard exercise clothing. The bloomer weighed much less and was considerably more effective for real activity. Opposition to bloomers came not because they weren't reasonable, but because they were considered ugly. Anything looking like pants simply could not be modest or feminine.

Women's clothes got far tighter before they got looser. In the 1880s, lawn tennis became the first real sport for women. Again, like croquet, girls approached it in their finest. Heavily corseted and bustled, they wore yards of material, hats, gloves, and even heeled shoes. They gently patted the ball. There was no running or strong serves. There couldn't be—their arms and shoulders were too restricted. Lawn tennis had to feel like upscale croquet. Newly invented lawnmowers kept the courts perfectly trimmed. Newly invented rubber-core tennis balls actually bounced on the firm turf. Tennis was so popular that it quickly moved off private estates and became a club event. As elite as tennis was determined to be, some 450 clubs appearing in Brooklyn suggest that the middle classes adopted it. By 1890, "Ladies Outdoor and Indoor Garments" reflected these "outing costumes." Readers were advised that tennis suits could be worn with ease until the evening.

The nature of the clothing of the second female who conquered Wimbledon is not known with accuracy, but one photograph suggests a young girl in a loose dress with no obvious corset. Her wide low-slung skirt was cut off around her knees. Tall, shorthaired, strong Charlotte, or Lottie, Dod amazed spectators with her aggressive play and powerful strokes. Because she was still a child, she was probably permitted leniency in her dress code. Her shorter, fuller skirts allowed actual freedom of movement. She lost only four games in her entire career, retiring in 1893 at the age of 21.

Not a teenager, May Sutton earned fouls at Wimbledon because of her shorter skirt, flash of ankle, and exposure of her bare lower arm due to a short-sleeved blouse. She was only allowed back on court by lowering her skirt. Sutton is credited with getting women out of trailing skirts, high-necked shirts, and long sleeves. Most women wore corsets well into the 1920s even while playing championship tennis. Younger women wore "health waists" or "duck shirts," which were simply stiff cotton bodices (a laced vest usually worn on the outside of undergarments). Wimbledon was a stickler for proper form. Any clothing that was not strictly traditional was seen as scandalous. Besides Sutton's shorter skirt—perhaps no more than 4 to 6 inches from the ground—Suzanne Lenglen's knee-length, sleeveless dress in 1919 caused furor. Tradition insisted that women should wear little dresses with skirts and underdrawers (equivalent to underwear but longer).

The same modified outfit that May Sutton wore at Wimbledon had evolved a good four years before newer, much less restrictive sportswear appeared on the lawns of women's colleges. Simple gym clothing in women's colleges evolved new comfort, practicality, and freedom—strictly kept from public eyes, but proudly worn in all-female competitions on campuses. But men enforced the rules of the game at their tennis clubs and they resisted any change. The United States Lawn Tennis Association was a powerful governing authority that kept strict rules about what women could wear in these public spaces. Not surprisingly, the clothing requirements for women remained more restrictive in sport settings in which men made the rules.

The activity that was the most challenging at protecting Victorian modesty and allowing movement was swimming. It took several layers of wool to prevent women's breasts from showing too much while swimming. The pull toward modesty was in direct opposition to practicality, as female swimmers were 40 pounds heavier due to the water-soaked wool. They sank to the bottom, and any kind of "swimming" beyond wading was impossible. Until women finally entered the Olympics, no sleek or strong fabric sensible swimming outfit had evolved. Nevertheless, girls enthusiastically played in the waters off Newport to mix with the boys, despite their swimming outfit failures. The famous painting by Winslow Homer, "The Bathe at Newport," depicts a happy frolic of men and women in the sea circa 1858. Despite all the efforts to keep women's bodies covered, Homer's painting is telling because he recorded what he saw, and what he saw was not women in straw bonnets, nor only long sleeves, nor all ankles and feet covered. Similar to other developments in women's sports, select women often simply did what they needed to do in order to participate in sport, leisure, and physical activity. In general, however, women were generally covered in tent-like canvas cloaks. Alternately, women donned baggy, blouse-topped dresses down to mid-calf, worn with a belt, and straight-legged trousers in the bloomer style, gathered at the ankles. A short cape or "talma" would provide warmth or coverage in case too much was being revealed. It was not a great-looking outfit, but made do for the next several decades. To avoid being seen, women changed clothes in "bathing machines" at the edge of the water.

By the 1870s, dressmakers produced a few less-ugly bathing dresses. One outfit had "darin" cap sleeves and a blouse top that barely covered the baggy pants below. The French introduced a trim design with or without sleeves. The trousers were to use the least material necessary. Wool was still the preferred fabric, but for the sake of health, corsets were not included, although "real ladies" still wore corsets. By the 1880s, the suit combined bodice and trousers into a single one-piece garment, over which the Americans added a separate skirt to conceal the figure. A woman who really wanted to swim left the skirt off. Long, piled high hair was held in check by oiled silk or waxed linen hats. Feet were protected by bathing sandals or slippers. This version of the bathing outfit was pretty much the same as the gymnasium suit that had emerged in women's colleges.

J. Parmly Paret declared in his 1901 *Woman's Book of Sports* that "Nothing tight should be worn for swimming, no matter how fashionable a dress may be for bathing." He didn't say to forget the skirt, but he did advise that it be above the knees. By 1925, women were wearing two-piece black wool-knit bathing suits with a long tunic over fitted pants covering the thighs. Both hit just above the knees. The body-baring aspect of this was that one worried about shaving legs and underarms for the first time.

Not surprisingly, American women had not been swimmers during the late 19th and early 20th centuries. By 1916, over 32,000 women had joined swimming classes at the Young Men's Christian Association (YMCA). The next year, the Women's Swimming Association of New York organized to promote national and international competition for women. Many were not as drawn to the *swimming* after the 1920s as they were drawn to the latest fad of having a tan to show off, spurred by French fashion. Bare arms, bare backs, and even cleavage on display in the emerging sportswear influenced eveningwear for the first time. The attempt to create a suit that wasn't scandalously revealing or dead weight led designers to find a better fabric. Lastex, created in 1934, was made of an elastic rubber core covered by cotton, or rayon, and was more practical than the rubber sheet that had split right down the middle when worn by Esther Williams, a competitive swimmer during the 1930s and three-time U.S. national champion, at the Los Angeles Coliseum. After World War II, Lastex yarn and nylon combined to create swimming suits that fit better, looked better, and improved swimming speeds.

Swimsuits kept evolving. The 1956 Melbourne Olympics was the event that first displayed Speedo suits. By the early 1970s, new "skirtless, second skin" Lycra suits were revealed at the world championship games in Belgrade. Speed records were smashed with each upgrade in design and fabric. While women were not permitted to wear functional clothing for most sports, the development of swimwear may have given way to the idea that sportswear for women should be functional. Athletes cannot win games without making every partial second count for them. Thus, competitors constantly pushed for better design and better fabric, comparing in great detail the differences in sport clothes that the different contestants wore. By the 2002 Winter Olympics in Salt Lake City, skintight ski racing suits were worn by both sexes. The changes have loosened boundaries not just in clothing, but also in women's lives in the first decades of the 20th century. Women have worked hard and succeeded in gaining their own lean outfits that permit them to compete and win.

Development and Importance of Title IX

Title IX was enacted in 1972 as part of the Education Amendments Act, and maintained that "no person in the United States shall, on the basis of sex, be excluded from participation in, be denied the benefits of, or be subjected to discrimination under any education program or activity receiving federal financial assistance." Previously, the Civil Rights Act of 1964 was passed in order to prohibit discrimination on the basis of race, color, religion, sex, or national origin; however, this act lacked specificity surrounding gender discrimination in public education. Thus, Title IX was enacted in order to address these issues.

Although Title IX was initially enacted to ensure equal educational opportunities for both males and females over a variety of areas (including counseling, access to classes, and admissions), it has most notably impacted the realm of athletics. Since the passing of Title IX, sport participation for high school girls has increased from fewer than 300,000 participants in 1972 to over 3 million in 2011. These statistics are also reflected in collegiate athletics as well, with participation increasing from 30,000 to over 200,000 female athlete participants by 2011. Similar trends are also seen at the elite level of sport with 44.3 percent of the participants in the 2012 London Olympic Games being women, the highest percentage to date.

Initially, Title IX did not have much impact as there were no regulatory measures in place to enforce the new law. In 1979, the Department of Health, Education, and Wellness (HEW) worked on a policy interpretation in order to address this problem. Under the interpretation, HEW outlined three components of Title IX, which provided a framework for assessing compliance. In order to be in compliance with Title IX, institutions are expected to achieve each of these three components. The first component is effective accommodation of interests. This component is measured by the three-prong test, which necessitates an institution to demonstrate at least one of the following prongs: (1) Athletic participation is proportionate to the gender enrollment of the entire institution, (2) the institution can show a recent history of expanding athletic opportunities for the underrepresented gender, or (3) the institution can prove that the interests of the underrepresented gender have been fully and effectively accommodated. If an institution satisfies one of these prongs, it is deemed compliant with the first component of Title IX. Component two requires that financial assistance must be proportional for males and females. This component primarily relates to collegiate athletic scholarships, but can also apply to private schools offering financial assistance. The third component of Title IX mandates that an institution establish "equivalence" in any other benefits and opportunities for males and females. This includes comparable uniforms, quality of coaches, facility access and quality, equipment quality and quantity, and sport offerings to name a few. An institution can only be in compliance with Title IX if it has satisfied all three of these components.

Since Title IX's enactment in 1972, its enforcement has evolved as numerous cases have helped shape how Title IX is utilized today. Originally, there was little legal controversy surrounding Title IX as enforcement was limited. However, since HEW began regulating Title IX compliance as outlined above through the policy interpretation, there have been numerous cases involving the amendment that have helped detail what Title IX entails. *Grove City College v. Bell* (1984) was one of many controversial cases in which an institution attempted to limit the scope of Title IX. Grove City College felt that it should be exempt from Title IX regulations because it did not receive any federal financial assistance. In the end, the Supreme Court maintained that any institution receiving federal funding was to be held to Title IX standards, and furthermore, this included Grove City College as it was an indirect recipient of federal financial assistance due to some of their student body receiving federal funds by means of the Stafford Federal Loan Program/ Pell Grants. The Court also ruled that only the financial aid and admissions offices had to adhere to these policies. In other words, only specific programs receiving federal assistance were required to comply with Title IX rather than the entire institution, a ruling that voided the HEW's earlier interpretation. This decision had major ramifications on collegiate athletics as most athletic departments do not receive federal financial assistance directly and, therefore, under this ruling, did not have to be held to the Title IX standard. In 1987, the Supreme Court reversed this ruling with the passing of the Civil Rights Restoration Act of 1987, which proclaimed Title IX covered all of the operations within an institution receiving any federal financial assistance, thus expanding the scope of Title IX.

Cohen v. Brown University (1992) was another first major court case in which a university was significantly challenged by Title IX legislation. Amy Cohen brought the lawsuit when Brown University planned to drop four varsity sports: women's volleyball, women's gymnastics, men's golf, and men's water polo, due to budget cuts. Cohen maintained that Brown's athletic department comprised only 36.7 percent female student-athletes, while the general Brown student body comprised 48 percent women. The court ruled in favor of Cohen and found Brown guilty of violating Title IX by failing to pass all aspects of the three-prong test. Because of this, universities then began to take Title IX compliance seriously. Over the next several years, there were many more attempts similar to *Cohen v. Brown* (1993) that aimed to find loopholes and weaken Title IX regulations. Most of these efforts have not succeeded. However, in 2005, Title IX was not in full effect for a short period of time when the Department of Education deemed it adequate for an institution to demonstrate full and effective accommodation of female athletes' interests by simply sending out a survey to its female students, asking what additional athletic opportunities they may be interested in. The hope was that the simple survey would be sufficient for satisfying one of the prongs of the first component, which is to prove that the interests of the underrepresented gender have been satisfied. If the results were not significant, the institution was not required to alter any of its programs, and it was presumed to be in compliance with

Title IX. While at first glance the survey seems legitimate, the issue was that sending surveys to students already at the college, who had clearly not attend the college for athletic reasons, was highly unlikely to show a significant unmet need. This loophole was rescinded during President Obama's first term, and the initial scope of Title IX was returned.

A long-held argument against Title IX is that men's sports are eliminated to make room for women's sports. Dr. Lapchick, director of the Institute for Diversity and Ethics in Sport, agrees that there was a period of time in which athletic directors were forced to cut men's teams in order to be complaint with Title IX. He notes, however, that due to the slow enforcement of Title IX, most athletic departments did nothing for a long time. Once athletic departments were finally being held accountable during the 1990s, things had to change fast to avoid lawsuits. While hundreds of men's sports have been eliminated, in the big picture "hundreds" is relatively few sports. As of 2012, there are more men competing in intercollegiate athletics than ever before, alongside more women than ever before. Furthermore, the cuts may not have been entirely due to making way for women's sports by discriminating against men's sports. One significant factor that has been pointed out by numerous Title IX experts is that National Collegiate Athletics Association (NCAA) rules regarding scholarship numbers favor football, especially in schools where football generates significant revenue such as in Football Bowl Schools (FBS). The NCAA sets the number of scholarships available to each sport. Football, for instance, currently has 85 full scholarships available to Division I schools. Football is a "head count" sport in which every player admitted receives a full scholarship. The limit of 85 easily allows the school to satisfy all special teams, offense, and defense needs. Many other sports are "equivalency" sports. In women's soccer, for instance, there are 14 scholarships available, a number just above the number of players on the field. However, the coach can give partial scholarships to athletes as long as the total equivalent is not exceeded. This system benefits high-revenue-generating sports, namely football, in that their high roster numbers are essentially protected. One outcome is that football is by far the most expensive sport for a college to afford. That is, with the stakes high in terms of revenue generation, a school is more likely to max out its roster with 85 football players, and "cuts" may need to be made elsewhere in order to keep the athletic department complaint with Title IX. Either those 85 male football players must be offset with female or male athletes, or teams must simply not use all 85 scholarships for football. Once Title IX was enforced more consistently, many athletic departments chose to eliminate smaller, non-revenue-generating men's teams rather than decrease their football rosters.

While Title IX has been successful at getting more equal opportunities for women to play collegiately and improved their experiences, there remain discrepancies. Often there are different accommodations for men and women, with women's teams frequently not receiving equal treatment with respect to what is known as the "laundry list," which includes the following items: travel expenses, equipment and supplies, practice times, access to tutoring, locker rooms, equal ease of access to athletic trainers, and housing, dining, and other support services. For instance, favorable scheduling and favors with respect to access to strength trainers and medical services are often allowed for high-profile men's teams such as football and basketball relative to the comparable women's teams. However, these aspects are often accepted by the female athletes themselves, who believe that a revenue-generating men's team *should* have greater access. Finally, there is much more room to improve when it comes to equal opportunities for women in athletic administration. Mentoring women to move into higher decision-making roles is the next step to improved Title IX compliance.

Title IX and the Changing of Women's Collegiate Sport Leadership: 1960 to 1982

As women's collegiate sport became more established, several governing bodies came into play between 1960 and 1990 in order to oversee the development of women's collegiate sports. The various interested groups were not always aligned philosophically. As noted above, professional sports owners, mostly men, supported women in competitive sport while mostly female administrators sought to keep women's sport anticompetitive. One result of the 1960s women's movement is that women began to gain greater access to educational institutions. This access was gained through the merging of women's and men's colleges as well as by predominantly male colleges and universities opening their doors to women.

As athletics had already been tied to education, bringing women and men together in educational institutions brought forth questions of how women's sport should be governed. In 1963, the Division for Girls and Women in Sport (DGWS) revised its position statement on women's collegiate sport from acknowledging that women's intercollegiate athletics exists to advocating that such programs were "desirable." With the growth of women's intercollegiate sport, the DGWS could not sustain oversight of the growing competitions for women. In 1966, the DGWS created the Commission on Intercollegiate Sports for Women (CISW), renamed the Commission on Intercollegiate Athletics for Women (CIAW), to oversee all competitions. Significant growth in competitions as well as female collegiate athletes resulted in national championships being established throughout the 1960s and early 1970s. Gymnastics and track-and-field national competitions for women were held in 1967. Shortly thereafter, swimming, badminton, and volleyball national championships were established in 1970 while basketball followed in 1972. As women's collegiate sport became more identified with competition, female administrators wanted to organize women's collegiate athletics in line with the NCAA, the governing body for men's intercollegiate athletics. In 1971, the AIAW formed under the jurisdiction of predominantly female leadership.

While the focus of the AIAW was to support competitive collegiate athletic programs for women, it remained influenced by earlier attitudes that emphasized participation. The organization promoted competition without the intense focus on winning that characterized the NCAA. Still, the AIAW was highly successful in organizing intercollegiate competitive sport for women and nearly quadrupled its membership over 10 years. During the first academic year of its existence, the AIAW had 278 member institutions. Ten years later, in 1981, its membership had reached over 800 institutions. However, the AIAW ceased operation on June 30, 1982. How did this highly successful advocate and organization for women's sports dissolve so quickly? What were the implications for women's leadership of female collegiate athletics?

Ironically, the answer lies in the aftermath of the passing of Title IX in 1972. As enforcement of Title IX became more consistent throughout the late 1970s, along with the fact that colleges and universities were more gender-integrated, the NCAA became highly interested in women's sports. As the governing body for men's intercollegiate athletics, the NCAA had a much longer history and a vested interest in retaining power over intercollegiate athletics. In particular, Title IX was a threat to its dominant status as it sought to equalize resources and opportunities among male and female athletes. In many ways, the NCAA was less concerned about allowing women to participate in sport than it was about maintaining its resources. The organization's first attempt to limit resources given to female athletics was to argue that athletic departments were exempt from Title IX mandates.

Although the narrow interpretation of Title IX was short-lived, the efforts of the NCAA to control women's sports gained greater traction as women's sports grew. Efforts to keep female athletic participation low proved nearly impossible. Observing this growth, the NCAA shifted its interest in women's sport from keeping participation minimal, to capitalizing on the potential financial gains as well as political power as it realized the potential of women's national championships. Hosting, as well as establishing the rules and regulations of those championships, was how the NCAA made money. Thus, the NCAA proposed bringing the AIAW into the structure of the NCAA, but hosting separate NCAA-governed national championships for women's athletics. However, it formed its own committee to determine how the AIAW should integrate as well as how the championships should be run. While the AIAW thought that the NCAA wanted to be a strong advocate for women's sports, it quickly learned that the NCAA had little interest in working together to promote women's sports. In negotiations to merge in 1974, the NCAA refused a 50–50 joint union with equal representation of the mostly female AIAW administration in all levels of policy creation and decision making.

Meanwhile, the merging of colleges and universities meant that athletic departments had to reorganize to become responsible for both women's and men's athletics. Prior to 1972, 90 percent of athletic directors of women's programs were female. However, after the reorganization, most of these women were demoted or simply forced out entirely. Given the cultural importance of men's sports, the women who remained conformed to the traditions and culture of men and male leadership. Women often had to outperform men in order to be recognized. As time went on, most women accepted the male norms within athletic departments and assimilated.

With the failed agreement, the NCAA decided to allow women to compete in its NCAA-sanctioned championships. It hoped to avoid Title IX lawsuits as well as keep the AIAW content. However, inclusion of women at these events was limited to a single female per event. This level of inclusion was clearly not about equal opportunity. However, once the NCAA realized that the federal government was taking equal opportunity seriously, it took significant steps to lure institutions into the fold of the NCAA. In the early 1980s, the NCAA put forth US$3 million to sponsor women's national championships. It offered to (a) pay all travel expenses for teams competing in a national championship; (b) waive additional membership fees for schools that added women's programs; (c) develop equitable financial aid, recruitment, and eligibility rules for women and men; and (d) show more women's sports on television. The AIAW could not compete with the wealth and prestige of the NCAA and ceased operation in 1982. As the NCAA took over managing all aspects of intercollegiate athletics, women found themselves less valued as policy and decision makers. As women's leadership roles quickly declined, the NCAA established the senior women's administrator (SWA) role. Today, every NCAA school must identify one woman in the administration as the designated SWA.

Endurance, Adventure, and Notable Symbolic Moments for Women in Sport

Pedestriennes: The Forgotten Women of Endurance

During the latter half of the 19th century, competitive endurance walking, named "pedestrianism," became a very popular spectator sport. These events took place in many forms including walking distances of 70 or more miles from point A to B. But one of the most popular forms was to walk around an arena for days or to attempt to walk 100 miles within a 24-hour period. Other forms of these endurance events consisted of participants walking 1,000 miles by completing 100 miles each day. While men certainly participated in this event, women did not shy away from these ultra-endurance events. These women went by the feminine form of the noun and were called "pedestriennes." As was the case for much of the history of women's sport, their participation was not recorded well in history. However, stories of the pedestriennes came to light during the 1960s and 1970s as scholars began to dig deeper into the history of women in sport. Based on newspaper accounts, the women who participated in these ultra-endurance walking events could draw spectators and compete with the men.

Two famous pedestriennes who competed in the United States were Bertha Von Hillern and Mary Marshall. Von Hillern immigrated from Germany in 1877 at the age of 20. She was a staunch advocate for athletics and physical activity for women. For two years, she competed as a pedestrienne in order to show the public that women were not fragile and had the capacity to endure as well as the men. Von Hillern walked in just over 25 events between 1876 and 1878. She became quite famous as she toured the country doing 1-day-100-mile walks. Some of those crowds were as large as 10,000 people, and her accomplishments drew many different conflicting opinions from the press, influential people, and medical experts. Von Hillern and Marshall competed against each other in a couple of famous six-day events. The first of these events was in 1876 in Chicago. The goal was to be the first to complete 300 miles within the time period allotted. When Von Hillern had completed 231 miles to Marshall's 234, Von Hillern decided to drop out of the race citing unfair refereeing. The women had a rematch in New York City. Marshall suffered from swollen feet and sore ankles while Von Hillern remained steady. By the end of the sixth day, Von Hillern had walked 323.5 miles to Marshall's 281, winning the six-day contest.

Despite her loss to Von Hillern, Marshall was not dissuaded from competition. Instead, Marshall became the first woman to challenge a man in a head-to-head competition. Shortly after her loss to Von Hillern, Marshall challenged Peter L. Van Ness, an endurance walker who could walk a mile in less than 10 minutes, to a three-day series of 20 miles each day. Whoever won two out of the three days would win the $500 prize money. Van Ness accepted, and Marshall stepped back on the track just a few weeks after her 281-mile loss to Von Hillern. Leading up to the event, the *New York Times* wrote that Van Ness was fairly quick, but speculated that he might not have the endurance. However, few believed that Van Ness would lose due to Marshall's compromised feet and ankles. During the first race, Van Ness took the lead early on; however, after having to break three times during the 20 miles, Marshall was able to keep steady and complete the 20 miles before Van Ness, who was a little over a mile behind Marshall at the time. Van Ness was more determined in the second race, and despite Marshall's signature steady pace, Van Ness completed the final 10 miles with a good pace and won the second race. For the third race, Van Ness went out fast and completed the first 10 miles in just over an hour. However, he took a 45-minute break while Marshall continued on steadily. The race was close during and up through mile 15, after which Van Ness ran out of energy. Marshall went on to win the third and final race. Some newspaper accounts varied. Some downplayed Marshall's victory by highlighting specific aspects of Van Ness's performance as "better" than Marshall's such as his speed at different points in the competition. Other articles applauded Marshall's achievement, noting it as an important step in the growing movement for women's equality.

Although pedestrianism was rather short-lived, pedestriennes became symbols for women's rights and helped shape new ideas about women's bodies, health, and physical capabilities that bolstered general efforts toward women's equality in society. Many women would come to watch these events, being in awe at the pedestriennes' display of endurance. Unsurprisingly, comments about the women's appearances and attractiveness were also part of the stories highlighting their athletic achievements. Because these events were lucrative, business owners helped publicize the events, and many of these women could easily make a living by endurance walking. Eventually, there were opponents to female participation. Religious groups and upper-class individuals who supported Victorian values and attitudes openly disapproved of women's participation claiming it as immoral and unhealthy. Doctors began to talk about how these women were being exploited by the entrepreneurs and should be protected. These arguments raised pubic doubt about the suitability of these races for women despite the fact that they were proving they could walk these distances on a regular basis and even outperform the men at times.

Outdoor Adventure and Extreme Sports:
Pioneers and Access

Tracing the pathways of women in outdoor pursuits shows the extent to which women have been part of a broad and rich history of women and sport. The accomplishments of women pioneers in outdoor pursuits reveal the various ways women were motivated to pursue or could gain access to these physical activities. Although often constrained by class, religion, and cultural practices, women found ways around such constraints. While there are a plethora of women who participated in outdoor pursuits during the 20th century, the three following accounts illustrate the typical ways that women approached outdoor pursuits as well as the ways they gained access to such activities.

For many women, access to the outdoors came through exposure to the outdoors during childhood and sustained by male companionship. For instance, Ruth Dyar, who became one of the most accomplished early female American mountain climbers, grew up exploring the outdoors as a child growing up in a small town outside of Spokane, Washington. She hiked on trails near her family's farm, climbed on basalt outcrops, and climbed apple trees. After obtaining a degree in journalism from the University of Washington, she moved to California for secretarial work. She became aware of the Sierra Club and began skiing with this group in winter and climbing in summer in 1938. In 1939, she was one of six individuals to establish a climbers' house named "Base Camp" for individuals who wanted a seamless interplay between life and climbing. Dyar met her husband within this context, and they spent many years heading off to remote places to climb. Love of the experience, easy-going attitude, and fun were central to her approach to climbing. She always viewed climbing as a cooperative venture fueled by the same desire as men to climb and achieve personal goals. When they had two children, they alternated climbing weekends, viewing their partnership fully as both parents and climbers. Together they achieved many first ascents in California.

For other women, the privilege of growing up in a wealthy family offered many opportunities not available to most working-class women. Canada's twins Rhoda and Rhona Wertele had such opportunities, but drew on their own personal desires to eventually excel in downhill skiing. Considered some of North America's women pioneers in extreme sports, the Wertele twins felt right at home trying to keep up with their older brothers from an early age. Rhoda and Rhona grew up in Montreal, Canada, and had access to one of the few ski hills located within a major city's boundaries. With money being no barrier, the girls enjoyed skiing every winter. By age 11, both girls had launched themselves off the senior ski jump, dared by their older brother to do so. Because ski jumping was not an option for women at the Olympic Games until 2014, the Werteles pursued downhill skiing. From 1942 to 1970, they competed in national and international competitions, sometimes being the only members of the Canadian women's Olympic ski team. Over the years, they accumulated many wins, not only over women, but also beating the men on several occasions. The twins even competed after having children, owing their participation to the simple idea that getting out and staying active are natural and normal parts of life. Later in their lives, they taught skiing to children and adults, especially women who were mothers.

Finally, another path for women who wanted to explore the outdoors was doing so much later in life, waiting until children were grown and marriages were dissolved. Emma Gatewood and Audrey Sutherland were two women who followed their desire to simply head outdoors at ages when most women were settling into sedentary lives. After leaving an abusive marriage, Gatewood became the first woman to solo hike the Appalachian Trail at the age of 67 in 1957. She repeated the hike in 1960 and completed it in sections in 1963. Gatewood traveled all over the United States, and hiked the Oregon Trail from

Independence, Missouri, to Portland, Oregon, as well. Gate-wood hiked with very little, taking a raincoat, drinking cup, plastic cover, and lightweight blanket. Her backpack never weighed more than 20 pounds as she relied on finding food along the way wherever she went. Such motivation to simply get out and explore was also evident in Sutherland's adventures. Sutherland spent over 25 years every summer paddling solo along the Alaskan and British Columbia coasts. She paddled an inflatable kayak over 8,000 miles of coast, inlets, and fjords. Her trips were always solo. Sutherland explains that her desire to go alone was not because of an antisocial personality. Rather, she just found the process much simpler. Sutherland planned her trips carefully and mailed food she had canned or dried herself to small towns she would pass through. Sutherland eventually wrote several books detailing her adventures. However, she never asked for sponsorship nor viewed her adventures as stories media should follow. She simply went for the experience and beauty of the wilderness.

These women are examples of how women approached outdoor activities during the 20th century. Certainly, these women were privileged, and all were white North Americans. These women challenged the belief that the outdoors was particularly appealing to men. Without any desire to be pioneers, these women just pursued adventure or extreme sport because they wanted to. Female outdoor adventurers persisted throughout the 20th century. All women expeditions such as the all women ascent of Annapurna led by Arlene Blum and the all-female expedition to the south pole led by Ann Bancroft were not commonplace, but they happened. Such persistent participation accelerated beginning in the 1970s and has only gained momentum. Research at the turn of the 21st century indicated that women more than men participated in outdoor sports more for the social reasons and cooperative aspects than the competitive or desire to be challenged. Such descriptions ring true for the women highlighted in this section. However, the idea that they did not desire to be challenged nor enjoy competitive aspects does not ring true for these women. There is evidence to suggest that these women both loved the fun and social aspects alongside the challenge. Outdoor sports continue to appeal to well-educated women, as the majority of women take up outdoor activities during college. In addition, women-only adventure groups have grown significantly, allowing women to experience these activities on their own terms.

High-Profile Symbolic Moments

Throughout the early 20th century, women's athletic achievements were rarely celebrated or highlighted at the national level. As was the case of the pedestriennes, these women's accomplishments were recorded in local newspapers but never made the history books. By the end of the 20th century, that trend was changing as scholars and women's right activists realized the importance of high-profile symbolic moments in women's sports. There are several high-profile moments in women's sport history during the latter half of the century, but the following two events stand out as examples of the ways in which the achievements of female athletes became much more than a simple sport achievement.

One of the most notable symbolic breakthroughs of women in sport was the competition between Billie Jean King and Bobby Riggs in 1973. Billie Jean King was the reigning Wimbledon champion and arguably the best female tennis player of the time, while Bobby Riggs had been on the top of the male circuit in his prime. Riggs challenged Billie Jean King and, with a crowd of 30,000 and television audience of nearly 50 million, King swept Riggs with a three-set victory (Wertheim, 2012). Huge strides were made with this victory as King fought to prove women were equal to men on the playing field of sport. King received mixed reviews after the match, with critics asking if beating a man twice her age made the match credible, while women fighting the same fight for equality praised King for her bravery and victory. The King versus Riggs match was the first of many strides women have made in the landscape of sport.

Following King's matchup against Riggs, the next societal phenomenon redefining societal norms of gender construction was the 1999 Women's World Cup Soccer Championship. The event was declared as the "largest women's sporting event in history" as every game was broadcast on national television with 40 million U.S. viewers (Longman, 2009. The final match was a battle between the United States and China with a 4–4 tie, leading into penalty kicks to decide the champion. With 90,185 fans in attendance at the Rose Bowl, Brandi Chastain smashed her final shot into the back of the goal, celebrating with ripping off her jersey (revealing her sports bra) and sliding to her knees followed shortly by a pile of teammates (Wahl, 2015). The United States was victorious and Chastain's shirtless celebration was the headline of every newspaper and magazine. While many praised the team for their championship title, several criticized Chastain's celebration with disproportionate presentation of the sexuality and attractiveness of the athletes rather than their athleticism (Messner, Duncan, and Cooky, 2003)—even though male soccer players removing their shirts in celebration was common. These highly public displays of female athleticism have impacted the current landscape for girls and women in sport. Role models are important, and seeing what is possible allows upcoming generations of girls and women to see sport and physical activity in a plethora of forms as normal.

References

Bell, Richard C. 2007. "A History of Women in Sport Prior to Title IX." *The Sport Journal*, 10(2). http://thesportjournal .org/article/a-history-of-women-in-sport-prior-to-title-ix/. Accessed on June 22, 2017.

Buchanan, Maggie Jo Poertner. 2012. "Title IX Turns 40: A Brief History and Look Forward." *Texas Review of Entertainment & Sports Law,* 14: 91.

Cahn, Susan K. 2015. *Coming on Strong: Gender and Sexuality in Women's Sport.* Urbana: University of Illinois Press.

Chatziefstathiou, Dikaia. 2008. "Reading Baron Pierre de Coubertin: Issues of Gender and Race." *Aethlon,* XXV: 2. http://library.la84.org/SportsLibrary/Aethlon/2008/AethlonXXV2/aethlonXXV2i.pdf. Accessed July 9, 2017.

Gerber, Ellen, et al. (Eds.). 1974. *The American Woman in Sport.* Reading, MA: Addison-Wesley.

Gipe, George. 1977. "Mary Marshall Was Strides Ahead of the Times When She Beat a Man." https://www.si.com/vault/1977/10/24/622007/mary-marshall-was-strides-ahead-of-the-times-when-she-beat-a-man#. Accessed on July 10, 2017.

"Girl Wrestlers to Perform for Balto, Frontier's Club." 1953. *Afro-American.* November 21.

Guttmann, Allen. 1991. *Women's Sports: A History.* New York: Columbia University Press.

"Key Dates in the History of Women in the Olympic Movement." 2017. https://www.olympic.org/women-in-sport/background/key-dates. Accessed July 11, 2017.

King, Ivora. 1931. "Feminine yet Athletic." *Baltimore Afro-American.* September 19.

Longman, Jere. 2009. *The Girls of Summer: The US Women's Soccer Team and How It Changed the World.* New York: HarperCollins.

Lucas, John, and Ronald Smith. 1982. "Women's Sport: A Trial of Equality." In R. Howell (Ed.), *Her Story in Sport: A Historical Anthology of Women in Sports* (pp. 239–265). West Point, NY: Leisure Press.

Mak, Jennifer Y. 2006. "The Impact of Title IX on Athletics Development in the United States." *Journal of Physical Education & Recreation*, 12(1): 34–38.

Markula, Pirkko. 1995. "Firm but Shapely, Fit but Sexy, Strong but Thin: The Postmodern Aerobicizing Female Bodies." *Sociology of Sport Journal*, 12(4): 424–453.

Martin, Michael. 2012. "Title IX Turns 40, but Has the Field Leveled?" NPR, Tell Me More. http://www.npr.org/2012/06/21/155504670/title-ix-turns-40-but-has-the-field-leveled. Accessed on June 27, 2017.

Messner, Michael A., Margaret Carlisle Duncan, and Cheryl Cooky. 2003. "Silence, Sports Bras, and Wrestling Porn: Women in Televised Sports News and Highlights Shows." *Journal of Sport & Social Issues*, 27(1): 38–51. doi:10.1177/01937325022395.

Paraschak, Victoria. 1990. "Organized Sport for Native Females on the Six Nations Reserve, Ontario from 1968 to 1980: A Comparison of Dominant and Emergent Sport Systems." *Canadian Journal of History of Sport*, 21(2): 70–80.

Park, Roberta J., and Joan S. Hult. 1993. "Women as Leaders in Physical Education and School-Based Sports, 1865 to the 1930s." *The Journal of Physical Education, Recreation & Dance*, 64(3): 35–40.

Parnther, Ceceilia, Jennifer Deranek, and Scott Michel. 2014. "Title IX and the Impact of Athletic Leadership," *The Hilltop Review*, 7(1): Article 8. http://scholarworks.wmich.edu/hilltopreview/vol7/iss1/8. Accessed on June 2, 2017.

Peacock, Louise. 2012. "Olympic Legacy Risks Failing Women." *Daily Telegraph*, October 24. http://www.telegraph.co.uk/women/womens-politics/9630230/Olympic-legacy-risks-failingwomen.html. Accessed on July 15, 2017.

Radford, Peter F. "Women's Footraces in the Eighteenth and Nineteenth Centuries: A Popular and Widespread Practice." *Canadian Journal of History of Sport*, 25 (1994): 50–61.

Sack, Allen L., and Ellen J. Staurowsky. 1998. *College Athletes for Hire: The Evolution and Legacy of the NCAA's Amateur Myth*. New York: Columbia University Press.

Wahl, Grant. 2015. "How the U.S. Women Won the 1999 World Cup." https://www.si.com/soccer/2015/07/02/si-vault-women-world-cup-1999. Accessed July 15, 2017.

Warner, Patricia Campbell. 2006. *When the Girls Came Out to Play: The Birth of American Sportswear*. Amherst: University of Massachusetts Press.

Wertheim, L. Jon. 2012. "When Billie Beat Bobby." *Sports Illustrated*, 116(19): 60–61.

2 Problems, Controversies, and Solutions

Introduction

At the 1928 Olympic Games in Amsterdam, women were allowed to compete in the 800-meter running event for the first time. The story of the final race was written in several newspapers upon completion of the race. *New York Evening Post* journalist, John Tunis, reported, "Below us on the cinder path were 11 wretched women, 5 of whom dropped out before the finish, while 5 collapsed after reaching the tape" (as cited in Robinson, 2012). The *Daily Mail* in England used the "spectacle" to make the case that women would age faster if they ran further than 200 meters. During the early 20th century, men wrote the stories about women's sport. Today, careful reviews of the photographs and film, along with personal accounts of people who attended those Olympic Games and witnessed the race, have a much different story to tell (Robinson, 2012). There were only 9 women competing in the final. All of them finished, and only one fell after she crossed the finish line because she was trying to edge out her teammate for fifth place. She got up within a couple of seconds. At the same Olympic Games, the men's 5,000-meter silver medalist finished, walked to the infield, and lay down for a while. Not one story was written about the "collapse" of the male runner.

The early stories of female athletes reflect strong cultural views about women. With the growth in women's sports and

---

Women compete in the "Tour de Gastown" bicycle race through Vancouver, Canada, in 2008. (Sergei Bachlakov/Shutterstock)

the increasing athleticism of female athletes, new stories are being told. While records and amazing athletic performances are at the heart of the modern story of women in sport, these long-held cultural views still shape how women experience sport. This chapter details some of these issues and problems. However, with new voices, perspectives, and attitudes, and increasingly raised awareness, women's sport is gaining legitimacy and solutions are emerging.

Gender Equality in Sports and Why It Matters

There is no doubt that sport is a powerful cultural institution in the United States. Sports matter as a symbolic representation of what it means to be an "American" (Morgan, 2006). For most Americans, sports are a visible reminder of meritocracy; that is, the idea that through hard work and fair play, a winner can be determined. Winning is the epitome of American "success." In the context of sports, winning carries psychological weight as well. Fans are sad when their teams do not win and elated when they do. Schools, universities, towns, cities, and nations rally around their favorite sports teams, coming together in ways that few other cultural institutions can. Coakley, Hallinan, and McDonald (2011) point out that not only do sports provide images of "success" to Americans, but they also support societal values such as hard work, toughness, resilience, perseverance, remaining calm under pressure, and self-discipline. Within this cultural backdrop, many scholars argue that attaining gender equality in sports matters to helping change larger societal views of women in general.

Specific reasons for why this change is needed emerge from the intersection of sports and business that are evident in everyday life. One of the most prominent ways that sports are embedded in everyday business are the sport metaphors prominent in business. Executives and managers often use language such as "winning" contracts, "stepping up to the plate," "coming down to the wire," "skate to where the puck is," and particular assignments as being "in your wheelhouse." If sport is universally associated with masculinity, these everyday terms and related values remain associated with male and men. Also, many businesses offer millions of dollars to get high-profile athletes to represent their products and services. Most of these endorsements are to male athletes. Perhaps most notable are the parallels between what is thought to bring about athletic and business success. Given the connection between sport and masculinity, these attributes are thought to occur naturally in men, especially men who have participated in athletics. These attributes are not by default attributed to women. In sum, the fact that "we embrace athletic achievement as more than it is, as a sign of human superiority" (McDonagh and Pappano, 2007, 234), and that the attributes associated with athletic achievement are culturally understood as male characteristics is problematic for women.

Achieving gender equality in sport is an important step to associating athletic success with girls and women. One first small step is to directly link successful female athletes to business success. Ernst & Young (EY) is one company that is doing exactly that. In its 2013 study about how sports participation connects to business leadership and working on teams, it found that 55 percent of executive-level women had a sports background, while 39 percent of female managers believed that their participation in sport helped them in business. In particular, survey results from both women and men revealed that executives and managers believed that their sports participation developed high-level teamwork functioning and the ability to problem-solve under pressure. However, realizing that female athletes did not benefit from these connections like men did, EY implemented a program to be more proactive about helping female athletes. EY created the Women Athletes Business Network Mentoring Program in partnership with the International Women's Forum. In this program, EY is purposefully bringing highly successful female athletes into the business world. The program connects 25 top female athletes each with female senior executives in businesses across the globe. However, linking female athletes directly to business success will be less impactful as long as men's sports continue to be viewed as the standard. Even though there *are* highly successful female athletes and there *are* many women in business who value their sports participation as part of their corporate success, until women's sports are valued on par with men's sports, the connections between sport and business will remain hidden and underappreciated. Despite recent gains in women's professional sport such as soccer, basketball, tennis, and golf, men's competition is viewed as more serious. Therefore, a critical second step is destabilizing the message that male sports are "the standard." When women's sports become equal in terms of legitimacy, women are more likely to gain parallel equal footing in other spheres of life.

Sex-Segregated Sport and Inclusion Initiatives

Sex segregation is pervasive in sports at every level. The primary argument against sex integration in sport (women and men playing on the same teams) is that girls and women are not as strong as boys and men. There are several assumptions at work here. First, the idea that girls and women would be injured is a protectionist attitude. Under the notion of concern for girls and women's general health, not directly tied to the fact that women are the childbearers, still lies the tendency to protect girls and women from harm. Recent data show that sport injury rates are different for women and men, and that each gender is prone to increased risk of injury in different areas. Sports medicine experts argue that attending to the differences is important, especially as girls and women have only been participating at high levels and in great numbers for a much shorter time than men. Thus, there is need to look at unique factors based on gender. The second assumption that undergirds the argument is that because girls and women are not as strong, they could never compete at the same level as men. This thinking has two outcomes. One outcome is that if girls and women could never compete at the level of men, then it is not worth supporting them in such efforts. The mentality is that girls and women are inherently less strong, and no amount of effort or training would help girls and women reach a comparable level of strength. The second outcome is that due to their lesser strength, the prevailing thinking is that girls' and women's sports are not really important or interesting. This attitude is pervasive when it comes to the "selling" of women's professional sports. The third outcome is the belief that women who are good enough to compete with men must want to be men or are suspected of being men.

Such suspicions drive policies around sex testing at elite sport events such as the Olympics. The efforts are aimed at ensuring sex segregation in sport. As such, there have been numerous efforts to confirm sex at elite sport in order to ensure that women and men are not competing with each other. The International Olympic Committee (IOC) has instituted several iterations of sex testing to confirm sex prior to competition. Due to the asymmetrical belief of male superiority, sex testing is only ever done on those who identify as female. The idea is that men would want to compete as a woman believing that their chances for success are far better because they would have a "natural" advantage. Prior testing has included physical examinations in which doctors verify that typical female organs are present. Another form of testing has been chromosome testing. Finally, the current form of testing has to do with testing testosterone levels. Given that testosterone is associated with muscle mass and strength, there are identified levels of testosterone foe males and females. However, at least one study by British endocrinologist Peter Sonksen has shown that about 25 percent of male Olympians did not test in the male range of testosterone. Furthermore, 5 percent of female Olympians tested in the male range and 6 percent of male Olympians tested in the female range. Therefore, testosterone, the strength hormone, may not matter at all for elite performance. Findings indicate that such is the case because not all sports rely mostly on strength. In fact, most sports rely on a complex mix of technique, strategy, agility, reaction time, and strength. Shaffer (2012) argues that even if some women have naturally higher testosterone levels, why should they be excluded when other types of naturally occurring physical advantages are allowed. Examples are variations among athletes regarding aerobic capacities and other conditions that make individuals tall and therefore better suited for sports such as basketball or rowing. Finally, biology professor Anne Fausto-Sterling has found a continuum of biology regarding sex, not two distinct categories. The variations occur with respect to testosterone, hormones, and physical features of anatomy and reproductive organs. Given these core beliefs about women's and men's biological differences, and the extent to which sex segregated sport is maintained, sex integrated sport remains an outlying idea.

In *Playing with the Boys: Why Separate Is not Equal*, McDonagh and Pappano (2007) argue that sex segregation is a problem on many levels. They note that there are two different types of sex segregation in sport. The first type is *voluntary* segregation. This type often emerges when a marginalized group decides voluntarily to create a segregated experience. Existing women's colleges today fall under this category. They are created out of choice, and women choose to attend based on the idea that they can gain strengths and knowledge in ways better than they could in a coed school. Girls' sport empowerment programs are another example of voluntary segregation.

The second type of segregation they identify is *coercive* segregation. This type is segregation based on criteria that everyone must follow without regard for choice. It is this type of segregation that McDonagh and Pappano argue sustains the belief that women are inferior to men. They make the case that as long as sex segregation in sport is institutionalized through legal means and concomitant organizational policies, unequal perceptions of women and men will prevail, most especially as sport is a highly visible and important social and cultural institution. McDonagh and Pappano argue that basing sports participation on a single factor (such as "female" versus "male") perpetuates inequities in profound ways. The fact that women must pursue legal means to get permission to play with boys and men "naturalizes" men's privileged position in society. Even if a girl has demonstrated an ability to play equal to or better than a boy, she is often denied access unless policies are changed or a court ruling allows it.

Critical to their argument is the idea that coercive sex segregation is based on three "flawed" assumptions: (1) women are inferior to men, (2) girls and women should be protected from injury in sport, and (3) it is "immoral" or simply "just not right" that girls and women compete with boys and men. McDonagh and Pappano note six different ways that sex segregation is institutionalized in sport. The three assumptions above are woven into the fabric of the various ways. The policies in place are thought to protect and preserve what exists as true sex differences. However, their point is that the current sex-segregated ways actually continually *construct* differences. The aim of highlighting the coercive ways that sex-segregated sport persists is to identify the underlying assumptions clearly so that they may be challenged in ways that help shift the reasons for sex-segregated sport from cultural constraints to purposeful opportunity.

First, there are often different sports for girls and boys. Baseball is for boys and men, while softball is for girls and women. Often this comes into play when schools must offer equal sports opportunities for women as men. The sports that are offered may end up being quite different. Such thinking has historical precedents. For instance, 17-year-old female pitcher Jackie Mitchell was contracted to play in AA baseball in 1951 based on her ability. During an exhibition game in 1952, she struck out Babe Ruth and Lou Gehrig, upon which her contract was canceled. The newspapers publicly stated that baseball was "too strenuous" and that Ruth and Gehrig did not really try. Other proof that girls and women do have the ability to play with boys and men is often met with similar resistance. Mo'ne Davis was the first female pitcher (girl or boy) to pitch a shutout in Little League history. Her accomplishments were embraced, with several commentators expressing the idea that "throwing like a girl" had taken on new meaning. Perhaps even more significant was the acknowledgment that it was Davis's precision, not her strength, that was her forte. Such acknowledgments reinforce the idea that strength may not be the most critical factor in sport success. The key is that the public view it that way instead of reinforcing the idea that women are not strong, and success through other means is less valid.

Second, when women and men participate in the same sport such as soccer, tennis, and golf, the competition is divided into women's and men's teams. In these instances, the men's game is often noted as the standard by which all other play is judged. This is reinforced by the fact that facilities for boys and men are often better. Facility differences are prominent in collegiate sports as well as professional leagues. For example, men's collegiate teams often have better locker rooms and better arenas, courts, or fields compared to the women's teams. The rationale is frequently that the men's teams will bring in more revenue, but there are fewer than 12 athletic departments whose men's teams fully support the athletic department and where the revenue and benefits of the men's program far outweigh the costs. Another way that men's teams are positioned as superior is by the pay differential in professional sports. The assumption is that the men's games are more valuable, marketable, and higher-level play and they are deserving of more money because no one wants to watch women play. Recent research shows this is not the case. The 2015 Women's World Cup soccer final was the most watched soccer game in the history of television in the United States. Research from the Tucker Center for Research on Girls and Women in Sport shows that people do want to watch women's sports, but the assumption of inferior play prevents substantial sponsorships and endorsements. In this case, it seems as though the lack of sponsorship and money put into women's sports is not market driven, but rather culturally driven.

Third, women and men may play the same sports, but often the rules for each sex are different. That is, women often still have different or modified rules than men. Often these rules do not make much sense, but the result is that the women's sport is generally considered "lesser." In Grand Slam tournaments in tennis, the women play two out of three sets while the men play three out of five sets. This has nothing to do with what women would be willing to play or even want to play. The rules were established at a time when society was protecting women from too much exertion. Other rules are simply different—such as in gymnastics, where the women's and men's events are entirely different. Even in the floor event that takes place on a tumbling floor, women do their routines to music while men do not. Finally, women's and men's teams may play for different amounts of time. For example, the National Basketball Association (NBA) teams play four 12-minute quarters, while the Women's National Basketball Association (WNBA) teams play four 10-minute quarters. Distances are different as well. The Olympic mountain bike race for women is 30–40 kilometers. The men's race is 40–50 kilometers. This occurred in a relatively new sport in which new rules could have been established. Other sports such as flatwater kayaking, rowing, road bike racing, and swimming have different distances for women and men, with the men's being longer. Other events such as archery and shooting are also segregated even though there is no sex advantage for men. One study showed that the most significant performance factor in shooting was the length of the barrel of the gun, not the sex of the competitor. There are a few sports that have been gender integrated for some time. These are typically sports such as equestrian events, because the performer is considered to be the horse, not the person.

The fourth way that sex segregation plays out in sport is in instances in which women and men participate in the same sport, but there are gendered expectations for how women and men present themselves. For instance, McDonagh and Pappano observe that in men's gymnastics, men are judged on their abilities to perform "substantial difficulty" whereas women are to adhere to "grace" and "dancer-like" movements. Such current thinking clearly extends from the turn-of-the-century efforts to keep women from looking too masculine when competing in sport or participating in physical activity. Other manifestations of this type of segregation are the various ways that women must appear as athletes in the rules and regulations. Figure skating requires women to wear outfits and wear makeup, all to accentuate their femininity and lend to the notion that they must appear graceful. While "graceful" is desired for women, it is not equally attributable to men or perceived as a worthy "male" athletic style. Men who exude this type of athleticism are "lesser" men and perceived as gay.

Fifth, many women's and men's pair events or coed competitive events frequently prescribe roles for male and female competitors that are gendered. For instance, in pairs figure skating, the rules state that a man must be able to hold and throw the woman into the air. This language seems innocuous at one level. As McDonagh and Pappano (2007) point out, the rules could as easily state that the stronger partner does the lifting and throwing. In that scenario, a stronger, taller woman could easily "throw" a smaller, lighter man. Further analysis suggests that eliminating the specific sex roles all together would be more fitting. As they note, "Why not let same sex-pairs compete in Olympic figure skating?" (14). A rule change to any kind of "pair" could open up a whole new way of competing, opening up numerous possibilities for all competitors. Finally, McDonagh and Pappano (2007) note that a sex-segregated structure prevails even in athletic events in which "men and women compete in the same sport by the same rules at the same time, but the event is structured as two distinct contests" (14). These events are often endurance or adventure-type events such as marathons, ultramarathons, and "Tough Mudders" in which women and men take off from the finish line simultaneously and complete the same course. An exception to starting simultaneously in these endurance events are at elite marathon races. Typically, at the international level, the women's and men's starts are staggered with the women starting earlier. However, all other competitors begin at the same time. In these events, final results are still posted by sex.

Benefits and Risks of Sport Participation for Girls and Women

Research shows that both benefits and risks are associated with sport participation for girls and women; however, the benefits typically outweigh the risks. Many of the benefits have been captured in the five Cs: competence, confidence, connections, caring, and character (Women's Sports Foundation, 2017). There are numerous physical benefits as well. However, sport participation is not risk free. One way to minimize the risks is to educate girls and women about possible risks so that they are more knowledgeable about what to look for when sport participation crosses the line from beneficial to problematic. In this section, the benefits and risks are organized by the following three categories: psychological, social, and physical.

One of the primary benefits of interscholastic or collegiate sport participation for girls is that female athletes tend to perform better in school. On the one hand, it is easy to understand that female athletes may simply be the type of girls who like to achieve, and thus the data are unsurprising. On the other hand, more recent research suggests that one of the benefits of sport participation for girls may actually give them an educational advantage over boys. Studies have noted that female athletes are more likely to be interested in and succeed in science and math. Although these relationships are merely suggestive at this point, there is the belief that such correlations may be the result of female athletes being more comfortable in male-normed social spaces, not only in the science, technology, engineering, and math (STEM) fields, but also in business. The latest survey of Fortune 500 executives (2014) showed that over 80 percent of the women in those roles had played sport throughout their high school days, and some even into college.

A second benefit is that female athletes often feel good *in* their bodies, and thus are more likely to have a stronger body image than girls who are not physically active. Very often this feeling good in their bodies translates to confidence. Notably, whether through perseverance, having achieved athletic goals, or feelings of having "given it their all," girls consistently report feeling strong as contributing significantly to their confidence and self-esteem.

Third, the Women's Sports Foundation reports that the process of developing sport skills allows girls to experience knowing that they can improve at anything given proper coaching and concerted effort. Furthermore, they note that sports also provide girls an avenue for practicing focus in a competitive situation. While boys have been able to develop these skills in organized sport for centuries, it is only recently that girls have been given similar opportunities. Even though there are other activities, such as drama and music, in which girls can develop the same skills, the cultural capital that sport carries in the larger society as well as its association with masculinity positions sport as uniquely beneficial for girls.

Female athletes may be at risk for psychological issues or poor mental health due to being overwhelmed by the demand of sport participation while also trying to be successful in school. Although not necessarily the cause of depression, girls and women already prone to depression may experience greater difficulty as a female athlete. While society in general is becoming more aware of depression as a biological and complex condition, the "toughness" attitude that prevails in sport can create the illusion that sport is not a safe place to talk about needing psychological help. The risk for depression is higher for female athletes than for male athletes. In particular, studies show that injured female athletes are more likely than male athletes to suffer from depression during a prolonged injury. Fortunately, many organizations such as the National

Athletic Training Association recognize that they play a key role in eliminating the stigma of mental illness or temporary bouts with depression so that athletes can get the help they need in order to return to their previous levels of confidence and performance.

In terms of the social benefits, studies conducted on youth and sport note that the primary reason girls and boys participate in sport is because it is "fun." Although "fun" comes from learning and developing new physical skills, fun is also derived from the social aspects of sport (Staurowsky, 2016). Even though it appears stereotypical, the socializing aspect of sport is particularly important for girls. This does not mean that sport participation is not serious for girls. Research shows that girls and women value both as an essential part of sport performance. The socialization aspect in sport allows girls to experience teamwork and support for each other. Such experiences also contribute to these girls' abilities later in life to support each other in workplaces. Some research shows that women in leadership positions in business often see other women as a threat to the few leadership positions that women seem to occupy. However, female athletes have the opportunity to develop socialization skills to support other women as adults in the workplace. In addition, socialization in sport results in strong social bonds. One outcome of these bonds for girls is that they can experience strong social support. Through strong social support while growing up, they learn to be resilient to the ups and downs of competition. Furthermore, these social connections support the positive sense of self more prominently for girls through participation rather than competence. As girls progress in their athletic abilities, however, competence becomes more valued.

Despite the many social benefits, there are potential negatives associated with the socialization processes related to sport. In particular, drinking and eating disorders are two behaviors that may pose more of an issue for female athletes. Isaac (2010) reported, "female athletes may drink in excess of 19 percent

more alcohol and experience greater drinking-related consequences than their peers who do not participate in college
athletic programs" (34) whereas male collegiate athletes drank
16 percent more. However, other research showed little correlation between female collegiate athletic participation and
alcohol consumption while still other research showed lower
consumption. Still, female athletes were more likely to engage
in binge drinking. Given the many factors that might explain
drinking behaviors, the data suggest that athletic participation is not necessarily a deterrent to drinking in college. In
2014, the NCAA conducted a survey among collegiate athletes regarding drinking behaviors, reporting that 33 percent of
female athletes participated in binge drinking. This percentage
was less than what was ten years earlier, when 41 percent of
female athletes reported similar behaviors. Some of the reasons
for binge drinking behavior in female athletes are (1) drinking is an easy form of "self-medication" in stressful environments such as collegiate athletics where students' schedules are
extremely busy, (2) certain sport cultures such as rugby, field
hockey, and lacrosse may encourage drinking, and (3) drinking
may help female athletes cope with injuries.

Furthermore, eating disorders for female athletes remain
a psychological risk. Among female athletes participating in
aesthetic sports such as gymnastics or figure skating, about
40 percent report issues with eating disorders. Approximately,
30 percent of female athletes in weight-class sports such as rowing, wrestling, and boxing suffer from an eating disorder while
that number drops to 15 percent in most team sports. Signs of
eating disorders include the following:

- Changes in attitude, being unhappy and impatient
- Drinking little water
- Excessive concerns regarding appearance
- Inability to recover normally from a workout
- More frequent muscle cramps and general fatigue

- Feeling faint or cold or having an increased inability to concentrate
- Withdrawal from social activities or not enjoying their normal social activities

For both of these possible risks, there are numerous resources available. Athletic departments already offer education and make resources known to athletes.

The physical benefits for girls who participate in sport include overall better health. Girls who are physically active tend to maintain healthy body weights. This remains true for girls and women who have larger bodies in order to participate in weightlifting or other sports that require larger bodies. "Health" can be achieved at many different sizes and weights for women. Being physically active reduces risks for diseases such as diabetes and heart disease. Studies show that many of the benefits of sport are more profound over the long term. Being physically active over a lifetime can benefit women. As more women are remaining physically active well into their fifties, recent research shows that these women are more agile and have better core strength that helps with overall movement and balance. In San Diego, there is a very active Senior Women's Basketball Association, which offers competitive basketball for women aged 50–59. Other activities such as yoga, gym activities, and walking are popular among older women. These aspects are important to being able to continue with daily activities as well as allow women greater enjoyment in sport throughout their lives.

The two most common physical risks for women in sport participation are anterior cruciate ligament (ACL) tears and concussions. Several differences in women's bodies make girls and women more prone to ACL injury. Studies show that women's muscle development is more varied, resulting in changes in their center of gravity as they become more physically active. Such changes require ongoing muscle development around the knee to accommodate for the different ways their bodies move. At the neuromuscular level, girls and women have less control in their knee movement. Compared to boys, they use their muscles to stabilize knees in asymmetrical ways. Female bodies tend to use their quadriceps more than their hamstrings to stabilize when jumping or changing directions. While female athletes tend to have more injuries than male athletes in similar sports, knowing the imbalances helps female athletes seek advice for how to strengthen and attend to neuromuscular differences. Although there is considerable information on concussions, less attention has been directed toward girls' and women's sports. However, recent research shows that girls and women take longer to recover from concussions than boys and men. The reasons for this difference are unclear, but muscle strength and hormones are thought to cause these differences. Nevertheless, gender-specific concussion protocols are developing as a result.

Black Female Athletes' Experiences, Marginalization, and Moving Forward

Black female athletes experience sport and physical activity in different ways than white female athletes. Different opportunities for athletic participation exist for black athletes for a variety of reasons. In addition, there remain negative stereotypes of black female athletes that constrain how younger black women might relate to athletics and physical activity. This section reviews the current state of collegiate sport for black female athletes and barriers to opportunities, and highlights some of the negative stereotypes reproduced in the media, the lack of black women in sport leadership, and possible ways forward to improve opportunities and experiences for black female athletes.

Since Title IX, black female athlete participation rates in college have increased almost 1,000 percent. As of 2015, black female athletes make up the majority of female athletes of color, representing 9.1 percent of all female athletes from

NCAA Divisions I, II, and III. Compared to their *nonathlete black* counterparts, they graduate from college at higher rates. However, they tend to graduate at levels lower than the *average* student body while white female athletes graduate above the national average. In addition, the number of sports in which black female athletes participate has remained limited. For the past two decades, over 65 percent of all black female athletes have participated in only two sports: basketball and track and field. Historically, these two sports have been offered and supported the longest in collegiate athletics. While there is growth in volleyball and soccer, black women appear to have much less support in pursuing a wide variety of sports. Although Title IX protects female athletes' scholastic and collegiate sport participation, federal law that supports educational opportunities for people of color is covered in Title VI.

Legal rights to pursue educational and athletic opportunities have provided more access to athletic participation for black women. Still, other barriers exist that narrow black women's choices. One barrier that exists is the fact that black female athletes experience both racism and sexism, which converge and intersect in unique ways. For instance, scholars have noted that feminism and efforts to bring more opportunities to women often do so without considering the unique challenges faced by women of color. Thus, race gets overlooked in many feminist movements and advocacy work. In addition, statistics show that black women are also overrepresented in the lower socio-economic class. These identities are experienced simultaneously for most black female athletes. In one study investigating the experiences of black female athletes (Harmon, 2009), findings revealed many ways in which black female athletes felt marginalized in the collegiate setting. First, they felt that the diversity of the student body was misrepresented during the recruiting process. For instance, they talked about how they met a few other athletes of color, but that when they arrived on campus, they learned they had met "all" of the minority athletes. Some athletes even experienced segregation practices such as eating in entirely different spaces as well as traveling in separate vans from white female athletes to track meets.

More significant are the different types of microaggressions that many female black athletes experience. Microaggressions come in three forms: assaults, insults, and invalidation (Allen and Frisby, 2017). An assault is a direct verbal or nonverbal act. For many collegiate female black athletes, research shows that racist assumptions are evident in their daily lives. Comments from teammates and coaches stereotype them as dishonest, lazy, poor English speakers, angry, not interested in academics, and loud, which were overheard on a relatively consistent basis, all of which negatively affected their collegiate and athletic experiences. One particularly offensive incident of assault occurred on sports radio when Don Imus and his cohost used overtly derogatory language to describe the Rutgers' Women's Basketball team during an NCAA championship game (Cookyet al., 2010). Following their loss to the University of Tennessee (predominantly white team), Imus and his host described the Rutgers University's female black athletes as "hard core hos" who look "rough . . . and got tattoos." The comparison to white female athletes became clear in the following statement by Imus: "That's some nappy-headed hos there. I'm gonna tell you that now, man, that's some—woo. And the girls from Tennessee, they all look cute, you know, so, like—kinda like—I don't know" (as cited in Cookyet al., 2010, 140). Initially, Imus contended that his comments were meant to be "amusing." However, given that "nappy" is historically a racist, derogatory word used to describe the texture of hair, and that "ho" is a shortened version of "whore," Imus's comments were clearly grounded in deeply held racist attitudes. On another level, talking about the appearances of both teams served to trivialize their athleticism and the importance of their performances in an NCAA championship. Imus eventually apologized, but ultimately kept his job with little to no penalty for such egregious comments.

Finally, black women are noticeably absent from sport leadership. During the academic year 2015–2016, only

10.9 percent of Division I women's basketball team were black women. This percentage is well below the percentage of black female athlete representation on basketball teams, which is close to 45 percent. In administrative positions, black women are virtually nonexistent. White women predominantly occupy the senior woman administrator position across all three divisions, representing between 84 percent and 94 percent, while black women represented between 11 percent and 3 percent. This trend is worse in other sport leadership contexts such as professional sports, youth sports, fitness, and outdoor pursuits.

Advocacy work for support of both black female athletes and sport administration positions begins with the understanding that marginalization occurs through small, subtle actions and behaviors. In particular, understanding how female black athletes are subject to at least two marginalized identities, female and black, is critical to advocacy work. Undoing these commonplace actions begins with understanding what those behaviors look like at the intersections of gender and race. Education about microaggressions and understanding the privilege of whiteness are critical steps. These efforts can be tailored to different ages and groups of people. In addition, the Women's Sports Foundation recommends taking several steps toward creating more racially and ethnically inclusive sport experiences and opening the doors for women of color to take on leadership positions. First, sport organizations should do a systematic analysis of how they currently represent female athletes of color in their media coverage. Specifically, athletic departments' promotional materials should include nonstereotyped imagery and language and should be authentically representative of experiences and contributions of athletes of color. Second, more women of color should be proactively recruited as coaches, administrators, and staff. These include making sure there is diverse representation among the candidates, but should also include training on hiring biases for those who make the decisions.

Homophobia, Lesbian Athletes, and Creating Inclusive Sport

Homophobia (intolerance or fear of sexual orientations other than heterosexuality) has persisted in women's sports because characteristics and desired values of sport are associated with male characteristics. This deeply rooted association of sport and masculinity creates tension for female athletes. The issue is that female athletes are thought to be presenting a masculine image, and traditional thinking about masculinity and femininity creates the assumption (conclusion) that female athletes must be lesbian. Of course, not all female athletes are lesbian, but heterosexual female athletes always *feel* the assumption. In many ways, this assumption would not create an issue for heterosexual female athletes except for the persistence of homophobia. In Pat Griffin's (1998) seminal book, *Strong Women, Deep Closets*, she puts forth the idea that homophobia has been employed as a "policing agent" to keep female athletes within gendered boundaries of ideal femininity. The "policing" takes the form of rules and policies about how girls and women should look when playing sport, from hair styles to uniforms. The key point here is that hyper-femininity reinforces the "ideal" female who is by default heterosexual. More subtly, homophobia can act as a "policing" force by creating the "desire" for heterosexual women to present themselves as clearly heterosexual. The desire not to be labeled "lesbian" runs strong throughout women's sport because the label alone can result in discrimination (Finket al., 2012). During the 1990s, lesbians were accepted in sport as long as they acted, behaved, and presented themselves as hyper-feminine (Anderson, Magrath, and Bullingham, 2016). More recently, remnants of homophobia in sport manifest in subtle comments about female athletes whose performances are exceptional or more aggressive in style. Often, their achievements are described as manly, and lesbianism is assumed. Such comments marginalize their achievements and reinforce heteronormativity because of the belief that if one is fully female, then high-level athletic performance is unattainable (Spaaij, Farquharson, and Marjoribanks, 2015). Put simply, the prevailing "logic" is that to achieve athletic success, a woman must be "manly" because men are naturally superior athletes.

Anderson, Magrath, and Bullingham (2016) trace the history of homophobia throughout the 1990s, noting a sharp decline at the level of society. Furthermore, their research shows an even steeper decline in homophobia in sport since 2000s, especially for men. Based on research conducted between 1999 and 2011, there is strong evidence that when gay male athletes come out in less aggressive sport such as cross country running, or in sports that are not high profile, it is "not a big deal." Research on openly lesbian athletes is nonexistent during this same time period, while there are a few studies conducted on lesbians in athletic departments as coaches and administrators. Insights from this gap in the literature come from a study conducted in 2015, in which Anderson and Bullingham analyzed interviews from lesbian athletes conducted in 2002. While findings showed a growing acceptance of lesbians on sport teams, unlike their male counterparts during this same time period, overt hostility was still experienced by openly lesbian athletes. This was not the case in Anderson's research, in which no openly gay male athletes experienced overt hostility. While there was increased acceptance, several lesbian athletes were ostracized from their teams in hostile ways. After coming out to her coach when he was complaining about her short hair, one lesbian athlete went back to her car to find that all four tires had been deflated and windows broken with a note left that said, "die dyke" (Anderson, Magrath, and Bullingham, 2016, 72). Other openly lesbian athletes recalled that they were left out of normal socializing with teammates unless it was directly tied to official team activities. In particular, no heterosexual female athletes would sleep in the same bed as the lesbian athletes on road trips. These findings contrast those found with male athletes in the United Kingdom, but align with male athletes in the United States. Furthermore, there were instances in which lesbians were out to teammates who were accepting, but not out to their coaches. One athlete recalls being called into the coach's office and being asked if she were a lesbian. She denied it at the time, and her instinct to hide this information was affirmed when the coach said he was relieved because it would be unfortunate if such "a nice girl from a nice family" (75) were homosexual. Finally, Anderson and Bullingham (2015) found some acceptance among coaches and teammates evidenced by general acceptance. One athlete talked about how she felt comfortable talking about her girlfriend and did not feel as though her teammates treated her differently after coming out. However, most of the interviews showed that tolerance was more prevalent than inclusive attitudes. A "don't ask, don't tell" mentality prevailed. One phenomenon attesting to the "don't ask, don't tell" mentality was the fear of negative recruiting. Negative recruiting happens in women's collegiate sports when other coaches tell their recruits not to sign on to another college or university because there are lesbians on the team and/or the coach is lesbian. Thus, silence was a strategic recruiting practice.

Research since 2012 indicates more favorable team climates for lesbian athletes in university settings, but administrations are slower to follow. Coming out to teammates seems to be much less of an issue than in prior decades. More recent studies (Anderson, 2014; Finket al., 2012) show increasing inclusivity and acceptance of lesbian athletes. What has changed is the idea of coming out. Prior studies indicate extreme apprehensions around coming out to teammates. Such decisions were difficult, causing much angst until which time lesbian athletes described that they simply could not tolerate keeping their sexuality quiet anymore. The emotional toll that being silent took on their psyche was significant in prior decades. However, in these more recent coming-out stories, they are hardly stories at all. Instead, the most common way of coming out has been simply to mention a girlfriend in regular conversations about romantic relationships. For instance, one athlete came out by simply telling them that her girlfriend had given her a new lacrosse stick. Another waited until she had a girlfriend before coming out. The same level of acceptance is not experienced at the administrative levels. In her 2010 study, Kamphoff found that homophobia remains fairly strong within the coaching context. Negative recruiting remains a real issue, and lesbian coaches still feel as though being silent is required, even when athletes know they are lesbian. Taking an intersectionality approach, Walker and Melton (2015) also found that sexual orientation compounded gender in athletic administration roles. Relative to male administrators, women felt less comfortable than their male counterparts. However, lesbian administrators reported the lowest levels of feeling psychologically safe in their workplaces. Experiences of isolation were even more pronounced for black lesbian administrators, who felt unwelcome in both the white lesbian community and black administrators' groups.

In women's professional and elite sport, more female athletes have come out in a wide variety of sports since 2012. Some research shows that there are greater levels of comfort among heterosexual teammates with respect to having lesbians on their teams. The area that previously brought up the greatest concerns was sharing beds on road trips. The little research conducted at the elite level suggests that open lesbian athletes experience much less homophobia than in prior years. For instance, in the case of one internationally competitive athlete, her openness about her sexuality brought forth less tension and enhanced acceptance. She noted, "A lot of my team say that by meeting me and by exposure to me it has broken down a lot of the myths and stereotypes they had about lesbians" (Anderson, Magrath, and Bullingham, 2016, 99). However, high-profile female athletes have been more reluctant to publicly make a statement about their sexuality. Several reasons for this reluctance are (1) little time to conduct thoughtful interviews in which sexuality may come up, (2) fear that coming out may somehow delegitimize women's sports, (3) fear of losing sponsorships, and (4) lack of understanding or willingness to acknowledge sexual orientation among administrators and coaches. The latter point is justified by these individuals because of the belief that sexuality has nothing to do with performance. While this belief is true, the tangential negative effects of having to be silent and "self-police" one's behaviors and personal life take an enormous psychological toll on lesbian athletes, which negatively affects their overall performance.

Prior research in recreational sport suggested that during the era when "don't ask, don't tell" was normalized for women's sports teams, being in the closet was the easiest path for lesbians due to the potential of a hostile environment. More recent research shows that lesbian athletes feel it is much easier being openly out on a team rather than hiding their sexuality. Anderson and Bullingham (2015) found that lesbians described being angry and ashamed before coming out to teammates. Participants in the study described how their internal bitterness "rubbed off on their teammates and friends" (as cited in Anderson, Magrath, and Bullingham, 2016, 83), creating tension and negative interactions among teammates. One participant described how she would retreat from a teammate's friendship if she believed the teammate thought she was lesbian. Upon coming out, the athletes talked about how much more relaxed they felt, and being accepted by the team not only strengthened their friendships, but improved performance as well. There is some evidence that suggests having other openly out teammates helps subsequent athletes feel comfortable with disclosing their nonheterosexual identities. Other findings also suggest that the current cultural shift in much more gay-friendly attitudes in society provides enough of a sense of safety that lesbians do not feel afraid to come out to teammates. They expect they will be accepted.

Creating inclusive cultures in sport and within specific sports teams depends on several factors and appears to be a continuum. While there are significantly fewer hostile and homophobic sport environments for female athletes, there remain cases and instances of continued silencing and expectations regarding silence. Tolerant team culture is described as a safe place in which lesbian athletes can be out to teammates, but the assumption is that they will keep all information related to their sexuality publicly quiet. Inclusive team and organizational cultures are characterized by being able to express all aspects of one's identities freely, without fear of discrimination and exclusion. Inclusive cultures are evident when (1) it is no big deal to come out to teammates; (2) friendships remain intact, and even deepen, because trust develops; (3) lesbian athletes' girlfriends are welcomed into social circles; and (4) heterosexual athletes are open to challenging their own stereotypes about nonheterosexual orientations. One of the most interesting shifts in thinking about inclusive cultures regarding sexual orientation is the role that "homosexually themed language" (McCormack, 2011) plays in bringing teams together rather than making gay/lesbian athletes feel unwelcome. McCormack suggests that within a gay-friendly sport culture, using homosexually themed language such as "that's gay" or when heterosexual teammates banter about physical appearance of female athletes or engage in similar banter with their lesbian teammates as they would with each other about sexual relationships, the banter actually bonds the team. However, if these comments are made within a hostile, homophobic environment, the effect is highly negative. As noted, with the ever-increasing openness toward nonheterosexual orientations in society in general, being openly lesbian on athletic teams is easier. Still, compared to the data on gay athletes, there is much to learn about openly lesbian female athlete experiences. Walker and Melton (2015) note that creating inclusive cultures begins with strong, overt support from leaders in sport organizations. The research to date suggests that leadership in sport organizations remains the final area for change. As scholars note, however, it may not be that people become less tolerant as they age, but rather that, as the older generation retires, the new attitudes and social inclusion

World Cup soccer tournament, 2015 marked yet another year of dismal attention paid to women's sports with 3.2 percent of all sports stories dedicated to women's sports. Of that percentage, over 80 percent was about women's basketball. Of the total sports coverage, 75 percent was devoted to three men's sports: football, basketball, and baseball.

As of December 2013, women receive 43 percent of available scholarships and interest in female sports is skyrocketing. Forty percent of all athletes are women, but only 2–4 percent are represented in the media—and too often how they look is highlighted than their skills. More coverage would give fans more excitement according to the Tucker Center for Research on Girls and Women in Sport (The Tucker Center). The pattern is that women are portrayed off the court, out of uniform, and in fairly sexualized contexts. The amount of coverage has declined over the past 20 years, even though interest is high. This underrepresentation may not have an immediate impact, but over a long period of time, it can influence public opinion. The Tucker Center argues that the media itself is creating the perception of low interest. Women's sports can provide good human-interest stories as well as it can for men. In general, sports fans like to follow winners. However, without the coverage, few people even know about the women's sports teams that are winning. For example, the Minnesota Gophers Women's hockey team's Final Four undefeated season should have been televised not only in the Twin Cities, but fans throughout the nation should have been able to view it. Only Twitter covered it. As Toni Bruce, a sport sociologist, notes about the relative absence of women's sport in mainstream media, "the overwhelming male focus of this coverage is seldom questioned" (Bruce, 2008, 56).

There is some evidence that social media may lead to more balanced coverage. Chen and colleagues (2016) studied whether equal coverage between men's and women's basketball programs on the athletic department's webpages and social media websites exists. The collected data included traffics for the athletic website, Facebook, and Twitter pages of Southeastern Conference institutions. The findings indicated that there was slightly more men's coverage than women's (53 percent versus 47 percent). That is not a statistical difference, however. Among those 14 schools, 8 schools had more content coverage for their men's teams. Only six women's programs received more official website coverage than their male counterparts. The exact tendency also occurred regarding the number of total Twitter posts.

While the quantity of women's sport coverage remains astonishingly low given the relatively high participation rates of women, the *quality* of the media coverage is perhaps even more discouraging. In general, female athletes are frequently depicted as conventionally pretty, passive, submissive, and dependent (Van Zoonen, 1994). They are frequently captured in ways that reflect these stereotypical portrayals of women. On the *Sports Illustrated* covers from 2000 to 2011, women were promoted in more socially acceptable gender-neutral or feminine sports. One common way that female athletes are depicted in the media is through sexualization of their bodies. A noteworthy example is the 2015 *Sports Illustrated* cover with Serena Williams. Williams is one of the most decorated tennis players of all time. Despite her athleticism and record-shattering accomplishments, the 2015 cover featured Williams in stiletto heels, black lace, and lipstick draped across a throne. Williams's depiction was sexualized by the style of clothing and makeup, emphasizing a particular heterosexual attractiveness. In the case of Williams, the additional layer of being a black female athlete comes into play. Due to the stereotype that black female athletes are "animal-like" and "physical," the hyper-femininity on display is reflective of the strength of the stereotype. Critics of her muscular frame commented that she was "unfeminine" and her powerful frame made them "uncomfortable" (Spies-Gans, 2015). *Sports Illustrated*'s cover was crafted to allay discomfort that viewers *presumably* would have experienced. In addition, "successful female athletes who appear to fit dominant cultural ideals of femininity, heterosexuality, and attractiveness tend to receive the most coverage" (Bruce, 2008, 60). As many sport scholars note, despite the opportunity to promote female athletes as talented performers worthy of respect and emulation, media continues the sex-role stereotyping and sexualization of their bodies, and in the process devalues and trivializes their athleticism.

While the paradox of female athletic empowerment and traditional female heterosexual appeal is regularly emphasized in the media's representation of women in sport, not all female athletes agree. In their book, *Built to Win: The Female Athlete as Cultural Icon*, Heywood and Dworkin (1998) found that younger female athletes embraced showing off their bodies with little clothing, an attitude that Heywood and Dworkin argue is part of third-wave feminism in which capitalizing on their bodies economically and socially is viewed as empowering. Ultimate Fighting Championship (UFC) fighter Ronda Rousey exemplifies this third-wave feminist view. In 2013, she was the first ever female fighter signed by the UFC. Despite being an athlete in a hyper-masculine sport, Rousey has become the face of the UFC and is arguably among the most marketable female athletes in the world (Raimondi, 2013). Rousey emphasizes an aggressive and violent persona in person but is sexualized in advertisements or in the media. Her inclusion in *ESPN The Magazine*'s Body Issue in 2012 and 2013 featured semi-parted lips, hair curled, and pink fighting hand wraps. Rousey has been criticized for being too "manly" and not fitting in the traditional stereotype of femininity, but also paradoxically critics on the other side of the gender debate denounce her overemphasized femininity in media. As Rousey points out, "women don't have to trade their femininity for athleticism" (Quinn, 2012).

Yet, the question remains: Does sex sell women's sport? Most sport scholars argue that women will remain second class if they permit being constantly objectified. Furthermore, it may not be what fans want. In a study completed by the

Tucker Center for Research on Girls and Women in Sport, participants were surveyed about what kind of female athlete image makes them want to attend the games. The types of images Kane and Maxwell (2011) showed the participants were as follows:

- Athletic competence (sportswoman portrayed in uniform, on court, in action)
- Ambivalence (some indication of athleticism is present, but the primary image features a nonathletic, off-the-court, feminine portrayal)
- All-American "Girl Next Door" ("wholesome" representation with minimal or no indication of athleticism)
- Hyper-heterosexual (image of well-known female athlete explicitly linked to traditional heterosexual role such as girlfriend, wife, mother)
- "Sexy babe" (image of "hot" female athlete, which falls just short of soft pornography)
- Soft pornography (representation that reinforces sexual objectification such as Olympic sportswomen appearing seminude in men's magazines) (205–206).

The participants consisted of eight focus groups with individuals in two age range categories (18–34 and 35–55), male and female, and two levels of sport experience (high and low). Women and older men across both levels of sport engagement by far preferred the action skill images and were offended by "sexy babe" images. Only younger men chose "sexy babes." Regardless, the top overall choice for participants who identified their sport level as "high" was the "real athlete" photo. Most female athletes believe that the athletic competence images were healthier than the sexy body images. The findings from this study suggest that sexualized images of female athletes do not "sell" sport, showing that there is indeed demand to view female athletes as athletes in media.

Main (Male) Stream Sport Media

There seems to be a disconnect between what viewers desire and what sports media content decision makers believe viewers want. In the only study in which top-level media decision makers were interviewed about their perspectives on women's sport media coverage, Gee and Leberman (2011) found that, indeed, male ideology dominates. Their study consisted of asking the male decision makers in French media how they chose to present female athletes. In short, their view was that media presentations of female athletes should emphasize their femininity, physical appearance, attractiveness, and heterosexuality. In short, female athletes are "gender-marked" against the male norm. Soccer (football) has the hold on French sport media attention. Sports are thought to be subject to the selection criteria of newsworthiness, nationalism, and notoriety for media spots. Yet, these same standards are not applied to women's sports, and football reigns supreme. The reason given is "After all, our target audience is 80% men" (331). Additionally, the French culture says that some sports are simply "a male domain and it shouldn't be any other way" (333). In this way, the sport media decision makers continually deflect their ownership in women's sports coverage. Either the audiences themselves or national sport federations were blamed for the subpar coverage given to women's sports, not the sport media decision makers.

It is a reality that 90 percent of sports editors are men, and within a male-normed culture like that of sports, men almost always tend to objectify women. Even when viewing a team of truly skilled female athletes, males are likely to remark that, "They're just not really pretty." Some argue that getting more women into media leadership helps, but the evidence so far does not unequivocally support that. The percentage of women in sports media across all outlets, including newspapers, broadcasting, radio, sport information, and even blogging, is less that 15 percent. Even lower are the percentages of women who achieve positions of leadership, like editor or news director.

Staurowsky (2016) suggests that an increase of women in the sport media industry would broaden the coverage of women's sports. Founded in July 2010, espnW is an example of how a site with women as the majority in production roles does equate with more coverage. The branch of ESPN produces content that provides unique points of view on the sports stories that matter most to women. Their social media access promises broader coverage and positive branding of the varied sports female athletes are playing. However, the evidence whether targeted female fans of sport on espnW are served well is unclear. Adding the "W" didn't jumpstart any demand for more female sports. Meanwhile, the WNBA has been persistent in its efforts and now is finally about females on court and in action. Also, collegiate women's sport in the "March Madness" NCAA Basketball Championship tournament *is* covered like the men's now. Industry experts are working to try to understand the women's sport media terrain more clearly. The annual espnW: Women + Sports Summit, now in its seventh year, brings together top athletes and industry leaders for meaningful conversations around women and sports, and is the leading event of its kind in the sports industry.

Social Media and Raising Awareness for Change in Media Representations

During the Rio 2016 Olympics, the general public engaged in feminist debates about the differential coverage of female athletes as compared to male athletes. Through social media channels, a wide array of individuals made comments about the sexism embedded in many of the mainstream media's treatment of female athletes. In many ways, this reflects a much more gender-aware public. It also reflects the power of social media to reach a large audience around which a movement builds. In response to these critics, a backlash ensued in which other stakeholders framed the criticisms as being overly sensitive. In an effort to uncover the extent of the bias, Allen and Frisby (2017) analyzed mainstream Olympic coverage of female athletes from the 2012 London Olympic Games as well as the 2016 Rio Olympic Games. Their intent was to find out if the public was exaggerating their claims of sexism or not. Their content analysis considered sexism through the lens of "micro aggressions," subtle ways that women are subordinated, trivialized, sexualized, or ignored. They found that the number of microaggressions against female athletes in the media *increased* by a staggering 40 percent between the 2012 London Olympic Games and the 2016 Rio Olympic Games.

They analyzed seven categories of microaggressions: sexual objectification, second-class citizen, racist/sexist language, restrictive gender role, racist/sexist humor or jokes, traditional physical appearance, and focus on physical body or shape (Allen and Frisby, 2017, 6). Sexual objectification was not a common microaggression. The most prevalent microaggression was second-class citizen (inferiority). For example, the positioning of female athletes as inferior was best evidenced by the reference to a female athlete's husband/male coach as the reason she performed so well. Sexist language and restrictive gender roles were evidenced by comments that talked about female athletes' behaviors and whether or not they met female/feminine expectations. Finally, comments about body or shape were common for all female athletes, but more prevalent for female athletes competing in more "masculine" sports such as weightlifting. For instance, despite Morghan King's impressive athletic performance in weightlifting, many comments were made about her 105-pound body and blonde hair. Taken together, most microaggressions were grounded in comments that focused on the "limitations of being a female rather than respect for the skill and talent of the Olympian and/or her team" (5). Female athletes of color were subject to more racist/sexist humor and jokes.

Allen and Frisby (2017) express a hope that their statistical data might be used to educate people as well as serve as a call to action for change. They suggest that

- media channels commit to nonsexist language,
- leadership in sport organizations should ask for a review of materials with an eye toward noticing and eliminating sexist language and portrayal of female athletes,

- all persons responsible for writing content should take training on how to avoid sexist/racist writing,
- media contracts should be made to give equitable coverage
  for women's and men's sports.

Mary Jo Kane at the Tucker Center for Research on Girls and
Women in Sport recommends listening to the athletes themselves in terms of how they want to be represented in the
media. In one of the center's studies, findings showed that
most female athletes prefer athletic on-court competence plus
medium classy nonactive images. The remaining athletes preferred simply court competence. If promised the same amount
of financial reward and commercial exposure, female athletes
preferred portrayals of athletic competence rather than portrayals of femininity in endorsement campaigns. The most
effective advertisements in endorsing events like softball games
or tennis matches were those featuring the competence of the
athletes. Of the participants, 94 percent picked competence as
one of their choices and 67 percent selected athletic ability as
their only choice. In addition, the Tucker Center suggests that
female athletes themselves use social media to control the ways
they want to be represented. They warn, however, that doing
so strategically is important in order to avoid detracting from
the focus on sport. For example, the push from teams to have
female players "tweet" while playing in order to engage fans
may in fact trivialize their athleticism.

Finally, media specialists can leverage social media platforms
to change the way women's sports are covered. In their analysis
of Facebook posts as part of a larger study, Chen and colleagues
(2016) found an unexpected result, as 13 schools had more
posts related to women's teams than men's teams. The results
tended to support the vital promotional role that social media
may play to increase the awareness and popularity of women's
sports. In general, the schools' official website still maintained
an accepted coverage proportion toward both genders without
heavily gravitating toward men's teams. Practical implications

are addressed for better utilizing social media to promote women's sports and maintain gender equity in media coverage. Collegiate athletic departments should consider having full-time staff or recruiting individuals aware of gender balance in terms of both quantity and quality to manage their social media pages.

Professional Female Athletes: Paths toward Equal (Better)

Professional male and female athletes receive despairingly separate treatment in their respective sports. Female athletes are not only paid significantly less than their male counterparts; the conditions in which they compete are vastly different. The only exception to this is professional tennis, as female tennis players have been paid the same as men in Grand Slam events since 2007 (Women's Sports Foundation, 2017). The dominant perception is that women have not earned the right to an equitable allocation of resources (Hardin and Whiteside, 2009). Brook and Foster (2010) argue that these differences are the result of the demand for women's sports and not systematic sex discrimination. In their analysis of head basketball coaches' salaries, they determined that there was very little discrepancy between male and female coaches when revenue generation, coaching experience, and productivity were controlled for. Furthermore, they pointed out that a salary difference does not in and of itself mean that sex discrimination is occurring. In the case of the WNBA, they suggest that it is the inability of women to meet the male standard of performance that is responsible for the differences in salaries. In 2015, the minimum salary was just under $39,000, but for the NBA players, the minimum salary was just over $525,000.

Another example of differential treatment is the 2015 World Champion Women's Soccer team from the United States. The U.S. Women's National Team received $2 million from the International Association of Federation Football (FIFA) and played on turf fields while the men received $35 million from FIFA and only played on well-kept grass fields. In soccer, women earn a minimum of $6,842; men's salaries are at least $50,000 (Harwell, 2015). The Professional Golf Association (PGA) and Ladies Professional Golf Association (LPGA) have also been known for discrepancies for as long as the two organizations have been in existence. The total prize money for the PGA tour in 2014 was over $340 million, which is more than five times the total prize money budget of $61.6 million for the 2015 LPGA tour (Pay Inequity in Athletics, 2015). Hardin and Whiteside (2009) argue that cultural change must begin at the individual level, but there must also be institutional and societal support to change the landscape of professional sport. Indeed, it seems that recent changes have involved efforts at multiple levels.

Major strides in gender equity for women's professional sport occurred with Wimbledon's announcement in 2007 that, for the first time, it would provide equal prize purses to both male and female champions. While the three other Grand Slam tournaments had given equal pay to female and male champions for years, Wimbledon had held out. All that changed in 2007, and the year 2007 marked the first time all four Grand Slam events offered the same prize money (Pay Inequity in Athletes, 2015). Other international and national tournaments still have vastly different prize money for women and men. With such public attention to women's professional sport's equal pay movement, the World Surf League made a similar announcement in 2012 that both men's and women's championship tours would have equal prize money. Much of the pay inequality and limited access to resources currently extends from sponsorship, television, and attendance at women's professional sporting events. Men's professional sports receive massive sponsorship and television contracts that are paired with ticket and merchandise sales for their sporting events. However, men's events are promoted significantly more as well. Fink (2015) found that less than 1 percent of sponsorship and less than 2 percent of airtime is dedicated to women's professional sport. Furthermore, the history of women's professional sport is a fraction of the history of men's sport. Although the interest in women's sports is currently much less than men's sports overall, there is growing evidence that women's sport spectatorship is growing. An example of this growing viewership was the United States versus Japan World Cup Final in 2015. Over 25 million viewers watched this final Women's World Cup Soccer match, making it the most watched soccer match ever (male or female) in the United States. However, as Fink (2015) pointed out, few sponsors took advantage of this opportunity. In addition, 3.1 million viewers watched the 2015 NCAA women's basketball championship, and the Women's College World Series viewership outdrew the Men's College World Series by 31 percent. As Fink noted, corporations and media are missing out.

The following three stories detail some of the efforts toward equal pay for women's professional sports noted above. Each illustrate a specific route that women took or are taking to bring women's professional sport to a pay level that allows women to pursue professional sports opportunities and for fans to enjoy the athleticism and sport drama therein.

Venus Williams Levels the Grand Slam Playing Field

In 1968, the men's singles Open Tennis champion, Rod Laver, won £2,000, while Billie Jean King, the ladies' singles champion, won £750, only 37.5 percent of the men's prize. For the next several decades, Billie Jean King advocated for women's prize money equal to that of the male players. In 1998, Venus Williams was outspoken about the pay discrepancy at Wimbledon, publicly calling out the organizers for not following the example of the other Grand Slam tournaments, Roland Garros, the Australian Open, and the U.S. Open, which had already equalized the prize winnings for women and men. In 2006, Larry Scott, CEO of the Women's Tennis Association, decided to give his support officially to Venus Williams and encouraged her to become the spokesperson for a cause about which she was already passionate. With a deep sense of obligation to the legacy of Billie Jean King, Venus Williams became more strategic about her efforts. She lobbied British Parliament, UNESCO, and Fleet Street for financial parity. After a poignant letter to the *London Times* in which she called Wimbledon on the "wrong side of history," Venus won the support of Tony Blair, British prime minister at the time. When Culture Secretary Tessa Jowell lent her voice to the cause for women's equal pay, Wimbledon chair Tim Phillips, who was previously unmovable on the issue, knew anything short of parity would prompt a very public backlash. With support on multiple fronts, Wimbledon officials finally relented in 2007. That year Venus became the first women's champion to earn as much as the men's singles winner (Roger Federer).

The All England Club had previously refused to back down on the issue. Primary among its inner arguments had been the fact that men play best-of-five-set contests, while women only play best of three. In addition, Wimbledon chairman at the time, Tim Phillips, also cited club polls, indicating that men's tennis gave better value for money. In rebuttal to these long-held reasons for unequal pay, Williams made five main arguments during her campaign for equal pay at Wimbledon: (1) The U.S. and Australian Opens had treated both sexes equally for several years, while the French Open had recently paid both singles champions the same sum. (2) Women's tennis is just as compelling to watch as men's tennis. In the documentary *Venus Vs.*, one rally between Williams and Lindsay Davenport in 2005 was showcased and compared to the 2010 now-legendary Federer–Nadal final. The strength of that rally showed how compelling women's tennis can be at its best, every bit as equal to the drama of the men's tournament. (3) Venus argued in her *London Times* newspaper letter that "The home of tennis [Wimbledon] is sending a message to women across the world that we are inferior." (4) She also stated that, "With power and status comes responsibility. Well, Wimbledon has power and status. The time has come for it to do the right thing by paying men and women the same sums of prize money." (5) She also drew on the women's rights movement globally and concluded, "The message I like to convey to women and girls across the globe is that there is no glass ceiling."

Gaining support from high-profile individuals combined with the publicity surrounding her efforts, Venus Williams was able to amass significant public support. While Williams did not see herself as a women's rights crusader, she eventually came to the conclusion that her success on the court and passion for tennis made her the best spokesperson for the cause. Many, including Billie Jean King, believed that Venus Williams had the personality, and is gregarious and highly sociable, to have picked up King's lifelong work. Public opinion backed her and the agreeable solution rolled out.

U.S. Women's Soccer Leverages Legal Courts and Solidarity in Public Opinion

After the success of the U.S. Women's National Soccer Team at the 2015 Women's World Cup championships, with both a gold medal performance and record-breaking viewership, the discrepancy in pay and resources between the women's and men's national teams had reached an untenable level. After years of receiving low pay and playing on poor fields at subprofessional-level stadiums, the U.S. Women's National Soccer Team decided to take legal action to improve the situation. On March 30, 2016, five players from the U.S. women's soccer team filed a federal complaint of wage discrimination to the Equal Employment Opportunity Commission against U.S. Soccer, the governing body that pays both the men's and women's teams. In June 2016, a federal judge ruled that the world champion U.S. Women's National Soccer Team did not have the right to strike to seek improved conditions and wages before the Summer Olympics, seeming to end the prospect of an unprecedented disruption.

After official legal actions were taken, several players spoke up in mainstream media. In November 2016, CBS news magazine

60 Minutes landed them a spot on the traditional post-NFL Sunday show, making the case that women deserve to be paid not just the same as the men, but more. The U.S. Senate voted in favor of a resolution calling for equal pay for the team. The labor deal came a day after Equal Pay Day. Appearances on the *Today Show*, followed by conference calls with media, helped to make the team a brand. Additionally there were posts on Facebook; polls taken of fans and younger soccer teams; an essay penned by Carli Lloyd, cocaptain of the U.S. Women's National Soccer Team, in the *New York Times*, "Why I'm Fighting for Equal Pay"; and a large feature story in *NY Daily News*. Some of the complications and intricacies to work out revolve around the radically different pay structures between the women's and men's leagues. Men get a bonus for playing, but not a steady salary. For men, if they're not called into camp with the national team, they don't get paid. Given this system, the men's national team has much more roster turnover in a given year than the women's team. FIFA awards World Cup bonus money on an exponentially different scale: $35 million for the last men's champions, $2 million for the women's. U.S. men usually get high pay from their local professional clubs, while women's professional soccer is still a low-revenue enterprise in the United States and globally.

In order to improve women's professional soccer, a new collective bargaining agreement was approved in April 2017 that will last for five years through the next Women's World Cup in 2019 and the 2020 Olympics. In this new collective bargaining agreement, several areas have been improved for the players. First, several salaries will be paid directly from the Women's National Soccer League to key players, which takes some financial burden off individual teams that are functioning under tight budgets. Second, the players' association will gain control over licensing agreements beyond national team sponsors so that players have more control and say in those types of media arrangements. Third, there will be significant increases in players' salaries so that they can have more time to train and compete without having to hold down several other jobs. Fourth, per diem compensation for traveling to matches as well as travel and hotels will be increased and improved to the level of the men as well as two years of back pay for unequal per diems. Finally, there will be more financial benefits for pregnant or adopting players. There's no question this is a battle won. The larger war, however, continues: Until FIFA starts paying U.S. Soccer the same bonuses for men's and women's World Cup wins—a gap that currently spans tens of millions of dollars—unequal pay in soccer will remain a problem.

U.S. Women's Hockey Goes on Strike with Clear Goals for Equality

In March 2017, the U.S. Women's National Hockey Team threatened to sit out a major international tournament unless it was making progress in their negotiations with USA Hockey, the sport's governing body. The issue at hand was the fight for fair pay. The major tournament was the International Ice Hockey Federation's (IIHF) Women's World Championships taking place in the United States. These championships had taken place since 1990 and run every other year or so until 1999 when they began to be held annually. The U.S. National Women's Hockey Team had been world champions in the three prior years. Here, they were competing for their fourth consecutive win against Canada, the team with the most number of world championships. The players used this platform to put pressure on USA Hockey to agree to a better compensation and marketing plan for women's professional hockey.

The players decided to strike just prior to the championships. Representatives from each side made public statements that reflected the players' resolve as well as the commitment to keeping the best U.S. team on the ice. Dave Ogrean, executive director of USA Hockey, said that he wanted to avoid bringing in replacement players and voiced his commitment to coming to an agreement. The attorney representing the players noted that the women were committed to sitting out the championships because they all knew that the situation would not improve without this kind of action. The demands were fairly straightforward. The women wanted a $68,000 salary and the same treatment that the men get, including the ability to bring a guest to competitions, business-class airfare, and disability insurance. They also wanted benefits such as childcare, maternity leave, and the ability to compete in more games throughout the year. They also wanted better marketing efforts to grow the sport.

Three days prior to the start of the world championships, USA Hockey crafted a four-year deal that the national team could accept. One clear motive was to resolve the situation so that the best players of the United States previously selected to play in the upcoming IIHF World Championship could play. From the outset, USA Hockey had been clear it would not employ players. However, USA Hockey agreed to allocate more resources for direct athlete support and training. Most of the demands of the players were met. In addition, there was significantly better compensation upon winning at the largest international stage, the Olympic Games. The players negotiated total player compensation in an Olympic year of approximately $210,000 per player if the team attains a silver medal and $237,000 for a gold medal. Additionally, in a non-Olympic year, the players' demands resulted in approximately $146,000 per player for a silver-medal performance and approximately $149,000 each for gold in a world championship. The women will also get better marketing and promotion. Additionally, there will be a special group designed to help advance girls' and women's hockey. In a *New York Times* article, Dr. Mary Jo Kane commented that this agreement was important not only from the standpoint of better compensation and treatment, but also because "it's how people, women in particular, understood what it was they were doing and why they were doing it" (Berkman, 2017, para 5).

Women's Struggle to Attain Leadership Positions in Sport

Across different sectors in the sport industry, women are significantly underrepresented in sport leadership. As competitive and recreational athletes, women make up nearly 50 percent of participants on average. Yet, female representation in the leadership of the organizations that govern the sports in which they participate is significantly lower. The WNBA does well with almost 55 percent of the head coaches and 40 percent of the front office filled by women. The remainder of the major leagues (NFL, MLB, NBA, and MLS) has nearly zero female coaches. One exception is with the hiring of Justine Siegal in 2015 by the Oakland A's as a guest instructor in the instructional league. Front office staff range from 14 percent to 19 percent women. Collegiate sport is slightly better with around 43 percent female head coaches. However, there are fewer than 23 percent female athletic directors, and just over 18 percent of all colleges and universities have no women on staff. At the Olympic level, the IOC recently met its 20 percent goal of female membership, bringing the female representation at the highest level of governance for the Olympics to 22 women. However, some progress was made when three women were elected to the IOC's executive board, selecting El Moutawakel from Morocco as one of four vice presidents of the IOC. Out of the 29 IOC commissions, women make up 19 percent of the 442 positions available. Gathering the data regarding female leadership in sport requires searching various reports such as Acosta and Carpenter's "Women in Intercollegiate Sport Longitudinal Study" last conducted in 2014, the gender report cards from the Institute for Diversity and Ethics in Sport, and data directly from the IOC's Women and Sport Commission.

The question remains: With the significant growth in sport participation of girls and women, why is it that men predominantly oversee sport? Several sociological concepts have been employed to explain this gap. The following seven concepts illuminate various influences or ways of thinking that function as barriers to women attaining and staying in sport leadership positions: hegemonic masculinity, role congruity, double bind, homologous reproduction, maternal wall, bias blind spot, and benevolent sexism.

Hegemonic masculinity describes the type of masculinity that functions as the "norm" by which all other behaviors, attitudes, and beliefs are judged. Dominant ideas of masculinity include strong, aggressive, tough, strategic, assertive, emotionlessness, invulnerability, and risk-taking. At almost every level of play, these descriptions align with the traits most valued in sport even though there are other aspects (such as teamwork, cooperation, and humility) that are part of high performance. As such, sport is powerfully associated with masculinity. Given that the leadership in sport is mostly male, the underlying association of masculinity and sport is even stronger. This phenomenon can make it nearly impossible for men in positions of power to even consider women for leadership roles in sport. For example, Walker and Sartore-Baldwin (2013) found hegemonic masculinity at work in men's collegiate basketball coaching staff. The men interviewed thought that a female coach would not feel welcome due to the regular use of sexist language, the fact that getting hired would be unlikely, that male athletes would simply prefer male coaches, and that being a female coach of a men's team "doesn't register as an opportunity and they are just doing what they see" (310), which is that women coach women, but men coach women and men. The authors also found that the coaches they interviewed admitted that women coaching men is "something you don't even think about because it doesn't exist. It's not even like it's rare, it's nonexistent at the Division I level" (311). In many people's minds, coaching and male go together without question. Other research shows that women do not advance as easily in sport organizations due to the influence of hegemonic masculinity.

Role congruity is another explanation for the underrepresentation of women at the highest levels of sport leadership. This concept describes the situation in which men are more likely to be considered for leadership positions because they are viewed as having the characteristics of leaders. That is, the attributes most associated with sport are also thought to be good leadership attributes. Thus, men are viewed as being "congruent" with leadership strengths whereas women are not. Furthering this belief is the importance of task-oriented and "instrumental" leadership in sport organizations, which is thought to be a male strength rather than a female strength. The idea that men and women are "naturally" better at certain tasks than others is another aspect of role congruity. Studies show that female board members for sport organizations were frequently assigned more clerical or kitchen work in meetings and served in roles such as marketing while the men oversaw maintenance of facilities, finances, strategy, and external relations. In intercollegiate athletic administration, women held a greater percentage of support roles such as administrative assistant (92 percent), academic advisor (60 percent), compliance officer (53 percent), life skills coordinator (69 percent), and business manager (60 percent) (Burton, 2015). Men held more positions with power and decision-making roles such as athletic director (20 percent), associate athletic director (34 percent), assistant director of athletics (33 percent), fund-raiser or development (32 percent), and promotions or marketing manager (34 percent) (Burton, 2015).

When women do take on roles traditionally associated with men, they face a situation called the "double bind." This phrase means that women get caught between trying to fulfill their roles as sport leaders and their gender roles as women. The "bind" comes into play when they display the same masculine traits that men display as leaders, but are then disliked or criticized for being "too bossy." If they display more feminine traits, they are viewed as less competent because traits such as empathy, compassion, and being nice are not associated with "good" leadership. Interestingly, the sport context may be more open to more assertive women working in leadership roles. For instance, Mazerolle, Borland, and Burton (2012) found that being assertive and proactive in communicating clear expectations with coaches prior to the season was extremely helpful in gaining respect. Furthermore, when female athletic trainers displayed competence and confidence in their abilities, they were able to garner confidence from coaches. This runs counter to findings in other contexts in which an assertive and confident-appearing woman may come across as "bossy." That is, these traits are respected in sport in general, so when women display them in this context, their behaviors align with what men expect in this context. Another possibility is that depending on the culture of the specific athletic department, men are simply more used to seeing competent women today than 20 years ago. Welty-Peachey and Burton (2012) found that women are not always subject to negative attributions when displaying leadership associated with more "feminine" attributes. Their results showed that transformational leadership, which emphasizes collaborative and personal attention approaches, was equally favored as a preferred leadership style for women and men. Thus, there was no "penalty" for female transformational leaders in the sport context. These examples point to a changing landscape for women who want to work in sport.

Although acceptance of women working in the sport context is growing slowly, there remain barriers to getting hired and being promoted. One major barrier is that with men still making most of the hiring decisions, they are simply more likely to hire people like themselves. Known as homologous reproduction, recent evidence suggests that this practice persists. The latter phenomenon can be explained through homologous reproduction as well. That is, people tend be around people who are like themselves. In the instance of sport, studies show that the "good 'ole boys' club" is less about purposefully excluding women as it is simply about hiring and promoting other men without really thinking about because "they [men] just keep promoting men in all athletics. As the money and salaries go up, the men were getting those position[s], and they just kept helping each other" (Mazerolle, Burton, and Cotrufo, 2015, 76). Still, there is growing perceptions that society is changing. However, the numbers do not reflect this reality.

One explanation for this kind of thinking is the *bias blind spot*. The bias blind spot is the belief that one can make decisions objectively such that when it comes to hiring and promoting, people believe they are really hiring based on objective measures such as experience, competencies, and willingness to work hard. Despite having achieved all of the above, women often find they are still not able to gain access to leadership. While more men are supportive of women moving into leadership roles, they often fail to address the tangible criteria set forth for hiring or advancement that privileges men. Studies show that men supportive of gender equality do not review policies or unwritten but spoken standards of employment. For example, in the case of one sport organization that wanted to recruit women to its board, it had rather strict guidelines for a good "fit" that were outside the boundaries of competence and experience. The "competencies" articulated were that the woman should not be overly feminist, should be committed to sport, should not have children, should be well educated, and should have experience in high-level corporate positions. Such criteria automatically leave out many women who are not only qualified to serve on the board, but also could bring valuable insights. Interestingly, other research shows that men who express a commitment to gender equality are valued over men who do not. The bias blind spot also manifests in the rationale that if women were interested in working in sport, there would be more women already present. Scholars suggest that a deeper level of raised awareness, one that is accompanied by the various concepts that explain why along with "what" is happening, can reduce bias blind spots. Such efforts are thought to bring more clarity around the term "gender inequality." In several studies conducted in the United States and Canada, there seems to be some confusion about whose responsibility it is to achieve gender equality. Debates over whether or not the institution was responsible for enacting proactive inclusive policies or whether or not women needed more training and education in leadership development persist in many sport organizations.

In instances where men are sympathetic to women working in sport, they often resist being strong advocates for women because they believe that the sport business environment would be too tough and unfriendly. These beliefs translate into protecting behaviors known as *benevolent sexism*, which leads to proactive behaviors of keeping women where they are or moving them into roles in which they feel are less hostile. Perhaps the most significant manifestations of benevolent sexism are the ways that motherhood negatively impacts women aspiring to be leaders in sport. Research shows that women carry the primary load when it comes to family and children. Despite the fact that there are notable exceptions, women are culturally expected to take care of family. As a result, women often are not considered for positions because it is believed that they would not "want" those positions because of family obligations. In fact, much of the recent data suggest that sport organizations are unwilling to accommodate women's schedules with respect to family commitments. Some constraints emerge from the nature of sport, where games and competitions occur primarily on weekends and in the evenings. Despite these radically different time commitments, sport organizations are neither highly flexible nor proactive when establishing work policies and family benefits. There are notable exceptions, and women with children have simply moved from organization to organization until they found a supportive culture.

Although often referred to as a "fix the women" approach, there are several steps that women can take to be more strategic about navigating working in sport. Staurowsky and Smith (2016) suggest that women develop greater business acumen through education or deliberately seek out specific knowledge such as finance or negotiation skills. In addition, women should be strategic about being competent in the areas valued by the organization with respect to their specific job. Once a leadership position is attained, they can attend to making substantive changes. In short, women cannot create change easily without being in positions of power, so they must first get there. Perhaps the most significant change needs to occur at the cultural and organizational levels. One strategy that women and men have used to create small changes in culture is the "nudge technique." For instance, women are often ignored when they offer ideas in meetings, only to have their idea repeated by a man, which then gets attention. A nudge technique would be for the leader to acknowledge the earlier comment, and ask how the man's idea is different from what the woman just said. Nudge techniques consist of noticing small instances of bias and acknowledging them in the moment of occurrence. Finally, proactive engagement with raising awareness around gender bias with the aims of reviewing hiring practices, reviewing professional development patterns, and analyzing who and how decisions are made would potentially lead to changed expectations. Such changes would not only benefit women, but also benefit men, who may also not fit nor want to be confined to the narrow construction of hegemonic masculinity.

Constraints and Possibilities of Feminine Beauty and Joy in Sport

Questions of beauty and joy in sport are points of tension for female athletes in ways they are not for male athletes. The imperative for female athletes to present as feminine while participating in sport is not an expectation for male athletes. Their participation in sport de facto presents male athletes as masculine. As noted previously in this chapter, media predominantly focuses on the appearance of female athletes, assessing their feminine beauty, more than it focuses on their athleticism. The constraints felt by female athletes manifest in the trivialization of their athletic achievements and pressures to wear clothing for the purposes of the "male gaze." As noted by many feminists, the ideal feminine beauty serves to oppress women. The argument is that if women work toward attaining a female ideal of beauty shaped by and approved by men, they remain subjugated. Furthermore, the idea of joy in sport has most often been articulated as "fun," which is often positioned as the antithesis of competitive sport. How can female athletes be both serious athletes and playful, still garnering respect as athletes?

In her chapter titled "Studying Sport, Feminism and Pleasure," Jayne Cauldwell (2015) explores the notion of feminine beauty, offering insights into the possibilities of how female athletes "own" their feminine beauty by "claim[ing] enjoyment via the feminine" (67). Acknowledgment of beauty that is defined by sexist assumptions is a critical first step. Drawing on feminist theory, she suggests that beauty as *a feeling* is entirely different. This *feeling* cannot be explained easily by language nor can it be understood entirely through the lens of gender politics. That is, as Cauldwell explains,

> it is clear that women, specifically sportswomen, are so much more than passive, one-dimensional objects for the male gaze. In other words, Bartoli's [female French tennis player criticized for her masculine appearance] feminine and sporting subjectivities are far more intricate and complicated than Iverdale [commentator who spoke negatively about Bartoli's appearance] is able to impose. (67)

Cauldwell's point is that feminism might frame comments about female athletes as sexist, but engagement of feminism should not be directed at the men who "have it wrong." Instead, a feminist perspective might help recover the complexity of feminine beauty, pointing out that the "male" view is narrow. Underlying this idea is that feminine beauty is not something that female athletes should necessarily eschew, but rather become conscious of the various sources of their feelings of beauty, which, as suggested, can be quite complex and individual and come from many aspects of who they are. One sport that brings these kinds of complexities to the surface is roller derby. In this sport, women assert femininity through makeup, tighter shirts, nail polish, and other display of femininity. However, roller derby athletes also wear kneepads, elbow pads, helmets, and skate aggressively. Studies show that these athletes consciously push feminine displays to the point of "parody and mockery," playing with what it means to be feminine. Through these actions and "play" with femininity, they create new ways to "enjoy" being feminine.

There is little argument that sport entails joy and fun. However, these concepts are complicated when looked at more carefully. For instance, joy is most often associated with "play." While most individuals say they participate in sport because it's "fun," fun becomes complicated by the "sport ethic," which is characterized by such masculine attributes as the will to win, toughness, and perseverance. Given the pervasiveness of sport as an endeavor in which winning through a particular means is prioritized, joy becomes much more difficult to talk about or figure into how it contributes to sport excellence. The most common way of integrating sport and joy is to define joy as the enactment of masculinity. That is, joy is framed as "pushing through" and "toughness." In extreme sports, joy is risk taking and "living on the edge." From this perspective, joy in sport remains tied to a male norm. Feminist scholars have brought attention to the fact that there are multiple ways of knowing and that exploring women's ways of knowing opens up pathways to understanding not simply "women's" ways of knowing, but rather ways not constrained by masculinity. That is, exploring women's experiences of joy in sport can open up new ways of talking about, and perhaps experiencing, joy in sport.

In a study of high-performance female ultrarunners, Hanold (2010) found that joy was integral to these women's performances. One of the most common ways that joy was experienced was the *feeling* of strength. All eight elite female ultrarunners spoke of wanting to compete because "I'm strong." Another runner stated, "I feel super positive about the fact that my body is strong, I can fall really, really hard and just get up and go." Joy is intimately tied to strong for these women, which means that "strong" is not uniquely a male athlete "joy." Additionally, the joy of ultrarunning was constructed as a way to achieve success in racing. Despite the demands of ultrarunning (distance and terrain), these women talked about having "fun" on the course because of the beauty of the trail or the unique, varied terrain that changed over the course of a long race. They also described the fun of running. At the most basic level, all the women expressed that they simply "love[d] being a body in motion" and loved the "aliveness" that they get from running. This joy has ties to high performance in various ways according to the participants. Some women feel as though the joy of running translates directly to good performances because as one says, "there's a feeling of speed over really technical terrain" that makes running fast enjoyable. For several runners, the idea that competition and joy were disconnected was challenged. As one runner explained, "you're not running fast to win, you're running fast because it feels good." In this way, the joy of running brings about a good performance. Still, the joy of actually racing was not always present as that kind of joy did not emerge from pushing hard or running in discomfort. However, all of them mentioned that the joyful feeling of running contributed to being motivated to put in all the training necessary in order to perform well. Finally, the joy of running ultramarathons contributed to another kind of joy. All of the runners mentioned how they believed they were creating a "better self" through ultrarunning. For instance, one runner notes, "when I start running I am just so happy and I love to talk. And I'm not that chatty when I'm not in motion." Several participants say that they are a "better person" when they run. For other participants, the joy of running crosses into the spiritual realm.

For another runner, "it's an energy outlet but it's also like a meditation type time. For me it's a calming period [. . . . and] a spiritual feeling where you're just at peace with everything around you." Female athletes in other lifestyle sports such as surfing, skiing, skateboarding, and mountaineering (to name a few) echo these sentiments (Wheaton, 2004).

The different concept of beauty and the ultrarunning example offer insights into the possibilities of rethinking feminine beauty and joy in sport. For the roller derby athletes and ultra-runners, expressing femininity and experiencing joy on their own terms were integral to their athletic performances and their "will to win," not in opposition to it. It also served to bolster how they felt about themselves. Certainly, sport has this kind of potential for women as they are already embracing this mentality in a few competitive contexts, which opens up new legitimate meanings in sport participation for women and men.

Shifting Beliefs about Women's Physical and Mental Strengths

There are clear differences between female and male bodies. These differences have long been used as an argument to frame women as inferior to men when it comes to sport. However, there are at least three questions that challenge the assumptions in this argument. First, McDonagh and Pappano (2007) consider the question, to what extent are male bodies superior to female bodies when it comes to sport and physical activity? They tackle this question by pointing out the ways in which female bodies may actually be an advantage in some sports while male bodies may also be disadvantageous in other sports. Second, to what extent do physical differences make in sports relative to other aspects? Sport requires a wide range of skills, of which technical, mental, and strategic abilities are critical. There is an assumption that men are better mentally and strategically, however, there is little evidence to support this belief.

Socialization processes as well as basic brain neurology may level the mental playing field. Third, does the current landscape of female performance versus male performances function as a blueprint for the future? Given that the mass participation of women in sport is a relatively recent phenomenon, female athletes may simply be playing catchup in terms of physical and biological strengths.

Female bodies may be an advantage in some sports. McDonagh and Pappano (2007) point out that one sport in which female bodies appear to have a clear advantage is in long-distance swimming. As they note, due to estrogen and the ability of women's bodies to have children, they tend to naturally carry more fat on their bodies, especially subcutaneous fat. This layer of fat has two distinct advantages. First, it allows women to float more easily in water, which then translates into less energy expenditure in order to stay afloat. It also results in "less drag" in the water because their bodies are floating up on the water more than men's bodies. Second, female bodies stay warmer in cold water. These advantages seemed to have mostly played out in performances throughout the history of long-distance swimming. Crossing the 21-mile English Channel has been an official swimming contest since 1875. Until 1926, only men had attempted to swim the channel, in water that ranges from 59 degrees to 65 degrees. In 1926, Gertrude Ederle became the first woman to complete the crossing and did so about 2 hours faster than the previous fastest male swimmer. When the first woman to cross the English Channel in both directions completed her swim in 1953, Florence Chadwick bested the prior men's record for two-way crossings by over 40 minutes. Currently a male holds the record for fastest swim across the channel by about 30 minutes. The fastest women's record was established in 2006, and the men's new record is from 2012. A woman holds the record for the most number of crossings. The various records tend to fall back and forth between men and women, and it may only be a matter of time until the fastest single crossing is once again held by a woman. In addition, of the four different long-distance swimming challenges between Catalina Island and the California coast, women hold three out of the four records. The history of the swimming records in both these iconic swimming challenges suggests that women and men have been evenly matched.

Ultimately, assessing advantages and disadvantages in sport is very complex, and substantial evidence suggests that there is no clear divide between women and men that gives men an unquestionable advantage. There are sports in which women's bodies are either an advantage or in which men's bodies are a disadvantage. For instance, in stock car racing, lighter, smaller drivers mean there is less weight for the car to move. Danica Patrick's small frame has been mentioned as an advantage. Her presence and consistent strong performances are reshaping the way society views women's capabilities in sport. Other sports, such as fencing and horse racing, favor lighter, agile bodies; larger and heavier male bodies (on average) are disadvantages. Wrestling is a sport in which advantages are shared by female and male wrestlers. Men tend to have a better strength to weight ratio, which helps in wrestling. They may or may not have a better strength to muscle mass ratio; however, the current weight classes are not determined by the latter ratio. Female wrestlers may have an advantage with greater flexibility and lower center of gravity. Wrestling is an example of the complex ways that "advantage" can be assessed in sport, implying that there is no singular physical advantage of male athletes over female athletes. Furthermore, mental and strategic skills account for significant aspects of sport performance. For instance, sailing and mountaineering require considerable judgment about what to do in any given moment. In sailing, skills such as knowing how the boat responds, sensing the winds, and determining the best strategies for how to trim sails and best heading to follow are all aspects related to areas of sport in which women and men have equal skills. Experience, practice, and training make a difference in excellence along these lines. In mountaineering, a sport long believed to be a "man's" place, similar skill sets are needed for success. Skills such as assessing the weather, setting up protection while moving across glaciers,

crew helping along the way with supplies) on the Appalachian Trail. She accomplished her goal, becoming the new Appalachian Trail record holder in a time of 46 days, 11 hours, and 20 minutes, averaging 47 miles daily. Her record held for four years through several other attempts by men. Eventually her record was broken in 2015 and again in 2016, both by accomplished male ultrarunners. Finally, when Nikki Kimball set out to break a record on Vermont's Long Trail, she was aiming for the men's record. Kimball's purpose in setting out, to publicly make a statement that women can compete with men and should set their sights high, was chronicled in the film *Finding Traction*. Although Kimball set the women's record by more than two days, she was just shy of the men's record. Although disappointed, Kimball remarked that if one girl was inspired by her run, the effort was worth it. As noted on the *Finding Traction* website, "this well-publicized run is more than a chance to inspire people to be active and spend time outdoors, it's her way of encouraging women and girls to take an equal place for themselves in professional sports" (2013, para 1).

References

Allen, Kara, and Cynthia Frisby. 2017. "A Content Analysis of Micro Aggressions in News Stories about Female Athletes Participating in the 2012 and 2016 Summer Olympics." *Journal of Mass Communication and Journalism*, 7: 334. doi: 10.4172/2165-7912.1000334.

Anderson, Eric, and Rachael Bullingham. 2015. "Openly Lesbian Team Sport Athletes in an Era of Decreasing Homohysteria." *International Review for the Sociology of Sport*, 50(6): 647–660.

Anderson, Eric, Rory Magrath, and Rachael Bullingham. 2016. *Out in Sport: The Experiences of Openly Gay and Lesbian Athletes in Competitive Sport*. London: Routledge.

Anderson, Eric. 2014. *21st Century Jocks: Sporting Men and Contemporary Heterosexuality*. New York: Springer.

Berkman, Seth. 2017. "U.S. Women's Team Strikes a Deal with U.S.A. Hockey." https://www.nytimes.com/2017/03/28/sports/hockey/usa-hockey-uswnt-boycott.html. Accessed July 7, 2017.

Brook, Stacey L., and Sarah Foster. 2010. "Does Gender Affect Compensation among NCAA Basketball Coaches?" *International Journal of Sport Finance*, 5(2): 96.

Bruce, T. (2008). "Women, Sport and the Media: A Complex Terrain." In C. Obel, T. Bruce, and S. Thompson (Eds.), *Outstanding Research about Women and Sport in New Zealand* (pp. 51–71). Hamilton, New Zealand: Wilf Malcolm Institute of Educational Research. http://researchcommons.waikato.ac.nz/handle/10289/3343. Accessed on July 14, 2017.

Burton, Laura J. 2015. "Underrepresentation of Women in Sport Leadership: A Review of Research." *Sport Management Review*, 18(2): 155–165.

Cauldwell, Jayne. 2015. "Studying Sport, Feminism, and Pleasure." In Richard Pringle, Bob Rinehart, and Jayne Cauldwell (Eds.), *Sport and the Social Significance of Pleasure*. London: Routledge.

Chen, Steve Shih-Chia, Terran Duncan, Eric Street, and Brooklyn Hesterberg. 2016. "Differences in Official Athletic Website Coverage and Social Media Use between Men's and Women's Basketball." http://thesportjournal.org/article/differences-in-official-athletic-website-coverage-and-social-media-use-between-mens-and-womens-basketball-teams/. Accessed on July 2, 2017.

Claringbould, Inge, and Annelies Knoppers. 2012. "Paradoxical Practices of Gender in Sport-Related Organizations." *Journal of Sport Management*, 26(5): 404–416.

Coakley, Jay, Christopher J. Hallinan, and Brent Douglas McDonald. 2011. *Sports in Society: Sociological Issues and Controversies* (2nd ed.). New York: McGraw Hill.

Cohen, Adam, E., Nicole Melton, and Jon Welty Peachey. 2014. "Investigating a Coed Sport's Ability to Encourage Inclusion and Equality." *Journal of Sport Management*, 28(2): 220–235. doi:10.1123/jsm.2013–0329.

Cooky, Cheryl, Faye L. Wachs, Michael Messner, and Shari L. Dworkin. 2010. "It's Not about the Game: Don Imus, Race, Class, Gender and Sexuality in Contemporary Media." *Sociology of Sport Journal*, 27(2): 139–159.

Cooky, Cheryl, Michael Messner, and Michela Musto. 2015. "'It's Dude Time!' A Quarter Century of Excluding Women's Sports in Televised News and Highlight Shows." *Communication & Sport*, 3(3): 261–287.

Daniels, Dayna B. 2009. *Polygendered and Ponytailed: The Dilemma of Femininity and the Female Athlete*. Canadian Scholars' Press.

Deitsch, Richard. 2015. "Panel: Young Women in Sports Journalism Share Their Experiences." https://www.si.com/more-sports/2015/02/23/panel-women-sports-journalism-30-and-under. Accessed July 6, 2017.

"EY Women Athletes Business Network (WABN) and International Women's Forum Continue to Connect Elite Female Athletes with Top Women in Business." http://www.ey.com/gl/en/newsroom/news-releases/news-ey-women-athletes-business-network-and-international-womens-forum. Accessed June 24, 2017.

Finding Traction. Directed by Jamie Jacobson and Charles Dye. 2013. Independent film. DVD available at http://findingtractionfilm.com/about.

Fink, Janet. 2015. Sponsorship for Women's Sports Presents Untapped Opportunity. *Sports Business Daily*. http://www.sportsbusinessdaily.com/Journal/Issues/2015/11/02/Opinion/Changing-the-Game-Janet-Fink.aspx. Accessed June 22, 2017.

Fink, Janet, Laura Burton, Annemarie Farrell, and Heidi Parker. 2012. "Playing It Out." *Journal for the Study of Sports and Athletes in Education*, 6(1): 83–106.

Gee, Bridget L., and Sarah I. Leberman. 2011. "Sports Media Decision Making in France: How They Choose What We Get to See and Read." *International Journal of Sport Communication*, 4(3): 321–343.

Gonzales, Laurence. *Deep Survival: Who Lives, Who Dies, and Why: True Stories of Miraculous Endurance and Sudden Death*. New York: W.W. Norton & Company, 2003.

Griffin, Pat. 1998. *Strong Women, Deep Closets*. Leeds: Human Kinetics.

Hanold, Maylon T. 2010. "Beyond the Marathon:(De) Construction of Female Ultrarunning Bodies." *Sociology of Sport Journal*, 27(2): 160–177.

Hardin, Marie, and Erin Elizabeth Whiteside. 2009. "The Power of 'Small Stories': Narratives and Notions of Gender Equality in Conversations about Sport." *Sociology of Sport Journal*, 26(2): 255–276.

Harmon, Noël Suzanne. "A Study of the Experiences of Black College Female Student Athletes at a Predominantly White institution." *Theses and Dissertations* (2009): 376.

Harwell, Drew. 2015. "FIFA Graft Scandal Could Touch Major U.S. Sports Brand." *Washington Post*. http://www.standard.net/frontpage/2015/05/28/FIFA-graft-scandal-could-touch-major-US-sports-brand.html. Accessed on July 10, 2017.

Heitner, Darrran. 2015. "Sports Industry to Reach $73.5 Billion by 2019." *Forbes*. https://www.forbes.com/sites/darrenheitner/2015/10/19/sports-industry-to-reach-73-5-billion-by-2019/#3fff14311b4b. Accessed on July 10, 2017.

Heywood, Leslie, and Shari L. Dworkin. 1998. *Built to Win: The Female Athlete as Cultural Icon*. Vol. 5. Minneapolis: University of Minnesota Press.

Isaac, Laufer Green. 2010. "High-Risk Drinking on College Campuses: College Life and Alcohol: Challenges and Solutions: A Resource Guide." http://www.rwjf

.org/en/library/research/2009/12/high-risk-drinking-on-college-campuses.html. Accessed on June 15, 2017.

Kamphoff, Cindra S. 2010. "Bargaining with Patriarchy: Former Female Coaches' Experiences and Their Decision to Leave Collegiate Coaching." *Research Quarterly for Exercise and Sport,*. 81(3): 360–372.

Kane, Mary Jo, and Heather D. Maxwell. 2011. "Expanding the Boundaries of Sport Media Research: Using Critical Theory to Explore Consumer Responses to Representations of Women's Sports." *Journal of Sport Management*, 25(3): 202–216.

Lapchick, Richard. 2017. "The 2016 Racial and Gender Report Card: College Sport." http://nebula.wsimg.com/38d2d0480373afd027ca38308220711f?AccessKeyId=DAC3A5 6D8FB782449D2A&disposition=0&alloworigin=1. Accessed on July 14, 2017.

Mazerolle, Stephanie M., John F. Borland, and Laura J. Burton. 2012. "The Professional Socialization of Collegiate Female Athletic Trainers: Navigating Experiences of Gender Bias." *Journal of Athletic Training*, 47(6): 694–703.

Mazerolle, Stephanie M., Laura Burton, and Raymond J. Cotrufo. 2015. "The Experiences of Female Athletic Trainers in the Role of the Head Athletic Trainer." *Journal of Athletic Training*, 50(1): 71–81.

McCormack, Mark. 2011. "Mapping the Terrain of Homosexually-Themed Language." *Journal of Homosexuality*, 58(5): 664–679.

McDonagh, Eileen, and Laura Pappano. 2007. *Playing with the Boys: Why Separate Is Not Equal in Sports*. London: Oxford University Press.

Media Coverage and Female Athletes. Directed by the Tucker Center for Research on Girls and Women. http://www.cehd.umn.edu/tuckercenter/multimedia/mediacoverage.html. Accessed July 12, 2017.

Morgan, William. 2006. *Why Sports Morally Matter*. New York: Routledge.

Patrick, Allen. 2016. "Sport Metaphors Used in Business, and Where They Really Came From." http://lifehacker.com/10-sports-metaphors-used-in-business-and-where-they-re-1782325688. Accessed on July 1, 2017.

"Pay Inequity in Athletics." 2015. *Women's Sports Foundation*. https://www.womenssportsfoundation.org/research/article-and-report/equity-issues/pay-inequity/. Accessed July 17, 2017.

Quinn, Sam. R. 2012. "ESPN Body Issue 2012: Ronda Rousey's Take on Her Body Is Great for Women." *Bleacher Report*. http://bleacherreport.com/articles/1255815-espn-body-issue-2012-ronda-rouseys-take-on-her-body-is-great-for-women?m=0. Accessed July 18, 2017.

"Race and Sport." n.d. *Women's Sports Foundation*. https://www.womenssportsfoundation.org/wp-content/uploads/2016/07/race-and-sport-the-womens-sports-foundation-position.pdf. Accessed on June 16, 2017.

Raimondi, Marc. 2013. "UFC Prez Says Rousey Shouldn't Do Movies until after Fight Career." *New York Post*. http://nypost.com/2013/02/27/ufc-prez-says-rousey-shouldnt-do-movies-until-after-fight-career/. Accessed July 19, 2017.

Rawjee, Veena P., Nisha Ramlutchman, and Nereshnee Govender. 2011. "Missing in Action the Portrayal of Women in Sport in the Print Media." *Loyola Journal of Social Sciences*, 25(2): 177–190.

Robinson, Roger. 2012. "'Eleven Wretched Women': What Really Happened in the First Olympic Women's 800m." http://www.runnersworld.com/running-times-info/eleven-wretched-women. Accessed July 18, 2017.

Ryan, Molly M. 2012. "Title IX and the Drive for Gender Equality in Sports." *Minority Trial Lawyer*, 11(1): 2–6.

Shaffer, Amanda. 2012. "Gender Games: The Olympics Has a New Way to Test Whether Athletes Are Men or Women. Is It fair? http://www.slate.com/articles/health_and_science/. Accessed on June 22, 2017.

"Social Media: What It Is and Why It Matters to Women's Sports." 2009. https://tuckercenter.wordpress.com/2009/09/21/social-media-what-it-is-and-why-it-matters-to-women%E2%80%99s-sports/. Accessed on June 12, 2017.

Spaaij, Ramón, Karen Farquharson, and Timothy Marjoribanks. 2015. "Sport and Social Inequalities." *Sociology Compass*, 9(5): 400–411. doi:10.1111/soc4.12254.

Spies-Gans, Juliet. 2015. "What Serena's SI Cover Reveals about How We See Female Athletes." *Huffington Post*. http://www.huffingtonpost.com/entry/serena-williams-cover-body-shaming_us_566efde0e4b011b83a6bf33a. Accessed on June 3, 2017.

Staurowsky, Ellen. 2016. *Women and Sport: From Liberation to Celebration*. Champaign, IL: Human Kinetics.

Staurowsky, Ellen J., and Maureen Smith. 2016. "Female Leaders in Corporate Sport." In Ellen Staurowsky (Ed.), *Women and Sport: Continuing a Journey of Liberation and Celebration*. Champaign, IL: Human Kinetics.

Van Zoonen, Liesbet. 1994. *Feminist Media Studies*. London: Sage Publications.

Venus Vs. Directed by Ava DuVernay. ESPN, Nine for IX. http://www.espn.com/espnw/w-in-action/nine-for-ix/. Accessed July 14, 2017.

Walker, Nefertiti A., and E. Nicole Melton. 2015. "The Triple Threat: Examining the Intersection of Gender, Race, and Sexual Orientation in Sport Organizations." *Journal of Sport Management*, 29: 257–271.

Walker, Nefertiti A., and Melanie L. Sartore-Baldwin. 2013. "Hegemonic Masculinity and the Institutionalized Bias toward Women in Men's Collegiate Basketball: What Do Men Think?" *Journal of Sport Management*, 27(4): 303–315.

Welty Peachey, Jon., and Laura. J. Burton. 2012. "Transactional or Transformational Leaders in Intercollegiate Athletics? Examining the Influence of Leader Gender and Subordinate Gender on Evaluation of Leaders during Organizational Culture Change." *International Journal of Sport Management*, 13: 115–142.

Wheaton, Belinda, ed. 2004. *Understanding Lifestyle Sport: Consumption, Identity and Difference*. London: Routledge, 2004.

Williams, Venus. 2006. "Wimbledon Has Sent Me a Message: I'm Only a Second Class Champion." https://www.thetimes.co.uk/article/wimbledon-has-sent-me-a-message-im-only-a-second-class-champion-f056h05hmzq. Accessed on July 15, 2017.

Women's Sports Foundation. 2017. "Benefits: Why Sports Participation for Girls and Women." https://www.womenssportsfoundation.org/advocate/foundation-positions/mental-physical-health/benefits-sports-participation-girls-women/. Accessed June 23, 2017.

Introduction

There is clear evidence that participation of girls and women in sport has experienced exponential growth. From scholastic and collegiate opportunities to extreme sports, girls and women are not only taking part, but also reaping numerous benefits. At the turn of the 20th century, views that women would become too masculine or risk their health permeated every aspect of sport. While those attitudes are virtually nonexistent today, there remain challenges for women in sport. Nonetheless, girls and women are benefiting from a wide variety of sports and physical activity for just as many different reasons. This chapter presents viewpoints on various challenges and benefits. The chapter begins with three essays related to the topic of intercollegiate athletics. The first essay is Kelli Rodriguez Currie's case against compensation for college athletes based on the argument it would lead to the decline of women's collegiate athletics. The next perspective showcases slight shifts in women desiring to be collegiate coaches. The next two essays dive into the ongoing complicated relationship that female athletes have historically had with their bodies. Two women with experience working with female collegiate athletes offer unique views on the ways women are developing and can develop their own relationships to their bodies. The next two essays take up the topic of empowerment through sport, while the final two essays

Two collegiate athletes vie for the ball during an NCAA women's soccer game in College Park, MD, on August 28, 2015. (Aspenphoto/Dreamstime.com)

offer viewpoints on transgender athletes and the path to sport leadership for two former collegiate soccer players.

Compensation of Student-Athletes Threatens Women's Collegiate Sports Altogether
Kelli Rodriguez Currie

At a time when participation in women's sports is increasing and the gap between male and female athletic participation is closing, many question whether Title IX is still necessary to provide increased opportunities for women in collegiate sports. I suggest that not only is Title IX necessary to promote increased gender equity in collegiate athletics, but it is perhaps the only mechanism protecting the future of women's collegiate athletics at all, as the National Collegiate Athletics Association (NCAA) and its member institutions are under increased pressure to compensate scholarship athletes participating in revenue-generating sports.

In August 2015, the National Labor Relations Board (NLRB) declined to determine whether the Northwestern University football players who received grand-in-aid scholarships were employees as defined under the National Labor Relations Act (NLRA). On January 31, 2017, however, the Office of the General Counsel of the NLRB issued Memorandum GC 17–01. The General Counsel's Office "determine[d] here that the application of the statutory definition of employee and the common-law test lead to the conclusion that Division I Football Bowl Subdivision (FBS) scholarship football players *are employees* under the NLRA, and that they therefore have the right to be protected from retaliation when they engage in concerted activities for mutual aid and protection" (Griffin, 2017, 23).

Essentially, the memorandum says that Division I FBS scholarship football players at private universities can negotiate increased benefits, compensation, and other terms of their employment with their respective private institutions, regardless of whether they seek to form a union. Notably, the memorandum is limited to Division I FBS scholarship football players. That is, it does not include scholarship athletes participating in other revenue-generating sports. However, the NLRB did acknowledge that "there are undoubtedly other sports that provide substantial financial benefit to colleges/universities and that involve scholarship athletes who are under significant control by the schools and the NCAA" (Griffin, 2017, 22).

The NLRB specifically calls out the monetary value that the scholarship Division I FBS scholarship football players deliver to the university as an important part of the analysis to determine if these athletes qualify for protection as employees:

> With regard to the question of whether athletes provide services for the college/university, the Northwestern football program, which is part of the NCAA Division I Big Ten conference, generated approximately $76 Million in net profit during the ten year period ending in 2012–2013, and provided an immeasurable positive impact to Northwestern's reputation, which in turn undoubtedly boosted student applications and alumni financial donations. (Griffin, 2017, 19)

This emphasis on revenue as "value" is problematic for women's collegiate sports in a culture that privileges men's sports. When the value of an athletics program is understood as measureable net profit and assumed increased applications and financial donations, well-established men's sports become the only sports in which student-athletes would be able to negotiate for compensation as employees in the current landscape. Arguably, there would remain little incentive to further support student-athletes in other sports should more money need to be redirected toward "athlete-employees" of revenue-generating sports. The athlete-employee classification of FBS scholarship football players heightens the inherent tension of supporting athletic programs that do not generate monetary value for the university. The impact on women's collegiate teams in these universities could be substantial. First, unless and until women's collegiate sports teams begin to generate revenue comparable to that generated by Division I FBS football and Division I men's basketball, traditional economic models do not support an argument to compensate female collegiate athletes, and the NLRA does not provide protection for female athletes to negotiate such compensation. Second, the reclassification further calls into question whether the university would support women's athletic programs at all if gender equity under Title IX were not required. In the absence of Title IX, institutions would likely favor the athletic contributions of the revenue-generating sports and be forced to make decisions about which programs it would continue to support, putting women's sports in particular at risk.

Thus, I argue that Title IX is the only regulatory authority that provides female collegiate athletes any opportunity for equity at the collegiate level. Under Title IX, any increased benefits afforded to the employee-athletes protected by the NLRA would be included in the list of benefits evaluated to determine whether the institution is providing equal athletic opportunities to members of both genders. Although Title IX does not require that an institution achieve precise equality between the genders, it does require that "where members of one sex enjoy more favorable treatment in one area, such benefit must be 'offset' by treatment in another area that favors members of the other sex" (NCAA, n.d.). Thus, if a university agreed to provide increased compensation to its Division I FBS scholarship football players, the female athletes at that university must also realize an equitable increase in their own total benefits or compensation.

Ironically, only in the collegiate athletics marketplace, where no employee-athlete is paid at all, is there equity in compensation between male and female athletes. Any increase in the compensation and protections as employees realized by male collegiate athletes must result in a similar increase for female collegiate athletes because it is required by Title IX, not because the marketplace independently supports such an increase for the female athletes participating in non-revenue-generating sports. In the professional sport marketplace, women's salaries and endorsements lag far behind those of their male peers despite recent progress made by U.S. Women's Hockey players and U.S. Women's Soccer players in negotiating salary increases in their new collective bargaining agreements. However, the "marketplace" is complex in sports because sport remains culturally male-dominated. Thus, market-driven compensation in sport is shaped by an inherent gender bias. Without the requirement that a university provide equity under Title IX, female collegiate athletes will meet a fate similar to that of their professional counterparts: at best, the gender pay gap in collegiate sports will increase, and at worst, women's collegiate athletics will cease altogether.

References

Brennan, Andrew. 2016. "Which Sports Have the Largest and Smallest Pay Gaps?" *Forbes.* https://www.forbes.com/sites/andrewbrennan/2016/05/05/the-pay-discrimination-in-sports-we-wish-didnt-exist-will-only-dissipate-with-womens-leadership/2/#18dd89031713. Accessed on May 15, 2017.

Brown, Anna, and Eileen Patten. 2017. "The Narrowing, but Persistent, Gender Gap in Pay." http://www.pewresearch.org/fact-tank/2017/04/03/gender-pay-gap-facts/. Accessed on May 15, 2017.

Dwyer, Colin. 2017. "In 'Important Step,' U.S. Women's Soccer Team Reaches New Labor Deal." http://www.npr.org/sections/thetwo-way/2017/04/06/522843140/in-important-step-u-s-womens-soccer-team-reaches-new-labor-deal. Accessed on May 15, 2017.

Griffin, Richard. F., Jr. 2017. "Report on the Statutory Rights of University Faculty and Students in the Unfair Labor Practice Context." https://www.nlrb.gov/search/all/Report%20on%20the%20Statutory%20Rights%20of%20

University%20Faculty%20and%20Students%20in%20
the%20Unfair%20Labor%20Practice%20Context%20.
Accessed on May 14, 2017.

Maese, Rick. 2017. "Women's Hockey Team, USA Hockey
Reach Agreement, Settling Pay Dispute." https://www
.washingtonpost.com/sports/olympics/womens-hockey-
team-usa-hockey-reach-agreement-settling-pay-dispute/
2017/03/28/a3823b28-13cf-11e7–9e4f-09aa75d3ec57_
story.html?utm_term=.83a001bd1b9c. Accessed on
May 12, 2017.

NCAA. (n.d.). "NCAA Gender Equity." https://www.ncaa.org/
sites/default/files/GE%2BEquip%2B%2BSupplies%2BBro
chure.pdf. Accessed on May 15, 2017.

"NCAA Sports Sponsorship and Participation Rates Report."
2016. Accessed on May 15, 2017.

Title IX of the Education Amendments of 1972, 34 Fed. Reg.
§ 106.41.

*Kelli Rodriguez Currie is Adjunct Faculty in the Sport Admin-
istration and Leadership master's program at Seattle University.
She regularly teaches the required sport law course and has taught
courses in ethics and operations management. With a background
in technology operations, student programs support, and biological sciences, Kelli has over 15 years of experience in operational
leadership, policy and program management, compliance, and risk
management. Her research interests include the student-athlete
experience and collegiate athletics compliance.*

A Shift in Perspective: Inspiring a New Generation of Female Coaches
Sara L. Lopez, Julie McCleery, and Hannah O. Olson

One of our faculty members clearly recalls a conversation that
took place five years ago with an incoming student in our
sports leadership graduate program. The pair was discussing

the student's career interests within athletics and where she might like to do an internship while enrolled in our program.

Faculty: You're obviously passionate about collegiate athletics and higher education. Where did this passion come from?

Student: My college coach was a major influence in my life and shaped me into who I am today. She helped me discover my love of athletics and passion for the game. I strive to impact others as she impacted me, you know?

Faculty: So it sounds like you are interested in pursuing coaching then? Following in her footsteps?

Student: Oh, I don't think I'm going to go the coaching route. I'm not sure that I'm qualified to coach. I imagine there are a lot of people out there with more experience than me.

Faculty: Maybe at this moment, yes. But experience and mentorship is exactly what you will gain as part of our program. Your internship will be a great entry point into the field and an excellent way to explore your interest in coaching.

Student: I just don't think coaching is a good fit for me long term. I don't see a lot of women like my former coach out there to learn from. And thinking long term, I want to have a family which I've heard just isn't possible as a college coach. I think working in an administrative position is a better idea.

In years past, we have observed narratives such as this during admissions interviews, class discussions, career mentoring, and many informal conversations. As women who have been collegiate and national team athletes and coaches, we are disheartened when young women, who demonstrate potential and promise in the area of coaching, are unwilling to pursue opportunities in the field, even for a short time.

These feelings of defeat are compounded as data and research illuminate the downward trend of women in collegiate coaching roles. While more women than ever are participating in college athletics, only slightly more than 40 percent of women's teams are coached by a female head coach (Stark, 2017). Likewise, the Institute for Diversity and Ethics in Sport released its annual report card in May, showing the all-time lowest score for gender and racial hiring in over a decade (Ryan, 2017). This trend is troubling (dare we say infuriating?); however, based on anecdotal conversations with incoming students more recently, we see a glimmer of hope on the horizon.

We have noticed a shift in the thinking of our female students. The shift is subtle, but important. The way we see women talk about the coaching profession is changing, and they show more interest and willingness to "try on" coaching as a career than as little as five years ago. We are hearing the following:

> I'm not sure if coaching will be my long-term career, but I'm interested in trying it and seeing where it will take me.
>
> I am confident in my ability to succeed as a collegiate coach.
>
> Someone is willing to give me a chance and I'm going to take advantage of the opportunity.

This shift not only is represented informally through conversations between our staff and graduate students, but can be seen in the increase in female application numbers to our coaching program and our graduates who are staying in the profession following degree completion. While the intention of these women may not necessarily be to remain in the field for the long haul, or perhaps they foresee challenges that could force an exit later in their careers, they are no longer immediately discounting coaching as a profession. Conversely, they are actively seeking coaching positions as an entry point into college athletics with a belief that there is a place for women and they, just as much as their male counterparts, are capable of success.

This shift is encouraging and gives us hope. This shift could be the movement that is needed to change the face (literally!) of coaches in collegiate athletics and reverse the current downward trend of women in coaching positions. While not all women who enter coaching will make it a long-term career choice, they are giving coaching a chance and potential challenges aren't being viewed as a reason to opt out from the outset. We feel that we are at a time and a place where real change can occur.

As faculty and educators, we have an obligation to play an active role in this work. First, we believe that actively engaging in research, education, and training that support women in the coaching space is critical to capitalizing on this shift. While we are aware of barriers for women in coaching, we also need to move toward understanding what kinds of programs, experiences, and advocacy work are needed to support them. Second, programs dedicated to cutting-edge education and professional development can proactively support women aspiring to be coaches by helping develop the skill sets needed to navigate not only coaching but the higher education landscape. Third, connecting this next generation of female coaches to current high-level female coaches as consultants and guest speakers allows for confirmation of their competencies and provides practical insights "from the field." Fourth, undergraduate education departments should involve sport-specific and coaching opportunities to students. Such efforts will give more students opportunities and exposure to coaching, thus deepening the pool of prospective women coaches. Finally, we believe there is much more work to be done in terms of educating coaches such that women see themselves "fit" for coaching. For example, projects such as our Ambitious Coaching research project, which highlights the skills necessary to be a successful coach, brings to the forefront nonsport-specific skills that we anticipate will resonate more with female coaches. The research project has several embedded goals, one of which is to illuminate for women that their existing skill set positions them for success within the coaching sector.

As true believers in the power of sport, we see a forward momentum that we must capitalize upon. With the above suggestions, perhaps future students will foresee challenges and barriers to entering a coaching career as a woman, yet not be dissuaded. Our hope is that they will understand the reality of these issues, yet choose the title of "Coach" nonetheless.

References

Ryan, Shannon. 2017. "College Sports Needs More Women—And Women of Color—In Coaching Ranks." http://www.chicagotribune.com.

Stark, Rachel. 2017. Where Are the Women? *NCAA Champion Magazine* (Winter): 33–40.

Dr. Sara L. Lopez serves as Co-Director for the Center for Leadership in Athletics and Program Director for the Intercollegiate Athletic Leadership MEd at the University of Washington where she teaches in the Intercollegiate Athletic Leadership MEd graduate program. Sara has an extensive background in sports administration and has been an active rowing coach for over 30 years.

Dr. Julie McCleery is a researcher and lecturer in the Center for Leadership in Athletics at the University of Washington. She rowed for the U.S. national team and coached high school and elite-level rowing for 20 years before turning her coaching attention to Little League baseball. Now she throws a mean batting practice.

Dr. Hannah O. Olson is a lecturer and administrator for the College of Education's Center for Leadership in Athletics at the University of Washington. Hannah's professional experience spans across recreational, professional, and collegiate athletics settings. She has coached softball for more than 15 years and is an aspiring tee ball coach for her two children.

Wearable Technology Helps to Inform and Improve Female Collegiate Soccer Players' Performance on the Field and Body Image off the Field
Allison C. Tenney

Wearable technology for monitoring collegiate athletes has helped to enhance and inform the decision-making process when it comes to athlete well-being and performance. We know that tracking performance metrics helps coaching staffs, athletes, and performance management teams make the best decisions for athletes to perform at the highest levels. But how do these technology systems affect *female* athletes? How do female athletes make sense of these measures and monitoring of their own bodies? Is technology simply one more mechanism through which women's bodies are controlled by individuals other than themselves?

From my work with female collegiate soccer players, I have found the use of wearable technology not only helps them connect better to what's going on with their bodies in positive ways, but also engenders trust that their bodies are being managed and handled in a way that puts them in the best position to be healthy and successful. As coaches, how we manage women's bodies from a performance standpoint shapes their feelings of success, not only from a performance standpoint, but also from a body image perspective. The intersection of performance and body image for collegiate female soccer players is improved by the use of wearable technology such as GPS (global positioning system) tracking, heart rate monitoring, and heart rate variability feedback to athletes.

Current technology is tracking all sorts of physiological as well as mechanical and physical metrics: heart rate, distance covered, high-speed sprints, maximum velocities, sleep, fatigue, recovery, and so on. The goal of technology is to close the gap between subjective analysis of a player and objective data to provide feedback in order to improve performance and the recovery status of a player. For female athletes in need of feedback, "having access to this data, and having a trusted staff member that is extremely capable of keeping track of it, thoroughly interpreting it, and responding to its indications in a way that is best for each athlete, is comforting beyond belief. It makes me feel safe, prepared, and at my best for high level performance" (I. Butterfield, personal communication, May 1, 2017). The combination of technology and the reliable interpretation of data to make informed decisions about athletes helps them to trust the decisions being made around their bodies and performance.

In some instances, there can exist a disconnect between the training methods of an athlete's body for peak physical preparation and the training necessary to push through perceived "mental blocks." The need to push physical boundaries in an attempt to also push players' mental capabilities is a training methodology that many coaches use. While mental preparation is a critical factor to consider when training athletes, it is not the only factor, and when used at the wrong time, can be devastating to athletes' health, performance, and success. Research in high-performance sporting environments reveals that a number of "social, organizational, and political stresses are placed on individual athletes and teams. Hence, in addition to optimal mental preparation, they need to develop a variety of coping and self-regulation skills to deal with the many stressors" (Gould, Flett, and Bean, 2009). Because of the wearable technology our collegiate female soccer players use, it is easier to be proactive about and deal with these stressors so they do not hinder performance. It also allows us to talk to players about these stressors, many of which are occurring off the training field. The technology provides a more objective platform to begin communication. This communication around technology helps players see they "are not just objects or athletes, we are people and our health matters more than the 'no pain no gain' [paradigm]" (J. Ray, personal communication, May 1, 2017). Wearable technology is able to quantify physical exertion so we can compare it with what a coach's' perception of that exertion actually is. A lot of times this can be skewed, and not in favor of the athletes, which can be dangerous to their health when not managed properly. The technology helps to build trust so that athletes can "feel like [they] can push [themselves] hard without having to worry about being too tired for the next day [or] getting hurt" (S. Spiekerman, personal communication, May 1, 2017). As a performance manager on a coaching staff, it becomes easier to communicate to coaches and players when fatigue has actually set in and create some realistic boundaries on how to properly train players within that fatigue. We are able to quantify fatigue and individualize recovery methods to optimize the recovery process in the athletes and allow players the space to recover properly to see success in the games, when it really counts. With our ability now to measure the response to chronic loading, our female athletes understand that more load past a certain threshold only results in more fatigue, not more fitness.

More interestingly, this technology seems to influence these athletes' body image in positive ways. Social norms governing female body image are those that are white, able bodied, cisgendered, long torso, lean, skinny, tan, and toned. This norm is an aesthetic standard for females that is very difficult, if not impossible, to attain. For athletes, this becomes even more problematic as you layer in a performance standard for their bodies that they must also live up to. In my own experience, wearable technology is helping bridge the gap between these ideals and their performance. Paradoxically, the reliance on concrete data as a metric for reliable feedback about their performance bodies is a welcoming and empowering form of feedback. The performance feedback grounded in data about their own bodies allows these female athletes to have a new relationship with their bodies because the guesswork in terms of what's "good" is removed. Concrete data and informative feedback to players about their body help them to tune in, access, and connect to their bodies in a way they can't without this type of feedback. It helps inform the type of training each individual player needs and mitigates coaches' individual biases around a player's perceived efforts. After certain feedback, one player reported "how much better I felt afterwards and thought about how the technology we use opened my eyes to that reality. I truly do think the technologies we used helped keep my body from becoming exhausted over the course of the season and kept me feeling ready to play each day" (K. Vogel, personal communication, May 1, 2017).

This way of relating to feedback about their performance bodies stands in stark contrast to the ever-evolving standard of beauty that society places upon women. One player reports feeling that "the technology elicits a sense of self-awareness to my own body. Doing HRV (heart rate variability) every morning during the season was a good way for me to do a self check-in about how I was feeling physically and mentally, and depending on those results, it would influence my decisions on how to better my body for the rest of the day" (J. Plummer, personal communication, May 1, 2017). It helped another player, "pay more attention to my body" (K. Vogel, personal communication, May 1, 2017). Developing this self-awareness through technology is in direct defiance to societal beauty standards. When all the messaging is telling women to be small and thin and to shrink in size, our athletes are learning how to tune in, listen, and take care of their body needs to enhance their performance capabilities. The technology has helped players to connect to their bodies in ways that are neither subjective nor outcome based. Instead, the technology helps these female athletes understand their bodies in real time because it reinforces what is already going on physiologically. Many times, the technology is simply confirming what they intrinsically already know and feel. This gives the athletes permission to acknowledge that they are physically fatigued or gives them the security to push their bodies without an increased risk of injury. This awareness empowers and enables them to make their own decisions about their bodies as well as provides a unique way for them to pay attention to how they feel *in their bodies.*

References

Gould, Daniel M., Ryan Flett, and Eric Bean. 2009. "Mental Preparation for Training and Competition." In Britton W. Brewer (Ed.), *Handbook of Sports Medicine and Science, Sport Psychology*. Hoboken, NJ: John Wiley & Sons.

Allison C. Tenney is the High Performance Manager and Strength & Conditioning Coach for Seattle University Women's Soccer team. After completing her playing career at George Mason University, she played with the Washington Freedom and after coached two seasons at Cornell University (2007–2009) before joining the Seattle U Women's Soccer staff in 2009. She has a master's degree in Sports Administration and Leadership from Seattle U and holds a CSCS (Certified Strength and Conditioning Specialist) along with a USAW (USA Weightlifting).

Navigating the Female (Athlete) Body Knowledge Gap
Anna Terry

The perfectly aligned human body exists only on anatomical charts. From birth, people crawl, walk, and run their way out of alignment. This is generally more pronounced in athletes. Consider what an athlete asks her body to do. Imagine a youth soccer player, who from a young age repeats a set of motions common to soccer thousands of times as she goes on to play in high school, college, and beyond. Every time she dribbles the ball and cuts left, she reinforces changes to her musculature, pulling herself further out of balance.

Now consider what happens when you add rigid ankle tissue to this scenario. When an athlete's ankle can't contribute, she is forced to find power elsewhere. It might be in increased range of motion in the knee or more rotation in the hip. Whatever the compensatory pattern, it will recur thousands of times, each time deepening an imbalance that will likely lead to injury. In this example, it would not be uncommon for the rigid ankle to force a change in hip rotation that ultimately leads to a compensatory injury in the opposite knee. The knee might require treatment. However, if it is not also viewed as a symptom, the injury will likely become repetitive and/or chronic. Until someone uncovers and alleviates the ankle rigidity, the pattern is bound to repeat itself—she has a bad knee after all.

If you ask an athlete what she needs to work on in the gym or on the field in order to improve, she will invariably have an answer. Ask her what she needs to do to restore balance to her body in order to reduce her likelihood of injury, and, chances are she won't have a reply. Through my work as the director of Integrative Health with Dartmouth Athletics, as well as my personal athletic experiences, I have seen many patterns impacting health and performance that emerge in young female athletes. Committed athletes receive an unimaginable amount of coaching, they practice for hours, they participate in strength and conditioning, and they often watch video in their free time. They do all of this work to improve their play. In this world of athlete preparation, there is an obvious gap—the overwhelming majority of athletes know their playbook better than they know their own bodies, and there are consequences. No matter how thoroughly an athlete has prepared, once she's torn her labrum, she will be temporarily sidelined and unable to perform at peak.

There is a significant need for programming that focuses on helping female athletes better understand their bodies. There is tremendous value in an athlete understanding her own body, knowing what will be expected of it in sport, and knowing what tools she should have in her toolbox to help her avoid injury and maintain peak performance. We all live in our own bodies and we often share the same goals. To reach those goals we need to first know what we specifically need. There is a clear need for individualized assessment that takes a holistic approach by analyzing an individual athlete's mobility and compensatory patterns set against the requirements of her sport. I have too often seen athletes arrive at college with biomechanical factors that, without support and correction, can lead to injury in college athletics. When conducting functional movement screening with these young women, it is found that they are infrequently aware of the risk factors present in their bodies unless they've suffered a significant injury. Even in those cases, young women often understand that they have a "bad knee" without realizing that their knee injuries are a symptom that traces back to a separate issue (such as a lack of ankle mobility).

The proof is out there. For example, research shows that "Female athletes with increased dynamic valgus and high abduction loads are at increased risk of anterior cruciate ligament injury" (Hewettet al., 2005, 495). There are resultant efforts under way to develop "simpler measures of neuromuscular control that can be used to direct female athletes to more effective, targeted interventions" (Hewettet al., 2005, 500). Unfortunately, the aforementioned body knowledge gap often means that this information is inaccessible.

How Can You Close the Gap?

1. You Must Know Your Body!

Do you have flat feet? Are your joints super mobile? Are your glutes firing properly? Is your breathing functional? Are your muscles locked short in your pecs, biceps, and scalenes; are they locked long in your traps; or are they underdeveloped in your midback? Your biomechanics matter. The time you spend sitting, your injury history, and genetics create patterns. Athletes must take the time to fully learn what is happening with their own bodies and the physical requirements of their sport. This goes beyond an analysis of soft tissue; female athletes must consider their menstrual cycle, sleep, and hydration. There are myriad health care professionals who can help, and it is often beneficial to step outside of the realm athletic trainers and physical therapists for support. Athletes should consider beginning with a conversation with their pediatrician or primary care provider, and should get referrals to therapists, nutritionists, sleep specialists, and others. Since, based on the very nature of high level sport, it is a given that athletes are going to push themselves as hard as they can physically, psychologically, and emotionally, it is worth considering setting up some of these conversations before acute or chronic issues begin to manifest.

2. Identify Barriers

Too often, the culture of sport itself is a barrier to self-care. This shows up in the "push through it" mentality. Understand that the "it" that you are often encouraged to push through is critical information that your body is sending you that, when acknowledged and analyzed, will help prevent injury. Don't forget that life outside of athletics has a significant impact on your body. Factors such as upcoming midterms or important social events often alter your rest and recovery time. Student-athletes who spend a significant amount of time sitting at a desk typing must consider the impact that that time has on their bodies. As an athlete sits in a lecture hall taking notes, at a computer at working, or behind the wheel on a long road trip, her hips will begin to lock short and her lower back will often bind. In order to make an effective plan, athletes must fully acknowledge all contributing variables, even those mentioned above that most athletes would never consider a part of their training plan.

3. Engage in Active Self-Care

Make sure to adopt a functional strength training routine and advocate for balance in your tissues before loading up your structure. When athletes matriculate from high school to college, it is not unusual for them to find themselves pipelined into a highly numbers-focused strength and conditioning program. It is easy to get swept up in a sport culture that values max squat above functional strength and mobility, even when there is little direct benefit on the field and can introduce an increased risk of injury. In these circumstances, it is critical that athletes understand the risks and self-advocate to ensure that they're being adequately prepared before more and more weight is loaded on the bar.

Ideally, once an athlete hits adolescence, she should be engaging in self-care education, studying up on the common injury patterns for your sport, and finding professionals and coaches who connect with in terms of mind, body, and spirit. Pushing the human body to the limit is not solely a physical pursuit; it requires an immeasurable amount of mental acuity and focus as well as emotional stamina. You must nurture yourself physically, intellectually, and emotionally in order to ensure peak performance. Remember, you're not the first person to walk this path—research what the best in your sport do, what those around you who seem like they have it together do, and be honest in your evaluation of self.

Perhaps most importantly, ensure that you build in adequate time for rest and recovery. When you push your body to the limits, it is going to need time to repair itself. Ensure that you are giving it the fuel that it needs through appropriate nutrition and hydration, and get plenty of sleep. Neglecting these often overlooked aspects of training and competing may result in all that hard work being for naught as you wrestle with chronic fatigue instead of improved performance. In short, love and take care of yourself—and whatever you do, don't forget that it's just a game, and that you are amazing!

References

Hewett, Timothy E., Gregory D. Myer, Kevin R. Ford, Robert S. Heidt, Angelo J. Colosimo, Scott G. McLean, Antonie J. Van den Bogert, Mark V. Paterno, and Paul Succop. 2005. "Biomechanical Measures of Neuromuscular Control and Valgus Loading of the Knee Predict Anterior

Cruciate Ligament Injury Risk in Female Athletes: A Prospective Study." *The American Journal of Sports Medicine*, 33(4): 492–501.

Anna Terry, board-certified and licensed massage therapist, yoga instructor educator, and NASM-certified personal trainer, has been assisting clients in eliminating pain and discomfort, increasing performance, and expediting recovery for over 15 years by resolving acute and chronic issues using hands-on assessment, movement pattern screening, and manual therapy. A former member of both the junior and senior U.S. Canoe Kayak Slalom teams, she has just completed five years as the director of Integrative Health at Dartmouth College athletics where she led a team of manual therapists and movement professionals in their treatment of the nearly 1,000 Division I student-athletes.

Sport Empowerment Programs for Girls
Erin Karner

Women have had to overcome many barriers to inclusion in the world of sport. Today, women are still fighting for equality in many areas of sport such as equality of opportunity, media coverage and representation, and credibility for athletic accomplishments. Despite these ongoing issues, females' sport involvement has increased dramatically in the recent decades. With the rising participation rate among all sports, sport has now become not just a domain for men but also an empowering place for women. Over the past 20 years, research has consistently shown that sport acts as a site of empowerment for women at all skill levels and ages across a wide range of sports. Women find empowerment through sport by feeling a sense belonging to a greater whole, through improved physical strength and body image, by achieving individual and group goals and finally, by simply developing relationships with other women.

While many sport programs focus on developing physical and technical skills, the rise of sport empowerment programs for girls has been increasing since the late 1990s. Sport empowerment programs purposefully use sport as the platform for young girls and women to develop non sport-specific skills such as confidence and self-esteem that are highly transferrable to everyday life experiences. According to Zieff (2006), adolescent girls adopt an athletic identity through involvement in sports. When they develop an athletic identity and continue to participate, they experience a sense of competence, enjoyment, and growth. Unfortunately, as girls reach late elementary school and early middle school, sport is often one of the first pastimes to be abandoned as more social pressures to be young women and feminine arise. Arguably, the aims of sport empowerment programs help prevent this dropout.

Many sport empowerment programs for girls operate in a mastery climate where growth is valued over proficiency. For example, Girls on the Run of Chicago described the programs' goal "isn't to turn girls into marathon runners but to inspire them to be joyful, healthy and confident individuals who can set a goal and then reach it" (Cary, 2013). Along with finding personal joy, sport empowerment programs emphasize that joy can also be discovered through helping others and being involved with a community. Using sport and activity as a vehicle, sport empowerment programs are able to reach girls with a myriad of backgrounds in ways that promote not only physical health but also social and emotional well-being. Volunteering and providing services to others are just ways that sport empowerment programs focus on building confidence, community, and joy within their participants (Cary, 2013; Pandolfo, 2016).

Perhaps even more importantly, at a time when adolescent girls experience negativity, programs like Girls on the Run take these challenging topics head on. For instance, Girls on the Run gets girls talking about bullying, friendship changes, and puberty (Cary, 2013; Feldman, 2015; Walton, 2015).

Discussion around these serious topics in group settings along with the team setting of sport helps to empower these young girls to stand up for themselves and others in the face of challenging social situations. The intentionality behind sport empowerment programs' lessons makes them stand out from traditional sport teams. In my own research, I encountered a Girls on the Run coach of 29 years, who talked about how one of her participants was using strategies that she learned from the Girls on the Run curriculum for combating bullying. She said that she learned from the teacher of one of her third-grade girls she was coaching that the lessons taught were useful and transferable to an everyday life of a third grader. The coach commented that the time she spent with the girls a couple of afternoons each week was valuable not only to girl participants but to the women leaders as well (Kramer, 2017).

More importantly, these transferable life skills taught in sport empowerment programs for girls stick with participants as they move into adulthood. Anna, a volunteer and past participant of Little Bellas, a mountain-biking empowerment program for girls, speaks highly of her experiences as a Little Bella herself and how the program set her up for success as an adult facing inevitable challenges. Anna noted, "Little Bella's has taught me what it means to grow from a student to a mentor, but also what it means to be an adult. Life is not going to be easy and there will be times I will want to give up, but I know I have to push forward. Whether you gather strength from watching your role models or by being a role model, perseverance is key" (LittleBellas.com, para 8). The transferable skills that Anna recognizes are found in many other sport empowerment program curriculums: dedication, confidence, and perseverance, which are all important qualities in many stages of life.

In my own recent study of sport empowerment programs for girls, I learned more about how these programs develop leadership aimed at both personal and social changes. Through teaching valuable life skills and creating welcoming environments for the participants, these programs are equipping young girls and women to not only deal with the barriers they face, but also own change and lead the conversation around what it means to be a girl or a woman. For example, Gritty Girls, an empowerment program derived from an athletic apparel company, Graced by Grit, incorporates leadership development through its acronym of the word "grit." "G" stands for guts and how being adventurous and learning from mistakes all take guts. "R" stands for resilience and the power in rising up after being knocked down in life. "I" stands for imperfection and how embracing imperfection allows girls to say "no" to the societal pressures of having the ideal body, never making a mistake, not trying new things out of fear of not excelling, and more. Finally, "T" stands for team or tribe. Gritty Girls focuses on the importance of having a strong support system whether that is through a sports team, family, or friends at school or in one's community. Teaching these concepts through small groups, exercise, yoga, or meditation, and through one-on-one counseling, Gritty Girls is changing what it means to be a leader:

> We absolutely incorporate leadership development. Usually it comes out [through] teaching that it takes guts to stand up for what you believe in. I think a lot of times, girls have this viewpoint that leaders have to be really outgoing, confident and popular. So I strive to present the different type of leaders . . . So the way that I've done leadership workshops as part of Gritty Girls is to have them look at their own strengths and what they are passionate about, to help them find out what makes it natural for them to lead. (Personal Communication, 9 March 2017)

Sport empowerment programs for girls focus on much more than just sport and physical activity. By utilizing sport as the platform to reach participants on a deeper level, sport empowerment programs seem to provide direct benefits to girls in the form of improved self-confidence, practiced leadership skills, engagement in the community, and developed relationships. By emphasizing the importance of sport for young girls, participants will ideally develop a conscious shift in thinking regarding their place in sport that stays with them as they move into adult life.

References

Cary, Joan. 2013. "Girls Running Program Makes Having Fun No Sweat." *Chicago Tribune.* http://articles.chicago tribune.com/2013-05-08/news/ct-x-girls-on-the-run-20130508_1_chicago-girls-5k-run-chicago-council. Accessed on January 9, 2017.

Feldman, Claudia. 2015. "Girls on the Run Program Is about More Than Athletic Accomplishment." *Houston Chronicle.* http://www.houstonchronicle.com/news/health/article/ Girls-on-the-Run-program-is-about-more-than-6222887 .php. Accessed on January 10, 2017.

Fuller, Linda K. 2006. *Sport, Rhetoric, and Gender.* New York: Palgrave MacMillan.

Kramer, Kenzie. 2017. "Girls on the Run Coach Changes Girls' Lives for 15 Years." https://www.girlsontherun.org/ remarkable/301/. Accessed on January 16, 2017.

Litchfield, Chelsea, and Rylee A. Dionigi. 2011. "The Meaning of Sports Participation in the Lives of Middle-aged and Older Women." *International Journal of Interdisciplinary Social Sciences*, 6(5): 21–36.

LittleBellas.com. "From Little Bella to Mentor: Meet Anna Singer." Little Bellas: Mentoring on Mountain Bikes. http:// littlebellas.com/little-bella-mentor-meet-anna-singer/. Accessed on January 10, 2017.

Pandolfo, Carolyn. 2016. How Girls on the Run Made Me a Joyful, Healthy, and Confident Woman. *Girls on the Run International.* https://www.girlsontherun.org/

remarkable/292/How-Girls-on-the-Run-Made-Me-a-Joyful,-Healthy-and. Accessed on January 4, 2017.

Roster, Catherine A. 2007. " 'Girl Power' and Participation in Macho Recreation: The Case of Female Harley Riders." *Leisure Sciences*, 29(5): 443–461.

Walton, B. 2015. "Girls on the Run a Joyful, Confidence Boosting Program." *Citizen-Times*. http://www.citizen times.com/story/news/local/2015/01/03/girls-run-joyful-confidence-boosting-event/21239985/. Accessed January 10, 2017.

Zieff, Susan G. 2006. "GirlSpeak: Adolescent Females Talk about Their Athletic Identities." In Linda K. Fuller (Ed.), *Sport, Rhetoric, and Gender*. New York: Palgrave Macmillan.

Erin Karner currently works for Girls on the Run of Puget Sound where she combines her two passions: education and sport. Erin played competitive soccer through college and enjoys playing in rec-reational leagues now. She also loves long-distance running and hiking.

"You Got This": Making My Way on the Confidence Journey
Séu Jacobi

It was September 7, 2016, on a warm autumn afternoon in Ljubljana, Slovenia. The leaves were vivid shades of orange, red, and yellow. "Alright everyone, get geared up and get on the water," my coach says. I had just arrived in this beautiful area, excited for the Whitewater Canoe Slalom World Cup Final. This particular day was for training, and the race would start just two days later, September 9. This was my first time seeing this whitewater course. The water was the brightest aqua-blue I had ever seen. This course is known for having the biggest wave-drop that is used in the entire canoe-race circuit. I had never seen anything like it. The water was loud and pumping hard. I took my first few runs, going under the cold, icy water every time. I was quite scared by this point, as were many others.

Many coaches, including my own, had told their younger athletes that there was not any pressure to race on a whitewater canoe course that was this big, and that the younger athletes did not have to race. The competition was mainly made up of the world's top senior-level athletes, so the group of young athletes was quite small. I was almost positive I would not race, as all of my practice sessions ended up with getting beat-up by this giant drop.

The day of the race came, and I had to make my decision. I accepted the risk, and said I would compete. Fast-forward to a few hours later, and there I am sitting in the start-gate surrounded by athletes having their final thoughts before their competition run. I could only hear the paddle strokes of the other competitors, with the occasional whispers of teammates discussing their race strategies. I had one last chance to get out of my boat and not compete. Then, I heard the judge say, "3 . . . 2 . . . 1 . . . GO!" My heart dropped. I paddled as hard as I possibly could, taking on this very first big drop. Water was splashing, my heart was racing, and then I heard my coach say, "YOU GOT THIS." Those three words changed everything. Maneuvering from different sides of the waves, I felt the rush, and I took advantage of it. It was the most perfect run I had the whole week. The race went fantastic, and I was so happy. I did not have a top-level winning run, but I felt like I had won myself in that moment. I overcame one of my biggest fears, and learned a new meaning for the word "confidence."

Being a teenage girl, confidence isn't something automatic. My mind *regularly* looks to what I do "wrong." I have had to teach myself that instead of looking at the bad, to look at the good and strive to make it better. This could be anything from one paddle-stroke or an entire race. Building on the "good" paves over the "bad."

Confidence, what *exactly* does this word convey?

The definition varies for each individual. I never truly understood the meaning until I felt it, thought it, and did it. I am not known for confidence. I never have been. It still is something with which I struggle to this very day, but I make small steps daily to gain confidence both mentally and physically.

Confidence is not an end state. It is a lifestyle, a process of moving in and out of "you got this." Confidence is the sum of many small experiences of doing and redoing, consistent support, the ability to step back and not take life so seriously, and being kind to myself.

During my training and competitions, I have experienced many emotional breakdowns due to my own confidence levels. I have worked and worked to change the way I think, train, and compete. On days when I felt like confidence was nowhere to be found, I would think "maybe tomorrow it will be different." It never was. Sometimes it made me want to give up, but I never did. Little did I know, someday my mind would change. Upside down, inside out, rotating 180 degrees in all directions like it did in Slovenia.

Throughout my entire life, I have had support from my amazing parents, coaches, teammates, family, friends, and even strangers, who give me the brightest smiles and the best laughter when I thought I just wasn't capable of anything. Strange how jokes about a platypus can turn your worst day of training in a positive direction! All of these people are part of my confidence journey. Because of them, I am more outgoing than I ever have been and am becoming more self-assured as each day goes by. I am beyond grateful for all the influential role models in my life who have taught me how to enjoy every bit of the journey. I have learned to give myself space—space to think, space to breathe, and space to accept myself. Having this space, my "me time," allows me to find the good in what I do and notice the improvements, however, small, on my own terms.

Confidence is a journey—a journey of paradox. It is about embracing one's own experiences, but accepting support along the way. It involves not taking life so seriously, but taking time to be with oneself and reflect on things that matter. It's when feeling, thinking and doing all come together in that moment you know "you got this."

Séu Jacobi is a competitive athlete in the sport of Whitewater Canoe Slalom representing the United States in international competition. Most of the year, Séu resides in Spain, in the town after which she is named. She enjoys reading and writing, and takes high interest in journalism.

Breaking the Gender Binary in Sport: Female-to-Male Recreational Athlete
Riley McCormack

At five years old, I did not feel comfortable saying, "I'm a girl." I have rejected every notion and every behavior on what it means to "be feminine." Twenty years later, I still despise these words. Every day, I live in a body that was assigned female sex at birth. I live in a body that is not mine.

For an elite athlete or a recreational one, such as myself, participating in any sport requires a certain level of mental and physical training. However, as an athlete and someone who identifies as transgender as well, I can say participating in sport entails an extra level of mental exertion. Reeser (2005) emphasizes it clearly that transitioning is not to gain any cultural reward or personal athletic advantage; it is about seeking personal harmony between body and mind. Transitioning is an internal experience and being an athlete happens with and among teammates and friends. I have to face obstacles and barriers that cisgender athletes do not. For example, transgender and gender fluid athletes, myself included, must navigate daily through spaces that are specific to the gender binary.

For most individuals, sex, gender, gender identity, and gender expression align on the same side of the gender spectrum, also known as cisgender. However, when individuals' gender identity, gender expression, inner feelings of self-gender, and the gender assigned to them at birth do not match, they may identify as transgender. People who identify as transgender may express themselves through their internalized gender identity. Transgender can be further defined as female-to-male individuals, transmen, transmasculine or male-to-female individuals, transwomen, or transfeminine. Individuals who choose to have sex reassignment surgery, currently on hormones, and have legally changed their gender may identify as transsexual (Semerjian and Cohen, 2006).

Sport has left me with a bittersweet taste. I love playing and teaching youth about sports. Playing on a sports team, I felt "at home" in sport and had a sense of community. However, the sports world became a frustrating and angry space during my social transition in college because my teammates would use female pronouns and/or say my birth name. In intramurals, we had to have a certain number of males and females on the field. I wanted to play as one of the guys, the way I saw myself. Yet, my body reflected differently and I had to count myself as one of the females simply because I had a chest.

Even talking about sports can make me feel sad because I have to either alter my sports experience as if I competed as a guy or come out and say I competed as a girl. For example, I played volleyball, basketball, and softball in high school. Often, I will replace softball with baseball because boys play baseball and girls play softball. Trying to find the balance is frustrating, so I tend to keep quiet about my sport experiences all together.

Reflecting on previous experiences of playing sports in high school, playing intramurals in college, and how much fun they were. I would feel comfortable playing in a lesbian/dyke softball league. However, I can't join because I pass as a guy by injecting testosterone once a week. I worry that people will think I'm "cheating" because I have some sort of physical advantage due to the testosterone. I feel sad that I can't be part of team sports because I do not feel comfortable playing on an all-male team.

I grieve the loss of my athletic identity in conjunction with the loss of sports community. There is a male team and there is a female team, I am forced to choose one or the other, or find an all-queer/trans team to play with. I just want to play with people.

Locker or changing rooms is another space that I have to navigate on the daily. If I want to shower after working out, the only space to shower is the male locker room. I remember the one and only time I showered after working out. The entire time I was showering, I feared for my life that someone would accidentally open the shower curtain. I had worst-case scenarios running through my mind on a continuum. I didn't even have time to enjoy taking a shower because I was scared. I felt shame, humiliation, and anger for entering a space where, according to society, my body does not belong. Since this moment, which occurred over two years ago, I refuse to take a shower at a gym because I do not feel comfortable in male locker rooms. The only space I do feel comfortable changing or showering is in a gender-neutral changing or locker room.

Running has become my sport because it is the one sport where gender does not make a difference. Running also frees my mind and body from the trapped feelings inside. It provides the space where I don't have to tear myself down. At times, I can feel the testosterone pumping through my veins. I feel powerful and more connected to my body when I run. I feel my body becoming more me with each run.

There is no singular experience of being a female or male and there is no singular experience of being an identified transgender male or female. Yet, the segregation of female and male athletes and the perceptions associated with gendered athletic ability leave little to no space for transgender and gender fluid athletes (Lucas-Carr and Krane, 2011).

In 2007, the Washington Interscholastic Athletic Association, which governs high school sports in the state of Washington, enacted a policy allowing students to participate in sports "in a manner that is consistent with their gender identity, irrespective of the gender listed on a student's records" (WIAA, 2007). When transgender and gender-nonconforming athletes want to play a recreational sport, they have to seek out a specific league that identifies itself as trans/queer-friendly. For example, there is a soccer club where an all-trans/queer team has had to fight to play without rules such as having a certain number of males and females on the pitch. Another rule that the team has asked to disregard while playing is the "macho rule" where if a "female" gets hit in the chest, it counts as a foul. For a transman with a chest, the latter rule can raise feelings of gender dysphoria, meaning how I feel on the inside is incongruent with how my body is read by society.

Policies around inclusion in sport organizations can be a good start toward transgender inclusion in sport, but attitudes need to change as well. Sport organizations with the least inclusive policies are likely those in which adopting inclusion policies for transgender athletes has not been considered. Next, there are some sport organizations such as in collegiate or Olympic sports that allow participation based on some degree of physical transitioning such as hormones or surgery. The most inclusive policies allow athletes to participate on teams that athletes feel are most appropriate for themselves (Buzuvis, 2012). According to Lucas-Carr and Krane (2011), sport psychologists should be leading the fight to create safe and receptive climates for gender nonconforming athletes by raising awareness, understanding, and compassion for gender-nonconforming and transgender athletes who face large obstacles in sport.

Transsexual, transgender, and gender-nonconforming athletes experience a great amount of marginalization, discrimination, and exclusion at all levels in sport today. This is particularly true for transwomen who want to participate on female sports teams or participate in female sport events. This is due to the persistence of the gender binary; that is, the belief that there are only two genders, and the commonly held view that men are stronger and better at sport. As transgender and gender-nonconforming athletes are becoming more visible in sport, these assumptions are being challenged.

While highly competitive sport seems like it's a long way from all-inclusive sport teams, there is much we can do to create more inclusive sport experiences and spaces for all genders. First, it is important to respect and refer to all athletes, specifically transgender and gender-nonconforming athletes by their preferred name and pronouns that correspond with their gender identity. Second, avoid making an assumption about how gender-nonconforming individuals feel about their body. Third, allow all athletes access to uniforms that they are comfortable wearing. Also, transgender and gender-nonconforming athletes should have access to their preferred gender locker room and shower area in a safe environment. Also, ensuring that sex-specific sports are not the only opportunities offered for youth and adults, but rather having sports that are open to anyone regardless of their sex. While coed sports may be good start, they still regulate the participation by sex, by having rules around how many females and males on the field or playing certain positions. Sport organizers should provide gender-free sports where athletes do not have to play based on their assigned sex at birth. Lastly, creating a space in sport that values diversity, acceptance, and inclusion, and creates compassion for transgender and gender-nonconforming athletes in the team atmosphere (Kauer and Krane, 2010).

In sum, I believe that raising awareness, compassion, and empathy around the obstacles and barriers transgender and gender-nonconforming people face in sport; creating transinclusive policies in recreational sports; and creating recreational leagues that are based on ability only benefit all athletes, especially those who identify as female or desire to play on female sports teams.

References

Buzuvis, Erin. 2012. "Including Transgender Athletes in Sex-Segregated Sport." In George B. Cunningham (Ed.), *Sexual Orientation and Gender Identity in Sport: Essays from Activists, Coaches, and Scholars*. College Station, TX: Center for Sport Management Research and Education.

Kauer, Kerrie, and Vikki Krane. 2010. "Inclusive Excellence: Embracing Diverse Sexual and Gender Identities in Sport." In Stephanie Hanrahan and Mark B. Andersen (Eds.), *Handbook of Applied Sport Psychology*. New York: Routledge.

Lucas-Carr, Catherine B., and Vikki Krane. 2011. "What Is the T in LGBT? Supporting Transgender Athletes through Sport Psychology." *Sport Psychologist*, 25(4): 532–548.

Reeser, Jonathan C. 2005. "Gender Identity and Sport: Is the Playing Field Level?" *British Journal of Sports Medicine*, 39(10): 695–699.

Semerjian, Tamar Z., and Jodi H. Cohen. 2006. " 'FTM Means Female to Me': Transgender Athletes Performing Gender." *Women in Sport and Physical Activity Journal*, 15(2): 28–43.

Washington Interscholastic Athletic Association [WIAA]. "Official Handbook," Section 8.15.0. http://www.wiaa .com/ConDocs/Con358/Eligibility.pdf. Accessed on May 3, 2017.

Riley McCormack is a recreational athlete who enjoys running, playing volleyball, and breaking the gender binary in sport. He is passionate about bridging the gap between the LGBTQ and sports communities. His dream is to open his own youth sports camp that is a queer-safe space. Riley has also written about his own transition experiences as a recreational competitive athlete in Transgender Athletes in Competitive Sport, *edited by Eric Anderson and Ann Travers.*

Gender Equality in Sport: (Un)Awareness, Education, and Resolve
Annie Sittauer and Sarah Tani

While supporters of women's sports point out the significant growth and gains that women's collegiate sports have made since Title IX, experiences vary. The culture of an athletic department seems to make an important difference in shaping those experiences. As former DI collegiate athletes, we have become aware of the ways that cultural differences hide or highlight the privilege of men's sport. One of us has little memory of gender discrepancies. In many ways, not sensing gender inequality, even in a university with a successful football program, was perhaps naïve. However, there can be a feeling of gratitude that emerges as well upon realizing that one of us got to play without the burden of gender inequality weighing in on an already busy life. For the other, gender inequality was felt in many ways through the observed cultural valuing of men's sports and relative nonvaluing of women's sports. In both instances, being a collegiate athlete was a way to continue doing what we had done our whole lives, and the privilege of that experience is not lost on us. Our different collegiate experiences, similar paths into graduate school, and now working for professional soccer teams (men's and women's) inspired the following reflections.

Hegemonic Masculinity

Hegemonic masculinity refers to the way that a certain type of masculinity is the established norm, or the standard by which all other experiences, activities, or ways of being are judged or are relevant to society. Masculinity associated with sport is *hegemonic* in that it is privileged in society at large. Such privilege plays out in collegiate athletics. For both of us, football was regarded as the primary sport, to which considerable resources were allocated. However, each of us felt football's privilege in very different ways. For one of us, there was the knowledge that the revenue from football *did* support most other sports in the athletic department. Although there are very few universities for which that is the case, the favoring of football did not seem to detract from women's sport nor was there the perception that receiving "less" than football was a detriment to women's soccer. However, we also know that there are fewer than 25 universities that have men's football or basketball programs that are that financially lucrative. For instance, in 2012 only 23 out of 228 NCAA Division I athletic departments earned enough money to cover their own expenses (Berkowitz, Upton, and Brady, 2013). It is much more common for athletic departments to operate in the red, relying heavily on subsidies from student fees, tuition, fund-raising, and other university-wide sources of income. Ticket sales and alumni donations rarely make up the deficit. As a result, when men's sports are given priority, very often that priority is felt by other sports, especially women's sports.

As was the case for one of us, the priority of men's sports was acutely felt by those of us in women's sports. For example, football was clearly the priority of the athletics department and the university, followed by men's basketball and baseball. Women's basketball, women's soccer, and softball followed in priority. In order to skirt Title IX requirements, universities will adopt a tiered system of priorities in which they designate two or three tiers of priority funding. This practice is accepted within the NCAA rules and usually justified as a university "choice" in terms of potential revenue. As noted, that revenue rarely plays out, and the tiered system functions as institutionalized hegemonic masculinity and sexism. These priorities are not only at the financial level, but permeate the culture of the athletics department and school. Despite the unfulfilled reality of revenue generation, one of us noted that wins and losses only mattered if they came from football or men's basketball. Other wins and losses seemed irrelevant. Resources such as stadium lights or better transportation were promised, but never fulfilled. Sports with the fewest allocated resources were often the first to receive less.

As student-athletes, there is much to be grateful for, as we were extended attention and privileges unlike other students. However, within this focused attention, the fact that men's sports were simply valued more became evident. Among the student-athlete community, it became clear how the male athletes dominated conversation and social interactions. They usually instigated social activities and their presence, or lack thereof, could change levels of participation. Additionally, our personal interactions with staff were limited to our coaches. Individual or personalized treatment only existed when we were checking in at the beginning of the season, if we were injured, or if we were in trouble. Such was not the case for the high-profile men's sports such as football, basketball, or baseball. Another way the privilege of men's sports is felt is by the fact that the administration pays little attention to knowing other athletes, learning their names, and being interested in their teams. A poignant example is the following memory: One staff member attended one practice for the women's soccer team and spent the entire time, 20 minutes, on the phone. He did not know our names, nor did he take an interest in our achievements and growth as athletes and individuals. Title IX paved the way for us to be able to participate, but it didn't necessarily mean we were equal once we got there.

Aspirations and Career Path

For one of us, the collegiate experience and a lifetime of playing soccer left as big a hole upon graduating as it had filling our lives. Career aspirations and the transition of our collegiate sports are captured well in Annie's following story.

After playing four years of Division I soccer, I felt lost. Soccer was the only thing I had known my entire life, and in a flash, it was over after exhausting my four years of NCAA eligibility. I remember sitting in my athletic director's office after my senior season, reflecting on my experience as a student-athlete. My experience was nowhere near perfect, but all I could think about was how I wished I could play those last four years on repeat. I did not want it to end. The director and I started talking about my plans after graduation, and during that time he took to talk, he offered me a glimmer of hope as he began to discuss how he too felt lost upon graduation and delved into his journey to becoming an athletic director. In that moment, I had no notion of the difficulty associated with becoming a female athletic director or the barriers women inherently face while working in sports; all I knew was that I wanted to help others experience the same positive impact of sports that soccer afforded me. In that moment I realized I wanted to become an athletic director and I had no idea what I was getting myself into. After two years of work experience and a graduate degree in sport administration, I am not only aware of the utter inequalities that exist, but I am determined to fight against them on a daily basis. My experience working in Division I athletic departments and earning an advance degree have illuminated the importance of understanding the ways in which our society perpetuates the notion that women and sports are inherently incompatible with each other.

Living the Divide and Finding Our Way

Each of us now works in professional soccer. One of us works for a men's team, and the other works for a women's team. Through our experiences and education, we both feel passionate about advocating for women's sports and empowering women through sports. Our tasks and daily lives are quite different in that respect. Working for a women's professional soccer team comes with many unique challenges that probably don't align with the typical glamorous image that people tend to associate with professional sports. The cultural value of women's sport affects our daily operations as we all wear many hats and function on little money due to the limited funds. While the men's professional soccer team is selling out stadiums and operating under a lucrative budget, the women's team is struggling to be recognized at all. While the male players have salaries that sustain their livelihoods easily, and they are taken care of on every level including access to the best technology and sport science and coaching available, the female professional players are receiving such limited salaries that most are forced to work multiple side jobs just to make ends meet. Which is more impressive? Selling out stadiums or working hard and going with very little just to be able to do what you love? On the other hand, working for the men's sports team comes with much of the glamor, albeit very hard, long working hours. Further, while the men's game garners more respect, being a female in that environment can be challenging. Small behaviors such as always "turning to the guy" to find an answer all add up to what Williams and Dempsey (2014) call "accumulation of disadvantage" (5). This is the phenomenon in which many small experiences of marginalization add up to create systems of marginalization.

Finding our way in sport leadership is balancing who we are with the culture of sports. Given that both of us are intimately familiar with the culture of sports, we realize that our organizational capabilities, understanding of teamwork, work ethic, and understanding of competition make sport a known entity for us. Leading within that context remains a path of self-discovery. One of the most critical realizations so far is that people can and do lead in a variety of ways and still be successful. First, it is important to realize that being oneself is more important than becoming like one's predecessor. This path is not always easy as support from above is important here. When there is little support from one's immediate supervisor, it is tough. However, when competency is recognized, more pathways open up. Emulating a leadership style that does not integrate well with your personality is ineffective. It's critical to understand that each person has her/his own unique leadership style and there isn't one "right" way for women to lead. We know that each of us has a slightly different path to advocating for women and women's sports, given our different roles in different organizations. Yet, we know that navigating our current environments in order to create change relies on being cognizant of barriers for female athletes and the ways in which women's sports are marginalized. This knowledge allows us to find the small ways to advocate on a daily basis. We are now neither naïve nor complacent.

References

Berkowitz, Steve, Jodi Upton, and Erik Brady, "Most NCAA Division I Athletic Departments Take Subsidies." https://www.usatoday.com/story/sports/college/2013/05/07/ncaa-finances-subsidies/2142443/. Accessed on July 15, 2017.

Williams, Joan C., and Rachel Dempsey. 2014. *What Works for Women at Work: Four Working Patterns Women Need to Know.* New York: New York University Press.

Annie Sittauer is team coordinator for the Seattle Reign FC, one of 10 teams in the National Women's Soccer League. Annie played collegiate soccer and still enjoys playing at the recreational level. Annie also enjoys working with and mentoring young female athletes.

Sarah Tani is game presentation coordinator for the Seattle Sounders FC, one of 22 teams in Major League Soccer, and current MLS Cup Champions (2016). She also volunteers for the community branch of the Sounder FC. She continues to play recreational soccer and gets out in the mountains, hiking and skiing as much as possible.

Introduction

This chapter highlights individuals and organizations important to the history, understanding, and advocacy of girls and women in sport. The brief sketches contain background information and descriptions of accomplishments and significant contributions. The list is not exhaustive, but includes a few well-known individuals and organizations as well as those typical of other individuals and organizations making an impact.

Association for Women in Sports Media

The Association for Women in Sports Media (AWSM) was founded in 1987. The acronym, AWSM, is pronounced "awesome," reflecting the role that it plays in advancing and supporting women in the sports media industry. It was established as a 501(c)(3) and is run through volunteer efforts. Its purpose is to provide support to women who want to pursue careers in sports media. Sports media entails sports writing, editing, public relations, and media relations, as well as broadcast and production. The organization was founded in order to channelize efforts around advocacy for women who want to enter into the sports media industry. It achieves this mission through various

Former CEO of the Women's Sports Foundation Donna Lopiano speaks at the Billie Awards, an awards ceremony celebrating female athletes in visual media, at the Beverly Hilton Hotel in California on April 11, 2007. (Vince Bucci/Getty Images)

support services and networking opportunities. The organization helps bring visibility to the role of women in sports media as well as sports media content. Comprised of approximately 600 members, AWSM welcomes both men and women as advocates for women in sports broadcasting. Functioning as a networking and support organization, AWSM membership consists of industry professionals and students aspiring to work in sports media. The AWSM board is made up of 16 women and men from the sports media. The work of the board focuses on fund-raising, developing internship opportunities, student development, facilitating awards, and organizing the annual convention. There have been 88 board members since 1987, demonstrating the broad support that AWSM has from industry professionals. In February 2005, AWSM redrafted its primary objectives. Its commitment is as follows:

> To serve as a positive advocate for women in sports media, through support services, networking and national visibility; to mentor and assist young women entering into sports media, through scholarships, internships and contact with experienced members; to serve as a watchdog, promoting fair portrayal of female professionals in sports media, encouraging diversity, positive workplace environments and equal access to opportunities.

AWSM offers several programs that help women launch their careers in sports media. AWSM partners with major sports media organizations to offer scholarships to 6–10 women annually since 1990. Scholarship sponsors currently include *Sports Illustrated*, MLB.com, *USA Today* Sports, ESPN, CNN and PRO Sports Communications, Golf Channel, and USA Softball. In addition to the organizations that support scholarships, AWSM has the support of the Associated Press Sports Editors and the Sports Journalism Institute to help with paid internship opportunities. Over 160 female students have benefited from scholarship awards and paid internships since 1990. To further support female students' access to sport media jobs,

AWSM partners with about 15 universities to host "chapters" on university campuses. Chapters are student-led and have one faculty advisor. No more than five chapters are approved each year. All members of AWSM student chapters receive the same benefits as members of AWSM. These include being able to access AWSM's directory of members, and receiving AWSM's monthly newsletter and job alerts. These student chapters are entry points for networking and mentorship. The approval process for becoming a chapter entails providing a list of potential members, officers, support from the university, and a vision and goals statement about how AWSM can support the efforts of the chapter.

In addition to helping young women enter the sports media industry, AWSM provides an ongoing network of professionals throughout one's career. Members note the value of AWSM as a network of individuals committed to helping each other. The positive camaraderie promotes being able to get career advice either in a current job or when switching specific jobs within the sports media industry. Specific areas of support are providing wisdom about resume writing, networking habits, and cover letter strategies. AWSM also offers a mid-career grant to women who have worked in the industry for several years and are looking to improve their skill sets and gain further knowledge. The grant is intended to directly support women already working in sports media further their careers by reaching the next goal in their career paths. The mid-career training grants are offered twice each year. These grants award each recipient up to $1,000 for professional development. In addition, the annual two-day convention features guest speakers, panels, and workshops aimed at improving specific skill sets in the various jobs within sports media.

AWSM also seeks to recognize important contributions of women to the sports media industry. The Mary Garber Pioneer Award has been given annually since 1999. It is named after Mary Garber, who began sports writing during World War II when most men were sent to war. After the war, Garber continued covering sports, especially topics that no one else wanted to cover such as athletics in black colleges and high schools. After being denied entry initially into sports writing associations, Garber became president of the Football Writers Association of America and the Atlantic Coast Sports Writers Association. In 2005, she received the Red Smith Award, which is given to the person who has made significant contributions to sports journalism. AWSM continues the legacy and inspiration of Mary Garber through honoring women who have made major contributions to the sports media industry. In 2013, AWSM created a second award, the Ann Miller Award, which recognizes those individuals who have made notable contributions in their service to AWSM.

Clare Balding (1971–)

Clare Balding is a leading sports broadcaster for the British Broadcasting Corporation (BBC) from the United Kingdom. Her coverage of the 2012 London Olympic and Paralympic Games earned her global recognition by receiving two distinguished awards. In 2013, she received the Special Award from the British Academy of Film and Television Arts for her expert and factual coverage that helped British viewers understand and relate to these Olympic events. In that same year, Balding received the Presenter of the Year Award from the Royal Television Society, an award that is not sports specific, but rather encompasses all television presenter performances in any given year. Since 2013, Balding has served as the senior presenter for horse racing and horse competitions as well as hosts her own sports talk show called *The Clare Balding Show*, which airs on two prominent sports television entities, BT Sport and BBC Two.

Balding began her career in sports radio for Radio 5 Live and Radio 1 in the United Kingdom. In 1995, she became a television presenter, providing highlights on famous horseracing events in the United Kingdom. She joined the BBC in 1997 to be the lead presenter for horse racing. Having family ties to horseracing as well as having been an amateur jockey, Balding was able to provide detailed, authentic coverage that resonated with audiences. Her on-air personality led to gaining presenter opportunities at many Olympic Games for BBC. She has been a presenter for six Summer Olympic Games, including Atlanta, Sydney, Athens, Beijing, London, and Rio de Janeiro. Among the Winter Olympics, She has covered the games in Salt Lake City, Turin, Vancouver, and Sochi along with four Paralympic Games associated with those events. In addition, she has covered three Commonwealth Games in Melbourne, Delhi, and Glasgow. The Commonwealth Games is an international multisport event held every four years among 52 globally recognized states or territories that were once a part of the British Empire and colonization. Her passion for rugby has also propelled her opportunities as a broadcaster for numerous world rugby events.

In 2013, Clare Balding was appointed Officer of the Order of the British Empire, an appointment that recognizes outstanding service and contributions in the arts, sciences, charity work, and public service. She has received numerous other awards for her ability to be engaging, authentic, and professional in both radio and television. Her versatility in the sports broadcasting industry is noteworthy. For these skills and accomplishments, Balding has received awards from *Attitude Magazine*, *Red Magazine*, *Tatler*, and the Horserace Writers Association. While Balding's first successes were in horse racing commentary, she has been able to move into other genres and formats. In 1999, she joined the BBC's Radio 4 "Ramblings" show. In these episodes, Balding supports walking as a pastime by joining and talking with interesting people all over Britain's countryside. In these episodes, walking is viewed as a healing activity, a way of being in motion that brings calm and peace. In 2010, she hosted a similar radio talk show called "Britain by Bike."

Most recently, Balding has written several books. Her first book, *My Animals and Other Family*, was published in 2012 and quickly moved onto the bestsellers list. In the book, Balding recounts what it was like growing up in a household entirely focused on horseracing. Her father was a champion horse trainer. Balding describes the family dynamics as horses were the first priority, her brother next, and then her. The biography follows her own growth as a young girl having to find her way and develop resilience through life challenges and proving her worth. As she noted in her book, "the running family joke was 'women ain't people.'" The book won biography of the year at the National Book Awards in 2012. Her second book, *Walking Home*, was published in 2014. The book draws from the "Ramblings" radio show and provides memoirs and stories of exploring the British countryside. In 2016, she published her first children's book, titled *The Racehorse Who Wouldn't Gallop*.

Based on her many accomplishments, Balding is sought after as a speaker. She continues to work toward inspiring women who want to work in the sport industry. In 2015, she worked with the United Kingdom's Women in Sport organization to encourage all sports organizations to become part of the movement to provide more opportunities for women in sport leadership.

Camber Outdoors

Camber Outdoors is a nonprofit organization dedicated to making the outdoors and the outdoor industry more inclusive for women. Founded in 1996 as the Outdoor Industry Women's Coalition, Camber Outdoors is a national organization comprised of individual members, industry organizations, and foundations. Bringing together outdoor industry constituents, Camber Outdoors aims to step up the efforts to increase women's participation in active-outdoor activities as well as support women on their paths to leadership positions in active-outdoor organizations. There are over 4,200 individual members and 190 corporate members. Corporate members enjoy full benefits of Camber Outdoors, including access to tools for sustaining executive commitment, assessment tools and best practices for recruiting and retaining women, access to a curated job board, and unlimited individual memberships for employees. Individual membership includes access to regional events, leadership development webinars, mentoring program, access to executive thinking, and a community committed to supporting women in the outdoors and related industries.

Camber Outdoors serves the outdoor industry by being advocates for diverse ideas and individuals. It stays focused on having an impact in business through helping corporate cultures leverage diversity in order to have an impact on innovation, business initiatives, and solutions. One of the primary ways it achieves its aims is through the CEO Pledge. The CEO Pledge is a promise from the CEO of a company to make women's leadership a strategic priority. Camber Outdoors provides materials and online spaces for organizational representatives to enact the CEO Pledge. It also facilitates networking events, hosts leadership development webinars, and hosts keynote speakers. Networking events are called "Camber Exchanges" and occur in multiple cities throughout the United States. The events are designed so that women from all areas of working in the outdoor industry can connect and exchange ideas. In addition, Camber Outdoors hosts webinars with industry professionals. These webinars are aimed at helping women think about and develop their own leadership skills. Finally, the speakers are experienced industry leaders who share their insights about how they have worked to solve problems and move their own organizations toward gender equality and inclusivity. The organization also tries to source and distribute key research on women in leadership positions. Capitalizing on the research from organizations such as the McKinsey & Company and Catalyst, it helps share the research and data that support the rationale as to why focusing on gender equality is a sound business decision.

Camber Outdoors has also developed several paths around mentoring. One path is its annual Pitchfest. Pitchfest is intended to support innovation and creativity in filling needs within the active-outdoor industry. Companies founded or cofounded by a woman and with at least one-third of female employees are allowed to apply. In the initial application process, founders must show their market value and revenue streams. If selected as a finalist to present at Pitchfest, founders work for two months with industry professionals to refine their ideas and business models. They are also guided on how to make a pitch for a business. The final pitch occurs the day before the annual Outdoor Retailer Summer Market tradeshow. The process is supportive and meant to help small businesses run and owned by women succeed and grow. A second mentoring path is the Mentor Program facilitated by Camber Outdoors. Mentors are women who have attained vice president level or above. Mentees are women who are in a manager or director position and lead a team of individuals. The program lasts for nine months.

In order to support women who embrace and live their values, Camber Outdoors presents two leadership awards each year. The Pioneering Woman Award has been awarded since 2002 and is given to a woman who has been recognized as creating positive change within the active-outdoor industry. The First Ascent Award has been in existence since 2005 and is awarded to a woman identified as having great leadership potential. Camber Outdoors also offers a curated career center. Both employers and job seekers can access this career site focused on connecting women to forward thinking and inclusive organizations.

Camber Outdoors serves as a model organization committed to the proactive engagement of helping organizations improve their policies, practices, and corporate culture to become a workplace in which women and people of diverse backgrounds feel welcome and are supported. Their strategy is to be the hub of connecting companies, individuals, research, and entrepreneurship and leadership development programming. This integrated approach not only serves its members well, but continues to raise awareness about gender equality as a critical business strategy that is integral for sustainable businesses.

Anita DeFrantz (1952–)

Over a span of four decades, Anita DeFrantz has been and continues to be one of the most influential women in sports policy making, especially with respect to the Olympic movement. In 1986, DeFrantz became the fifth woman, first American woman, and first black woman to be elected to, at the time, the 93-member International Olympic Committee (IOC). DeFrantz had served on the board of directors for the U.S. Olympic Committee for 10 years prior to her being elected in 1986 to the IOC. In 1987, she became president of the LA84 Foundation, and from 1993 to 2013, she served on the International Rowing Federation.

DeFrantz's desire to work in sport was fueled by her participation in the 1976 Montreal Olympic Games in rowing. Not only did she win a bronze medal, but she was profoundly changed by that experience. She recognized the power of sport to bring people together and serve as a positive place for growth and development, especially for women and women of color. DeFrantz had taken up rowing as an undergraduate at Connecticut College. Upon completing her undergraduate degree, DeFrantz enrolled in law school at the University of Pennsylvania. She continued to row with the national team throughout her entire law school experience and up until 1980.

One of DeFrantz's early roles in the Olympic movement was serving on the U.S. Olympic Committee's Athletes Advisory Council. She joined the council in order to help fight against the 1980 Olympic boycott. With a law degree in hand, DeFrantz sued the U.S. Olympic Committee regarding the legality of the boycott. While this move made her unpopular with many influential individuals, her advocacy work never faltered, and she was later awarded the Bronze Medal of the Olympic Order for her support of the 1980 Olympic Games. Her dedication to Olympic athletes' well-being earned her the position as chief administrator of the Olympic village for the 1984 Olympic

Games. Since this event, DeFrantz has served on subsequent local organizing Olympic committees including Barcelona in 1992, Atlanta in 1996, and Salt Lake City in 2002.

DeFrantz's appointment to the IOC in 1986 marked the beginning of a long history of advocacy for athletes as well as women in sport leadership. DeFrantz has served in many roles within the IOC. She served on the IOC's executive board from 1992 to 1997. In 1997, DeFrantz became the IOC's first female vice president. Then in 2013, she was elected for second time to serve on the executive board for the IOC. DeFrantz became chair of the IOC's Women and Sport Commission in 1995, a position she held until 2014 at which time she became an honorary member. Throughout her work, DeFrantz has worked toward gender equity for female athletes and women in sports management and leadership. She helped lobby for the successful inclusion of women's soccer and softball in the Olympic Games. She has also led the way in terms of policy making aimed at improving women's representation on sport policy-making committees. She was instrumental in setting the initial goal of having at least 10 percent of the IOC board and all National Olympic Committees be women. More recently that goal has been raised to 20 percent of Olympic governing bodies be comprised of women. Other advocacy efforts include being a member of the IOC's Sport and Law Commission and as an arbitrator for the Court of Arbitration in Sport.

From 1987 to 2015, DeFrantz served as president of LA84, a grant development and educational foundation for sports in the Los Angeles area. LA84 was founded with $93 million from some of the profit generated from the Los Angeles Olympic Games, a rare occurrence. LA84 has been supporting youth sport development through giving grants, hosting conferences and special events, training youth coaches, and commissioning research.

DeFrantz has received many awards and recognition over her longtime dedication to sports and women in sports. Highlights of her numerous awards include being named as one of the "10 Women Who Changed Sport" by *L'Equipe Magazine* in 2009, one of "The 20 Most Powerful Women in Sport" by *SportsPro Magazine* in 2007, and one of "The 100 Most Influential Sports Educators in America" by the Institute for International Sport. The Sporting News has named DeFrantz one of the "100 Most Powerful People in Sports" nine times (1991–1999). Her influence in sport and sport policy has also earned her to be named as one of "10 Women Making a Difference in Los Angeles" while *Newsweek* included DeFrantz as one of the "150 Women Who Shake the World" in 2011.

Tony DiCicco (1948–2017)

Tony DiCicco is most well known for being the U.S. Women's National Soccer Team's (USWNT) head coach from early 1995 to 1999. DiCicco established a winning percentage of .899 with a record of 108–8–8. This record is the best in U.S. Soccer's history. DiCicco's first coaching job with the USWNT was assistant coach in 1991 with his primary duties being a goalkeeper coach. In 1995, he stepped into the role of head coach, and later that year led the USWNT to third place in the Women's World Cup in Sweden. From there, he continued to make improvements in USWNT's playing strategy and celebrated the team's first Olympic gold medal in the 1996 Olympic Games in Atlanta. He continued as head coach through the 1999 Women's World Cup in which the United States defeated China.

DiCicco went to Springfield College where he played soccer for four years, earning the position of captain and most valuable player his senior year. After graduating in 1970, he went on to earn his master's degree in physical education from Central Connecticut State University. He played professionally for five years and earned a spot on the 1993 Men's National Team. Other coaching positions he held were goalkeeper coach for the 1993 Under-20 Men's National Team for the Men's U20 World Cup.

After retiring as head coach of the USWNT, DiCicco founded the Women's United Soccer Association (WUSA), and served as commissioner from 2000 to 2003. WUSA was the world's first women's soccer league. All players earned salaries, marking the first professional soccer league for women. The league folded in 2003, but DiCicco continued to be a strong advocate for women's professional soccer in the United States. Following the folding of the WUSA, DiCicco founded a youth soccer club in Connecticut called SoccerPlus Elite. He added to his coaching resume by becoming the technical director for Adidas's Elite Soccer Program and founded and directed the National Soccer Coaches Association of America's Goalkeeper Academy. In addition, he coached the SoccerPlus Connecticut Reds, leading the U23 Women's Team to a national championship. At the international level, DiCicco led the U20 Women's National Team to a 2008 FIFA World Cup Championship. From 2009 to 2011, when the league folded, DiCicco coached the Boston Breakers, a women's professional soccer team in the Women's Professional Soccer league.

With his depth of experience and breadth of knowledge about soccer and women's soccer in particular, DiCicco has been the commentator for several international events. He worked with NBC as a soccer commentator for the 2000 Olympic Games and for ESPN during the 2003, 2007, 2011, and 2015 Women's World Cup events. For regular season play, DiCicco offers play-by-play insights for women's soccer games on both ESPN and Fox Sports. Adding to his work with women's soccer, DiCicco coauthored a book in 2003 with Colleen Hacker and Charles Salzberg titled *Catch Them Being Good: Everything You Need to Know to Successfully Coach Girls*. The book features many anecdotes and examples from DiCicco's own career about how to motivate, nurture talent, create team cohesion, and even assess one's own coaching style. In addition to sharing what works for young girls and women in soccer, example workouts and specific team-building activities are included. The book is highly accessible and offers much practical advice.

DiCicco shares his thoughts about knowing your strengths as a coach and surrounding yourself with other talented individuals and letting them fill in where you are less strong. He believes in working hard and always playing to win, but being humble and open to vulnerability as a coach. Knowing how to validate his players' feelings through honest and open conversation was one of DiCicco's strengths. He details how to conduct team tryouts, develop self-esteem, give feedback, and how to foster talent.

Althea Gibson (1927–2003)

Althea Gibson was the first woman of color to be invited to play at the U.S. National Championships (now the U.S. Open) in Forest Hills, New York, in 1950. Although she lost in the second round to the reigning Wimbledon champion, Gibson would go on to win 11 Grand Slam titles. She made her international debut in Jamaica in 1951, winning the Caribbean Championships. In 1956, she traveled extensively in Europe and Asia, competing in 18 tournaments and winning 16 of them. One of those tournaments was the French Open, making Gibson the first black woman to win a Grand Slam tournament. On this tour, Gibson became a symbol of strength and hope for other people of color. In 1957, the following year, she won two other Grand Slam titles by winning Wimbledon and the U.S. Nationals (later renamed the U.S. Open). Her victory at Wimbledon marked the first time in the 80-year history of Wimbledon that a black individual had claimed the championship. She also won the U.S. National title that year. In 1958, Gibson defended her Wimbledon and U.S. National titles. Gibson was named Female Athlete of the Year by the Associated Press in both 1957 and 1958. Because of her success and the fact that she continued to achieve "firsts," Gibson was the first black woman to appear on the covers of *Sports Illustrated* and *Time* magazine.

Althea Gibson was born in South Carolina, but her family moved to Harlem in New York City when she was three. While

Gibson was from a poor family, there were blacks who began to appreciate the upper-class status of tennis, and negro tennis clubs emerged in the early 1950s. These clubs were associated with the American Tennis Association (ATA). The Cosmopolitan Tennis Club was the ATA-affiliated club in Harlem. In 1940, neighbors collected money so that Gibson could get a junior membership. In 1941, Gibson won her first ATA tournament. She won several other titles, and by the late 1940s, she was noticed by male black leaders in the tennis circuit. They saw that Gibson could be a way to gain respect among whites and pride within the black communities. Gibson had access to technical training, and her coaches made her go through "social" training. Gibson recalled that she was uncomfortable with the formal rules and etiquette of tennis, but she understood how tennis became that way.

The more Gibson won, the more she became a hope for blacks and an example of how difficult it was for a black woman to play in a white, upper-class sport. Some newspapers compared her to Jackie Robinson, claiming Gibson as an important figure not only in the history of tennis, but in the history of female athletes of color. However, being a public representative for race and as a figure who could speak out against racial injustice was not easy. Gibson backed away from playing for a cause, and turned her focus on simply playing tennis. She received criticism from the black community for not embracing her responsibility as a successful black athlete and was alienated from her own community. Later, she admitted that she would have taken on that responsibility, but that at the time, she felt that focusing on her own playing was more important. Gibson was able to play through charitable donations of money, plane tickets, clothing, and food. She decided to quit in 1955 because she was tired of people having to support her efforts. However, plans changed in 1956 when the State Department sent Gibson and three other athletes to Asia and Europe to showcase a successful black woman. That year Gibson gained considerable experience. The following years were her most successful.

In 1958, Gibson had won 56 national and international titles in singles and doubles combined. She retired from the amateur circuit as there was no money and finances were a struggle. While other white players, whom she had defeated multiple times, were getting offers to play professionally in exhibitions, Gibson was not getting similar offers. Instead, Gibson took up professional golf and played from 1964 to 1978. While she was able to earn money in the tournaments and through a few sponsorships, she was often banned from hotels and clubhouses because she was black. Gibson was inducted into the International Women's Sports Hall of Fame in 1980. Gibson had to face segregation and being an outsider in an upper-class sport. Fewer than 5 percent of tennis players were minorities when she started. While predominantly white, about 30 percent of tennis players are people of color today.

Pat Griffin (1963–)

Pat Griffin has devoted much of her life to the LGBTQ social justice movement in sport. Griffin retired early from the University of Massachusetts, becoming a Professor Emerita, in order to pursue advocacy work for LGBT athletes and coaches. Emerging from her own experiences as a lesbian coach and seeing her athletes struggle to live fully themselves, Griffin became outspoken against homophobia. Her work for over 30 years has been to eliminate fear, hatred, and misunderstanding of athletes and coaches based on their sexual orientation and gender identity. One of Griffin's avenues for advocacy has been disseminating information through writing. Griffin consults regularly with the National Collegiate Athletic Association (NCAA) and other college and high school athletic programs as they shape policy and education around LGBTQ inclusion in athletics. Griffin coauthored *On The Team: Equal Opportunities for Transgender Student-Athletes, the NCAA Guide for the Inclusion of Transgender Athletes* and *Champions of Respect: NCAA Guide for the Inclusion of LGBTQ Student-Athletes*. She published *Strong Women, Deep Closets: Lesbian and Homophobia in Sports* in 1998. The book was the first to reveal and examine homophobia in women's sports. From 2005 to 2009, she served as director of It Takes a Team, a project of the Women's Sports Foundation (WSF) aimed at eliminating homophobia in sport by providing practical educational information and resources to athletic departments, athletes, and parents. In 2007, she coedited *Teaching For Diversity and Social Justice: A Sourcebook for Teachers and Trainers* that provides theoretical perspectives for inclusion along with detailed, practical activities that are ideal for workshops. In addition, she created a blog in 2007 called "Pat Griffin's LGBT Sports Blog," which is featured regularly in the *Huffington Post*.

Griffin's involvement in sport has been a lifelong endeavor. She was a collegiate athlete at the University of Maryland where she played basketball and field hockey as well as competed on the swim team. She also coached several sports at both the high school and college levels. At the high school level, Griffin coached basketball, field hockey, and softball. At the University of Massachusetts, where she worked on her advanced degree in sport, she coached swimming and diving. Griffin stayed active as an athlete while supporting LGBTQ inclusion in sport by participating in several Gay Games. In 1994, she won a bronze medal in the Gay Games Triathlon. Later in 1998, she won a gold medal in the Gay Games Hammer Throw.

Girffin's activist work began in 1981 after years of being the coach in whom lesbian athletes would confide as they struggled to constantly closet themselves within sport and their college communities. Because of seeing that many of her athletes were facing these issues, Griffin spoke about homophobia and lesbians in sport at a national conference in Washington, D.C., on the New Agenda for Women in Sport. At the time, no one was speaking out about these kinds of issues female athletes were facing. Griffin recognized the work to be done and launched her activist work by combining her passions and areas of expertise as an athlete, coach, educator, and organizer. She is recognized as one of the most important people in champion-ing LGBTQ sports equality over the last three decades.

In addition to the extensive writing projects, Griffin founded Changing the Game: The Gay Lesbian Straight Education Network (GLSEN) sports project in 2011. GLSEN focuses on providing educational materials, conducting research and sup-porting students in K–12 schools to create safe schools where all students can learn and grow without fear of being bullied or harassed for their sexual orientation and gender identity. While the focus is on the broader inclusion of all LGBT students in K–12, Griffin joined these efforts to specifically champion safe spaces for LGBT students in physical education classes as well as on sports teams. In order to launch the project, Griffin was able to gain the support of a wide array of individuals from sport to support overall inclusion efforts. The advisory group consisted of Olympic and national champion athletes, journal-ists, former college athletic directors, and current professional, college, and high school coaches. Griffin helped bring in sup-port from the corporate world in 2012 by co-organizing the first National LGBT Sports Summit. The summit was hosted by Nike and drew together prominent activists and organizers to learn about each other's efforts and brainstorm ways they could collaborate. As a result, a nationwide network focused on making sports respectful and inclusive of LGBT coaches and athletes emerged. In 2011, Griffin was named Outsports' Person of the Year for her longtime activist work at the high school, collegiate, and national levels for fighting homophobia and sexism.

Nikki Kimball (1971–)

Nikki Kimball is best known for her accomplishments as run-ner of ultramarathons, and the length of time she has been able to perform at a high level. She ran her first 100-mile race at Western States 100 Mile Endurance Run in 2004, winning it that year. She won that same race in 2006 and 2007, becoming only the third female to ever win Western States three times. In 2007, Kimball won the Ultra Trail du Mont Blanc (UTMB). UTMB is a trail-running race that circumnavigates Mont Blanc going through France, Italy, and Switzerland. It is 103 miles long and runners gain and descend over 30,000 vertical feet. Then, in 2014, Kimball won the Marathon des Sables, which is a multiday race through the Moroccan desert. Runners cover a total of 156 miles in six days. Over the span of her ultramarathon career, Nikki has set numerous 50-mile course records.

Kimball was an unlikely runner because of being born pigeon-toed. Her legs pointed inward, making it difficult to run. She wore casts on her leg as an infant and slept with braces on her shoes for over a year in the hopes that her feet would straighten out. When she learned to cross-country ski, she found that it helped force her feet and legs to be parallel. Given the physical difficulty, Nikki did not begin life as a talented athlete. In school, challenges were even more difficult. Nikki was diagnosed with dyslexia, and had to work hard to overcome that. She learned that cross-country skiing actually helped her focus in school. She always could focus well after training or races, and used sport as a way to balance out and actually help her complete the academic work. Kimball learned that she could always reach a goal, but that she might have to work a bit harder and take a bit more time than others. Due to her success in cross-country skiing in high school and her perseverance in academics, Kimball attended Williams College, competed in biathlon and, upon graduation was aiming for the Olympic Games in 1998. However, her life took a different turn when she found herself sleeping 18 hours each day, not eating, and unable to work. She lost over 30 pounds and spent much of the time crying and overcome with hopelessness. Kimball knew the signs of depression and sought help.

In 1996, Kimball decided to quit biathlon and go back to school to become a physical therapist. With the help of a psychiatrist, Kimball went on medication, which relieved some of her symptoms, but she also took up trail running. For Kimball, trail running was unlike biathlon because she was able to embrace running for the sake of running. Although Kimball was never able to make the JV cross-country team at Williams, she learned that she could run forever on the trails. For Kimball, running was a type of meditation. In 1999, Kimball ran her first 50-mile race at the Vermont 50 Miler. She won and set a course record. For Kimball, however, trail running has simply been about pushing her own limits, seeing what the body can do, and believing that she could get though anything.

While Kimball's running success has been an inspiration for many girls and women, her story of overcoming adversity throughout her life has had a greater impact. In 2012, Kimball set out to set a new overall record (men's) for the fastest time with support from crew in Vermont's Long Trail. The Long Trail is 273 miles. While Kimball did not reach her personal goal of breaking the men's record, she set a new women's record of 5 days and 42 minutes. The documentary film *Finding Traction* captured her lead-up and record-breaking journey. Kimball's aim in making the film was to raise awareness about gender equality and mental illness and empower girls and women. Kimball wanted to be able to show young girls and women that they have a legitimate place in sport. Through the film, Kimball raised money for the nonprofit girl empowerment program, Girls on the Run. She also wanted to tell her story about her own struggles with depression and overcoming obstacles. In conjunction with the film's promotion, Kimball conducted numerous interviews and gave presentations about her life with depression, the role that trail running plays, and the way of eating she has adopted that helps. In sharing her story and continuing to push her own physical limits, Kimball hopes that she can inspire young girls and women as well as de-stigmatize mental illness.

Billie Jean King (1943–)

Billie Jean King is one of the most influential female athletes in the modern history of sport. Not only was she one of the most winning female tennis players during the 1960s and 1970s, but also she continues to be one of the strongest voices for women's opportunity and equality in sport. Her win over Bobby Riggs in the "Battle of the Sexes" match in 1973 has stood as a symbol of women's abilities in sport and served to empower women in sport. The match was televised and reached over 50 million viewers. At 30,000 spectators, the match remains the largest live audience for a tennis match to this day. While the match was important at the symbolic level, it was her work at the organizational and policy levels that helped push forward equal pay and respect for women in sport. King founded several organizations focused on inclusion and respect from women in sport. She cofounded World Team Tennis, a pioneering coed professional league, and the WSF in 1974. In 1973, King was the first woman to be named "Sports Person of the Year" by *Sports Illustrated*. In 1987, she was elected to the International Tennis Hall of Fame. King won the 2009 Presidential Medal of Freedom, the highest civilian award, for her dedication and many years of advocacy for gender equality in sports and other areas of life. *Life* magazine named her one of the "100 Most Important Americans of the 20th Century."

King first learned tennis at the age of 11 in the late 1950s through the free tennis instruction offered at the public courts in Long Beach, California. She worked odd jobs in order to save money for her first tennis racket. She won her first championship by age 14. King won 39 Grand Slam titles over her playing career. King dominated women's tennis in the 1960s, and was ranked number one in the world five times between 1966 and 1974. She was ranked in the top 10 for over 17 years. In 1971, she became the first female athlete to win more than $100,000 in one season.

As King became successful and dominant in women's tennis, she saw large disparities between what women could earn as professional tennis players compared to men. By the end of the 1960s, King was regularly speaking out about the differences in prize money awarded to men and women. In 1970, her drive for equal pay led to the establishment of the Virginia

Slims Tour, an offshoot tour that offered better prize money for female tennis professionals. King was instrumental in gaining financial backing and promoting the tour. While King played tennis, she still kept an eye on equal rights for women in sport and society. She supported and lobbied for Title IX legislation that eventually passed in 1972. In 1973, King led a meeting at Wimbledon to spur the creation of the Women's Tennis Association (WTA), bringing all of women's tennis under one organization. Through the WTA, King helped push for equal prize money and recognition. Finally, in 1973, the U.S. Open awarded equal prize money to both women and men. It took another 34 years before all Grand Slam tournaments followed suit.

After King retired from tennis, she continued to be involved in the sport. She captained the United States Fed Team, the equivalent of a World Cup team for a total of five years from 1995 to 2001. In 1996 and 2000, she also coached the U.S. Olympic Women's tennis team. Her leadership for social justice and equal opportunity continues through her membership on the President's Council on Fitness, Sports and Nutrition committee and board membership on the WSF. In 2014, King founded the Billie Jean King Leadership Initiative, which is a global initiative focused on helping leadership understand and learn how to promote and recognize talent, contributions, and diverse viewpoints so that organizations can prosper.

Donna Lopiano (1946–)

Donna Lopiano was an athlete, coach, director of the women's athletics at the University of Texas from 1975 to 1992, CEO of the WSF from 1992–2007, and the president and founder of Sports Management Resources, a consulting firm that draws on experienced individuals to guide high school and collegiate athletics departments through problems and issues they face today. Her involvement in sports prior to Title IX sparked her interest in leading a life dedicated to improving women's sports opportunities. For her persistent and pervasive influence on gender equality for girls and women in sport, Lopiano was named one of "The 10 Most Powerful Women in Sports" by Fox Sports in 2007 and has been one of "The 100 Most Influential People in Sports" by the Sporting News several times. Lopiano has been inducted into 13 halls of fame for both her time as an athlete and her consistent leadership in women's sports.

As a youth, Lopiano loved to play baseball. When she was 11, she was the first pick at Stamford's Little League draft day. While Lopiano had been playing baseball regularly as a kid, she was denied the opportunity to play for the little league team because the rule book expressly prohibited girls from playing. Lopiano took up softball and at 16 was offered a position with the Connecticut Brakettes, a national women's softball team at the time. She played for 10 years with the Brakettes, traveling to Europe and Asia to compete. She was a highly versatile player, earning All-American designation at four different positions over her career. She also held top 10 performances in those various positions including runs batted in (RBIs), hits, and home runs. She was a six-time National Champion and three-time American Softball Association MVP. Despite playing softball at a high level, Lopiano completed a bachelor's degree in physical education from Southern Connecticut State University and a doctorate from the University of Southern California.

Once Lopiano retired from softball, she became an assistant athletic director at Brooklyn College. Not only did she work on the day-to-day activities of running an athletic department, but she also coached softball, volleyball, and basketball. She held that job until 1975 when she became the first director of Women's Athletics at the University of Texas. Her budget that first year was $70,000. Lopiano worked tirelessly to create respect for women's sport and bring much-needed funding to the women's athletics program. By 1992, Lopiano had grown the program significantly such that it was known as one of the most successful women's collegiate athletic programs in the United States. Part of her success was being able to bring in over $4 million annually. The financial support was critical to the overall success of the program because Lopiano could attract the best coaches and athletes. During Lopiano's 17-year tenure at the University of Texas, women's athletics won 18 national championships.

Early in her collegiate administrative career, Lopiano fought against amendments to Title IX aimed at making exceptions to the law. Only two weeks into her job as Women's Athletics director, she testified against a proposed amendment to Title IX that would exempt sports like football from the Title IX regulations. While doing so could have easily jeopardized her job, Lopiano made sound arguments and stood by her resolve to keep Title IX a driving force for women's equality in athletics. Lopiano continued gender equality in sport advocacy by becoming CEO of the WSF in 1992. Having served on the board since 1987 combined with her success as athletic director, Lopiano was an obvious choice. Lopiano's ability to connect people, advocate for women's sports, and articulate a business perspective on the value of women's sports proved invaluable during her 15-year leadership at the WSF. Under Lopiano's leadership, the WSF moved from being merely an advocacy group to the leading authority on gender equality in sports. She was able to bring in support from Reebok, Nike, Ocean Spray, Gillette, and Merrill Lynch. Individual donations quadrupled during her time as CEO, going from $1.7 million annually to over $8 million in 2007. She also spearheaded the establishment of the foundation's Long Island headquarters.

Lopiano's advocacy work extends to public speaking at high-profile events and writing academic articles as well as opinion pieces in numerous popular platforms. She has published scholarly articles in the *Journal of Physical Education, Recreation, and Dance* as well as the *Roger Williams University Law Review*. Other writing includes short essays in newspapers and newsletters on sport, gender equality, and collegiate athletics administration. Her book, *Athletic Director's Desk Reference*, is a comprehensive guide to leading a collegiate athletic department. It provides an overview of leadership principles, the importance of mission and vision, organizational structures, staffing, operations, student athlete support, managing events, fund-raising, and media relations. Practical insights and lists provide useful starting points for the implementation of many of the ideas.

Upon retiring from the CEO position at the WSF, Lopiano founded Sports Management Resources. Through this platform, she consults with a wide range of organizations and individuals. Some of her work was aimed at media coverage of women's sports on ESPN. She held conversations with ESPN executives regarding the coverage of women's sports and the possibility of creating a network dedicated to women's sports. In 2010, ESPN created ESPNW, a dedicated platform for women's sports coverage. While the debate about the role ESPNW plays in promoting and legitimizing women's sports continues, the intent to give media space to women' sports that was not occurring on the ESPN site remains rooted in gaining respect for women's sports. Lopiano has also helped female athletes connect with various sports agencies and brands as the growing movement to align brands with female athletes as part of overall marketing efforts increases. She has also been advisor to prominent female athletes such as Julie Foudy, member of U.S. women's national soccer team, on issues of pay equity. In 2002, Lopiano found herself once again defending Title IX when the Bush administration decided to revisit the law. She organized town hall meetings in four major cities and lobbied against the changes that were once again aimed at providing exceptions to big-time men's sports. Although the commission created to review Title IX proposed the changes, the Bush administration rejected them, and the law remains as originally written. Her efforts have more recently taken her to the Middle East where she has helped bring recognition to the value of girls' sports programs to a male-dominated culture.

Kim Ng (1968–)

Kim Ng is a pioneer in executive management in Major League Baseball. Currently Ng is senior vice president for Baseball Operations with Major League Baseball. She served as the Los Angeles Dodgers' vice president and assistant general manager from 2001 to 2011. With a long history in baseball operations, Ng was the first woman to ever be interviewed for a general manager position with the Dodgers in 2005. While she has not yet attained a general manger position, she was interviewed several other times, including being a finalist in 2008 with the Seattle Mariners. Honors include making the "10 to Watch" list by Baseball America in its 25th anniversary issue as well as "Who's Next" in *Newsweek* in 2006. She served a total of 12 seasons combined with the New York Yankees and Los Angeles Dodger as assistant manager, reaching the postseasons 12 times and winning 3 World Championships.

Ng attended the University of Chicago, majoring in public Policy and playing softball for all four years. Her senior thesis was on Title IX and its impact. During her senior year, she interned with the Chicago White Sox and, upon graduating in 1991, went to work for them full time. Her job title was Special Projects Analyst from 1991 to 1994. Ng possessed a solid ability to look at players' worth not only in terms of their stats, but also in terms of their attitude and leadership potential as well as assess players' talent relative to other players. Ng compiled statistical research for contract negotiations and moved into the role of overseeing team's salary arbitration. Her ability to work from an analytical standpoint and be comfortable with computers gave her an edge over ex-baseball players. In 1995, Ng was promoted to assistant director of Baseball Operations. She also served as director of Waivers and Records in 1997 for the American League, a role that allowed her to gain knowledge about player transactions and contracts. This role also gave Ng direct access to the American League General Managers. In 1998, Ng was hired as the vice president and assistant general manager for the New York Yankees, becoming the youngest in the league at the age of 29 and only the third woman to hold this position. She stayed with the Yankees for four years. During her tenure, the Yankees advanced to the World Series four times and won three championships.

In 2002, Ng left New York to be assistant manager with the Los Angeles Dodgers. In this role, she was involved in player acquisitions, trading, signing free agents, and negotiating all contracts. With her arbitration experience, Ng oversaw all arbitration efforts and managed the daily baseball operations, including team travel, video, clubhouse, and research. In 2004, Ng moved into the interim position of director of Player Development and managed the Dodgers' Minor League department, including developing and evaluating all players in the farm system, appointing managers, coaching staff, and solidifying relationships between the Dodgers and its minor league teams. Ng's contributions helped the Dodgers earn the 2006 Organization of the Year by Baseball America.

In 2012, Ng went to work the Major League Baseball in New York as the senior vice president. In this role, she is the highest-ranking female in Major League Baseball. Although Ng still has aspirations to become a general manager one day, Ng has been adept at influencing baseball on an international level. She has been part of the growth of player development facilities and programs in Latin America, the Dominican Republic, Puerto Rico, and Venezuela. The abilities Ng leverages in this role come from her broad experiences. She has a deep knowledge of baseball and the language of baseball. Her negotiation skills are excellent, her organization allows her to handle a demanding schedule, and her communication skills are strong. Ng understands how various individuals in baseball see the game and operations, and she is able to connect with people from their perspectives. More importantly, Ng is known for her intense curiosity about why and how operations work. Not only does she engage with the details, but she is also adept at investigating strategies and outcomes of various strategies.

Wilma Rudolf (1940–1994)

Wilma Rudolf was an American track-and-field athlete, whose accomplishments inspired young athletes. Rudolf achieved athletic success at a time when there were few opportunities for black athletes and even fewer opportunities for female black athletes. Equally inspiring is how Rudolf overcame a physical disability induced by an early childhood illness. In 1960, Rudolf was the first American woman to win three gold medals in a single Olympic Games in track and field. Her success resulted from her determination to overcome challenges and barriers that seemed insurmountable. Rudolf's athletic success was a platform from which she worked to empower and inspire young athletes. For over 20 years, she helped open and run innercity sports programs, consulted with university track teams, spoke to amateur athletes, and founded the Wilma Rudolf Foundation, a foundation dedicated to promoting athletics. Rudolf also spent time lecturing across the United States. In 1991, she served as an ambassador from the United States to celebrate the dismantling of the Berlin Wall. Her success as an athlete and efforts beyond the track enhanced the visibility of and respect for women's track.

Rudolf was the 20th of 22 children from her father's two marriages, born in rural Tennessee and weighed in at 4½ pounds. Her siblings took care of her in the early months. When Rudolf was four, she contracted polio, a disease that attacks the central nervous system and often causes developmental problems in children. Due to the disease, she caught double pneumonia and scarlet fever. Although Rudolf survived, she was left with a paralyzed left leg. Upon advice from doctors in nearby Nashville, Rudolf went to weekly heat and water therapy and received massages four times daily from her siblings for two years. The weekly travel to Nashville was by bus, which was segregated. Rudolf and her mother had to always sit in the back of the bus and stand when they were forced to give up their seats to whites. At five years old, doctors fitted her with a steel brace to use during the day. Wanting to be like all the other kids, Rudolf often took off the brace and tried walking without a limp. When she was nine years old, she stunned doctors by taking off her brace and walking by herself. According to an interview with the *Chicago Tribune*, by the time she was 12, she was running and playing, challenging all the boys.

Basketball was a popular sport for girls and women during the 1950s. Rudolf's first athletic dream was to play basketball for her high school, but the coach refused to put her on the team. Rudolf eventually asked for a tryout, and the coach worked with her for 10 minutes each morning. While she earned a spot on the team, she was cut her freshman year. Rudolf ended up attending a different high school where she made the basketball team primarily because the coach wanted her sister to play. While Rudolf eventually became a good basketball player, a basketball referee who was also a track coach at Tennessee State University noticed her running ability. Rudolf began training with the girls track team at Tennessee State during her summers while still in high school. In her first big track meet, Rudolf did not win a single race. In her autobiography, Rudolf notes that the losses were devastating, but that she realized that talent alone was not enough. As a result, she learned how to focus on training and work toward incremental improvements. The next summer, Rudolf competed in the National Amateur Athletic Union (AAU) meet in Philadelphia. Rudolph entered nine races and won all of them.

Before training and competing in track and field, Rudolf had no idea the Olympic Games existed. At 16, however, Rudolf qualified for her first Olympic Games in 1956, winning a bronze medal. In the fall of 1957, Rudolf officially entered Tennessee State University with a desire to pursue elementary education. The stress of training, running, and school left her ill most of the season in 1958. She recovered for the 1959 track season, but pulled a muscle at a crucial meet between the United States and the Soviet Union. By 1960, Rudolf had healed and made the 1960 Olympic team. Her 1960 performance at the

Rom Olympics was unparalleled. She won three gold medals, finishing both the 100-meter and 200-meter races three yards ahead of the silver medalists. Her third gold medal came in the 400-meter relay team, where she anchored the relay team and came from behind to win the gold.

Rudolph's athletic accomplishments gained her celebrity status across Europe and the United States. In the United States, she was invited to appear on television and be a guest at multiple dinner celebrations, and received accolades and awards. She was invited to the White House by John F. Kennedy and received ticker tape parades. Her hometown in Tennessee hosted a homecoming parade that was attended by over 40,000 people. Upon Rudolf's insistence and refusal to participate otherwise, the parade was the first racially integrated public event in the history of the town. In 1961, Rudolf earned the Sullivan Award as the top amateur athlete in the United States, and won the Associated Press's Female Athlete of the Year Award. Rudolf broke more barriers by being the first woman invited to compete at some of the most prestigious track events at the time, including the New York Athletic Club Meet, the Millrose Games also hosted in New York City, the Los Angeles Times Games, the Drake Relays, and the Penn relays, which is the oldest and largest track-and-field competition in the United States.

In 1963, Rudolf decided to retire from racing. Given that she still made little money for her success coupled with the desire to leave her sport at the height of her career, Rudolph decided not to train for the 1964 Olympic Games. Rudolf went back to college, finished her degree, and became a school teacher and athletic coach. Rudolph was a member of the U.S. Olympic Hall of Fame and the National Track and Field Hall of Fame. Using her accomplishments as inspiration, she traveled frequently and became well known and sought after for her motivational speeches to youngsters. In 1963, she traveled to Africa as a goodwill ambassador for the U.S. State Department. She stayed for a month in Africa, serving as U.S. representative to the 1963 Friendship Games in Senegal. She also attended sporting events, visited schools, and appeared on television and radio in Ghana, Guinea, Mali, and Upper Volta. Just after her return from Africa, Rudolf participated in a civil rights protest to desegregate public facilities and restaurants in her hometown of Clarksville, Tennessee. Shortly following these protests, the mayor of her hometown announced plans for desegregation. In 1967, Rudolf worked on a national project called "Operation Champion," which brought top athletes to innercity youth to train and coach them in athletics. Rudolf continued to make a difference in the lives of youth and young athletes for the remainder of her life. She chronicled her story in her 1977 autobiography titled *Wilma*. She died of brain cancer in 1994 in Brentwood, Tennessee.

Barbara Slater (1959–)

Barbara Slater currently serves as the director of sport for the BBC. She has been in that role since 2009. Slater has worked for the BBC since 1983 and been in several roles prior to becoming the director of sport. As director of sport, Slater oversees 20,000 hours of sports broadcasting on the global level. Coverage platforms include television, radio, and online. One of her major roles is to negotiate media rights to different sports and events. The coverage rights vary from live sport events, sports news, special magazine features, and sport highlights. During her tenure, BBC Sport moved from London to Salford, United Kingdom. BBC Sport has approximately 450 staff throughout the United Kingdom, and reaches 40 percent of the country's population. Throughout her career, Slater has been an advocate for media coverage of women's sports. In 2014, BBC Sport devoted over 30 percent of its live television broadcast time to women's sport. Slater cites the growth in women's soccer as one indicator of the growing interest in women's sport. She firmly believes that putting female athletes on mainstream media is critical to the growth and legitimacy of women's sports. For these efforts, BBC Sport was awarded Media Outlet of the Year in the Women's Sport Trust's inaugural #BeAGameChanger Awards. Slater was awarded the Order of the British Empire in 2014 for her leadership and service to sports broadcasting.

Slater grew up in a sporting family in Birmingham, United Kingdom. Her father was a soccer player and her uncle played cricket. Slater was an athlete as well, competing in gymnastics for a period of time. She representing Great Britain in the 1976 Olympic Games and served as the flag bearer for Great Britain. Eventually, she earned two university degrees and became a physical education teacher at Loughborough University, a highly regarded institution for the teaching of sport and sports-related majors. Her teaching career was not long, and Slater began working in television broadcasting in 1978. In 1983, she became a trainee in broadcasting at BBC. One year later, she joined BBC Sport as an assistant producer. Slater worked her way up the hierarchy until she became head of sport production. Her work in this role was to produce large, widely viewed sports programs such as the Open and Master's golf, the Commonwealth Games, and horse racing. In 2009 she became the first female director of sport for the BBC.

As director of sport, Slater was responsible for covering several large-scale sport events. She oversaw coverage for the 2010 Men's World Cup soccer in South Africa. In that same year, she also directed BBC's media coverage of the 2010 Winter Olympic Games in Vancouver, British Columbia. In 2013, she negotiated the media rights to the Football Association Challenge Cup (FA Cup), a men's British soccer tournament. There is a Women's FA Cup tournament as well.

Perhaps Slater's most prominent broadcasting event was the 2012 London Olympic Games. Slater was responsible for all of the BBC Sport's coverage on all platforms, television, online, and radio. The 2012 Olympic Games was the largest national televised event in BBC history. Slater also believed that the 2012 Olympic Games was an important year for women's sports. She was at the forefront in insisting that female athletes should get the media attention they deserved. She believed that the many female athlete performances and the BBC coverage of them left a legacy to how and why women's sports should be in the spotlight. Slater was awarded the "Inspirational Woman Prize" at the Women in Film and Television Awards in recognition of women's sports coverage. In 2014, she was also appointed to the International Olympic Committee Radio and Television Commission to help guide future Olympic coverage of female athletes.

Salter continues to lead the way with respect to women's sports media coverage. As part of these efforts, Slater secured the rights to the 2019 Women's World Cup soccer, and BBC will cover the event across all its platforms. She views it as much as a business decision as championing for female athletes. She cites the growth of women's soccer viewership as a driving factor. In 2011, the UK audience for the Women's World Cup soccer was 5.1 million. The UK audience more than doubled for the 2015 Women's World Cup with over 12 million viewers. Slater knows that the viewership is still a quarter of what men's soccer might draw, but she has been following the trends. In 2015, more UK viewers watch the UK women's soccer play in the semi-finals on BBC than the men's Open Golf Championship, a premier event in the United Kingdom.

Ellen Staurowsky (Birthdate Unknown–)

Ellen Staurowsky is a professor in sport management at Drexel University. Prior to this appointment, Staurowsky taught for over two decades at Ithaca College. Her area of expertise is at the intersections of sports, educational institutions, and gender. She is an often-quoted authority on the business of college sports, being an advocate for athletes who are responsible for successful on-the-field or on-the-court performances that bring universities, the NCAA, and their related conferences millions of dollars. In 2014, Staurowsky was an expert witness in the *O'Bannon v. NCAA* court case in which athletes fought for rights to gain financially from their images used by the NCAA for commercial purposes postgraduation. In addition, she has lobbied for gender equity and LGBT inclusion in sports. She writes op-eds for several media outlets including *Forbes* online, *Huffington Post, Indian Country Today Network, New York Times, News from Indian Country, Sport Litigation Alert, Street & Smith's Sports Business Journal, The Atlantic, The Chronicle of Higher Education*, and *U.S. News & World Report.*

Staurowsky served as director of athletics at William Smith College and Daniel Webster College in the mid-1980s to early 1990s. She has coached collegiate men's soccer and women's field hockey and lacrosse. She has been a professor in sport management since 1992. Her teaching and research has focused on Title IX, intercollegiate athletics, gender equality, media and sport, and sociology of sport. In addition, Staurowsky was the lead author on the 2015 report for the WSF titled, "Her Life Depends on It III: Sport and Physical Activity in the Lives of American Girls and Women." The report is compiled from the insights of over 1,500 studies on girls and athletic participation. These insights focus on the ways that sport and physical activity are important to the health and well-being of girls and women. Contents include findings regarding academics, coaching and athletic administration, injuries, the female athlete triad, and women's sport leadership. Staurowsky is a coauthor on another forthcoming report sponsored by the WSF on workplace climate for women in intercollegiate athletics.

Staurowsky is coauthor of *College Athletes for Hire: The Evolution and Legacy of the NCAA Amateur Myth*. Written in 1998, Staurowsky and Sack take an historical critical look at the NCAA's policies and practices. The authors make the point that the NCAA made significant shifts in policies during the 1950s that allowed it to function under the guide of amateurism, but promote professional practices and policies that result in wealth creation for the NCAA. A major contribution of the book is the perspective on the role of women in collegiate sports and how female athletes are affected by the professionalism of the NCAA. They show how the philosophy of women's collegiate athletics during the 1950s more closely aligned with the vision of amateurism. While the women working in college athletics at the time were outspoken in opposition to such rule changes, they were not taken seriously. With the rule changes, Staurowsky and Sack argue that women's sports continued to be subordinate to men's sports because of the focus on sport for entertainment and the belief that women's sports were not a commodity. In 2016, Staurowsky edited a comprehensive book on women and sport titled *Women and Sport: Continuing a Journey of Liberation and Celebration.* The book provides a strong historical perspective on Title IX as well as discussed the landscape of girls and women's sport participation and leadership in sport in the current context.

Staurowsky not only publishes on gender and sport, but she also has worked extensively to bring together activists, researchers and participants through a wide variety of platforms. In 2011, Staurowsky founded and launched the "LGBT Issues in Sport: Theory to Practice" blog. She worked with colleagues from various universities to create a space for bringing together activism and research regarding LGBT inclusion in sport and physical activity. The goal is to connect researchers and activists so that there is a raised awareness of how to transform and create inclusive policies for these marginalized groups. In 2017, Staurowsky brought a multiplatform documentary titled *TOMBOY* on women in sport to the College of Business at Drexel University. She coordinated the showing of the documentary with a discussion including a panel of experts prior to the showing. The goal of the symposium was to raise awareness about what sport means to women in order to shape the future of sport participation on girls' and women's terms.

Tucker Center for Research on Girls and Women in Sport

The Tucker Center for Research on Girls and Women in Sport was founded in 1993. Its purpose is to bring together scholarship, education, and community initiatives focused on girls and women in sport. The center sponsors research and promotes positive practices and policies that emerge out of the research to help create more opportunities and positive experiences in sport for girls and women. One of the primary goals is to disseminate latest research findings to the larger efforts regarding gender equality in sport. In 1996, the Tucker Endowed Chair was established through a $1 million contribution. The chair brings national recognition to the Tucker Center, helping to attract quality graduate students and engagement in ongoing high-quality scholarship. Dr. Mary Jo Kane has held the endowed chair position since its inception in 1996. Dr. Kane continues to be an integral part of the Tucker Center's efforts. Dr. Kane has received the highest honor within the field of kinesiology by being recognized as a fellow in the National Academy of Kinesiology in 2002. Her work for girls and women in sport through the center earned her accolades from the WSF, who named her Scholar of the Year. Other distinguished awards include the Distinguished Service Award from the Minnesota Coalition of Women in Athletic Leadership in 2012 and one of the 100 Most Influential Sports Educators by the Institute for International Sport in 2013. Through the support of the Tucker Center, Dr. Kane has been able to contribute significantly to breaking barriers for women and girls in sport. Dr. Nicole LaVoi joined the Tucker Center in 2007 as codirector, and has been instrumental in realizing the mission of the Tucker Center. Her research and advocacy work has centered on female coaches and the support they need to be successful, the coach–athlete relationship, promoting physical activity among underserved girls, and media representations of girls and women in sport. Dr. LaVoi was a contributing author to the "2007 Tucker Center Research Reports: Developing Physically Active Girls." Not only does the Tucker Center for Research on Girls and Women in Sport allow for focused research and advocacy work to be carried out by two highly acclaimed academics, but the center also serves as a focal point for researchers, policy makers, educators, parents, and practitioners to collaborate for the betterment of the lives of girls and women in sport and beyond. The center has 11 affiliated scholars from the University of Minnesota from various departments who collaborate on research projects and initiatives. The center also maintains external relationships with sport scholars specializing in girls and women in sport across the United States and New Zealand.

As part of their research efforts, the Tucker Center provides internship opportunities for students whose passion is gender equality in sport. The summer internship was created in 2013 through a grant in honor of the 20th anniversary of the Tucker Center. The internship experience is for those students desiring to pursue graduate studies. The internship involves playing an active role in specific research projects in which interns learn about the research process of literature review, data collection, data analysis, and reporting data. The aim of these internships is to promote the ongoing research around girls and women in sport as well as foster future researchers in this area. The Tucker Center also awards various fellowships and scholarships to undergraduate, master, and doctoral students at the University of Minnesota. These awards are for those students whose academic pursuits are contributing to the center's overall aims. These awards are for students who examine issues related to the following: gender equity in sport and physical activity, girls and women in recreational sport, deeper understandings of sport and physical activity experiences, and issues around leadership, leadership development, and gender in the sport context.

The Tucker Center hosts five events. On campus, it hosts the Tucker Table on a monthly basis for open discussions on research and findings. Since 2010, the center has hosted an annual film festival, featuring films about women and sport and female athletes. The Distinguished Lecture Series is for community outreach and intended to bring latest research to a wider, public audience within the Minneapolis–Saint Paul area. Since 2014, the center has hosted a women's coaches symposium. This conference-style gathering aims to provide education, facilitate networking, build community among female coaches, and support women who desire to have coaching be a long-term career.

One of the Tucker Center's most significant research aims has focused on media and women's sports. Significantly, the center has been able to support free access to all their research and data. Much of the research has been made available in highly accessible forms. When the center launched the #HERESPROOF project to proactively dispel the myth that no one is interested in women's sports, it did so with the aim of creating highly accessible content to be used in advocacy work. The Tucker Center provides reports, infographics, and other media as open resources to help organizations make the strong case that people are interested in women's sports. In 2014, the Tucker Center coproduced a documentary titled *Media Coverage and Female Athletes*. The center won the Upper Midwest Emmy Award in the Sports Documentary category for its research and evidence-based exemplary coverage of the amount and type of media coverage of female athletes. The video is available on its website via streaming. The center also distributes the DVD free of charge.

Donna de Varona (1947–)

Donna de Varona is an Olympic swimmer, sports broadcaster, and longtime advocate for women's sports. De Varona was 13 when she competed in her first Olympic Games in 1960. Her performances four years later at the 1964 Tokyo Summer Olympic Games resulted in two gold medals, an Olympic record and world record holder. De Varona became the best-known female swimmer both nationally and internationally. She appeared on the covers of *Sports Illustrated*, *Look*, and *Life* magazines, becoming a model for female athletes. In 1964, de Varona was voted the "Most Outstanding Woman Athlete in the World" by the Associated Press and United Press International. By the time she retired from swimming, De Varona had broken 18 world records and earned 37 national titles in swimming. De Varona's accomplishments are noteworthy because, during her competition days, there were no collegiate athletic scholarships or support for female athletes. De Varona grew up in a sports-minded family, who supported her efforts through her teenage years. In 1999, *Sports Illustrated for Women* ranked her as one of the "100 Greatest Athletes." She has been inducted into multiple halls of fame including the International Swimming Hall of Fame, U.S. Olympic Hall of Fame, Bay Area Hall of Fame, San Jose Hall of Fame, and Woman's Hall Of Fame.

In 1965, de Varona decided to retire from swimming because there were no scholarships for women to compete on the university swim team and she was gaining more experience and knowledge from the work she was doing in the broadcasting world. De Varona successfully launched a career in sports broadcasting at 17, signing a contract with ABC. De Varona was the first female sportscaster in the United States. In 1965, de Varona provided swimming commentary for ABC's Wide World of Sports with Jim McKay. Following her early success in sports commentary, she became the first woman to cover the Olympic Games for ABC during the 1968 Olympic Games. From there, her sports broadcasting career took off. She became a host, special reporter, and analyst for many programs such as ABC Sports and ABC News. Her coverage of the Summer Olympic Games continued, and she worked as a commentator for the 1972, 1976, 1984, 1996, and 2000 Olympic Games. From 1978 to 1983, De Varona also worked for NBC SportsWorld and covered sports-related stories for the *Today* Show. De Varona also worked as a journalist and reporter for the 1984, 1988, 1994, and 1998 Winter Olympic Games.

De Varona's accomplishments as a sports broadcaster helped bring recognition to women within this sector. Her features on female athletes during the 1998 Nagano Winter Olympics for Turner Network Television contributed significantly to the network's outstanding ratings. In 1994, de Varona kept the nation updated on the series of events and controversies between American figure skaters Tonya Harding and Nancy Kerrigan. Given the unusual circumstances around this feud, de Varona worked tirelessly to unearth the story. She appeared on ABC's *World News Tonight, Good Morning America, Weekend News*, ABC's *Wide World of Sports*, and various talk shows to keep America and the world updated in the midst of an unprecedented event. She continued to provide coverage of the story through 1994 Winter Olympics in Lillehammer, Norway, while also providing coverage for many other athletic events at those Olympic Games. Two years later, de Varona was the key reporter for the 1996 Olympic Games in Atlanta, anchoring *Good Morning America*'s Olympic coverage and broadcasting daily events on ABC Radio. With experience in radio, de Varona became a weekly commentator for Sporting News Radio in 1998. During her broadcasting of the 2000 Olympic Games in Sydney, Australia, de Varona was awarded the IOC's highest honor, the Olympic Order. She was awarded the Gracie Allen Award for excellence in broadcasting in both 2000 and 2001.

Throughout her lifetime, de Varona has worked for women's and female athletes' rights. De Varona faced many constraints and worked hard to be a pioneer for women in sports broadcasting. In April 1998, ABC did not renew de Varona's contract. The public reason for not renewing her contract was that ABC felt that de Varona was no longer able to appeal to the 18- to 39-year-old male viewer. De Varona's experience and knowledge of the industry gave her confidence to fight back. She filed a $50-million lawsuit against ABC. De Varona felt strongly that men in the business received preferential treatment through better, more high-profile assignments. In 2002, ABC settled out of court and de Varona rejoined ABC as a sports reporter and commentator. Because of her experience as a female swimmer, being denied the same opportunities to compete for UCLA, de Varona became a staunch advocate for Title IX. From 1976 to 1978, she consulted with the U.S. Senate as it worked toward drafting and passing the Amateur Sports Act, which aimed to give women and minorities greater and better access to training facilities and money. De Varona has served on President Ford's Commission on Olympic Sports and President Carter's Women's Advisory Commission. She also served five terms on the President's Council on Physical Fitness and Sports. De Varona served as the WSF's first president from 1979 to 1984. In 1984, she served as a consultant to Peter Ueberroth, who headed up the highly successful 1984 Los Angeles Olympic Games. Her work directly impacted the creation and direction of the "Olympic Spirit Team."

Other notable contributions to sport include her involvement on boards and special media projects. De Varona served many years on the board of directors for Special Olympics, helping to raise awareness of Special Olympics and work toward creating more sport opportunities. In 1991, she produced a poignant story of a 1991 Special Olympian. She received a prestigious Emmy Award for her coverage of one athlete's journey and participation in the 1991 Special Olympics. De Varona is a member of the IOC's Women and Sports Commission. She serves on the U.S. Department of State's Empowerment of Girls and Women through Sports Council. From 1997 to 1999, de Varona chaired the organizing committee for the 1999 Women's World Cup Soccer Tournament Organizing Committee, the most successful women's sporting event in history. In 1998, de Varona wrote, narrated, and coproduced *Keepers of the Flame*, an award-winning ABC Olympic television special. Her sport advocacy work has also extended to policy making about performance-enhancing drugs and serving as an advisor to the White House Task Force on the World Anti-Doping Agency. In 2017, de Varona was awarded the 2016 Theodore Roosevelt Meritorious Achievement Award by the U.S. Sports Academy, which recognizes individuals who have made significant contributions to both sport and society over at least a decade.

Venus Williams (1980–)

Venus Williams is an American tennis professional player, whose consistent performances have earned her seven Grand Slam titles, including five Wimbledon championships. She has played on the singles and doubles circuit, often teaming up with her sister, Serena Williams. Part of Venus's success is attributed to her friendship and rivalry with her sister. They have won 13 Grand Slam doubles titles and have competed for singles championship titles more than 20 times, including the finals of 8 Grand Slam tournaments. In 2011, Williams was diagnosed with an autoimmune disease, Sjogren's syndrome. She changed to a vegan diet and adjusted her training to allow for more recovery time. In 2012, she and Serena won their 13th Grand Slam doubles title at Wimbledon. Between singles and doubles matches, Williams has earned four Olympic gold medals and one silver medal, leaving her tied with the all-time most number of tennis Olympic Medals.

Venus Williams was born in the Los Angeles area, growing up in a lower-income and high-gang activity municipality of Compton. Her father read tennis books and watched videos, coaching both Venus and Serena on the public tennis courts. At the age of 10, Venus could serve at 100 miles per hour. Such powerful play set her apart from other junior players. She won 63 out of 63 matches in her first U.S. Tennis Association's junior tour. At age 14, Venus turned professional in 1994. She beat the number 50 seed player in her first match as a professional in the Bank of the West Classic in California. Three years later, Williams became the first unseeded tennis player to make it to the women's finals at the U.S. Open Championships. While she lost that match to Martina Hingis, Williams improved steadily and won both the U.S. Open and Wimbledon singles championships in 2000 and 2001.

In 2000, Venus Williams made history when she signed a $40-million, five-year contract with Reebok. The contract marked one of the largest in sports history, and the most significant contract ever negotiated with female athlete of color. Billie Jean King remarked on the significance of the contract, citing the importance of equitable endorsements–based athletic performance for women. At the time of the contract, Williams had won seven single championships and nine doubles titles. While Williams's performance had waned by 2003, ending the season at No. 11, Reebok cited various reasons for not renewing the last two years of her contract. Reebok struggled to gain traction in the overall tennis market and was critical of the appeal of some of the clothing Williams designed and wore. Still, Williams earned over $21 million over the first three years of the contract. Venus Williams regained her momentum in 2007 by winning the Wimbledon singles tournament and a gold medal in the 2008 Olympic Games in doubles with her sister Serena. In 2016, Venus Williams became the oldest female Grand Slam semi-finalist at the age of 36 in the singles event at Wimbledon since Navratilova in 1994.

While Venus Williams has been one of the most dominant female tennis players in the history of the sport, she has paved the way for many athletes of color. Although her career intertwines with her sister Serena Williams, who has won more singles titles in recent years, Venus stands out for her persistent advocacy for women in sport. Venus Williams was instrumental in the fight for equal pay for women. In 1998, the U.S. Open was the only tournament that offered equal prize money to women and men. In 1998, after the first round play at Wimbledon that year, Williams publicly spoke out about the need for all Grand Slam events to offer equal prize money to women and men in tennis. By 2005, all Grand Slam tournaments except Wimbledon offered equal prize money to women and men. Prior to the championship match at Wimbledon in 2005, Williams took a proactive role in these efforts by meeting with the All England Lawn Tennis and Croquet Club, the organization that runs Wimbledon. In this meeting, Williams simply asked each member to visualize what it might be like to be in the shoes of a female athlete. As told in the documentary,

Venus Vs., that traced Williams's fight for equal pay at Wimbledon, she asked those present to close their eyes and imagine being a little girl who trains for years only to "get to this stage, and you're told you're not the same as a boy."

While this approach was unorthodox, her actions got the attention of CEO of the Women's Tennis Association, Larry Scott. Scott reached out and asked Williams if she would be the voice and activist for pursuing equal pay. Williams embraced this role, actively seeking support from other female tennis stars. She also reached out to Billie Jean King and asked for advice and guidance. The primary argument against equal pay at Wimbledon was that the men played the best of five sets while the women played the best of three sets. One of the counterarguments Williams made was that women were only constrained to three sets not by their own choice, but by the rules and regulations set forth by tennis associations. According to *London Times*, Williams viewed equal pay at Wimbledon as an important step in breaking barriers for female athletes. She based her arguments on the principle of meritocracy, pointing out that unequal pay sustained the subordination and devaluation of not only women's tennis, but also women's sport. The *London Times* article caught the attention of Tony Blair, the British prime minister who made a public statement in support of equal pay. In 2007, the chairman of the All England Club at Wimbledon announced that Wimbledon would be offering equal pay for women and men.

Williams has also developed interests beyond her athletic accomplishments and identity. She earned a certificate in interior design, launching her own interior design company called V*Starr Interiors for residential. She started a clothing line called EleVen and oversees a collection of women's apparel for Wilson's Leather. In 2009, she and her sister Serena Williams became part owners of the Miami Dolphins. In 2010, she coauthored *Come to Win: Business Leaders, Artists, Doctors, and Other Visionaries on How Sports Can Help You Top Your Profession*. Williams has also worked with the United Nations

Educational, Scientific and Cultural Organization on gender equality at the global level.

Women in Sport (United Kingdom)

Women in Sport is a nonprofit organization located in London, United Kingdom, whose mission is to make sport an empowering endeavor for girls and women. The organization aims to transform sport in the United Kingdom so that all girls and women have the opportunity to participate in sport and physical activity as well as benefit from their participation over their lifetimes. The specific aims are to increase participation, facilitate women's leadership in sport organizations, and bring more visibility to women's sports in the media. As a charity organization, Women in Sport accepts individual donations and works to bring in additional funding by aligning organization funding with specific projects and the patron program. The patron program is a recent effort to bring high visibility to the work of Women in Sport. As of April 2017, there are two patrons. Mark Sampson, the England Women's National Soccer Team manager, became a patron in 2015 after leading the team to a bronze medal in the 2015 World Cup. Just prior to the 2016 Rio Olympics, Women in Sport named Rebecca Adlington as its second patron. Adlington is a four-time Olympic swimming medalist for Great Britain from the 2008 and 2012 Olympic Games. She mentors and works with elite athletes in their medal quest as well as helps children learn to swim. As patrons, both Sampson and Adlington publicly lend their support to the efforts of Women in Sport.

Women in Sport has several programs aimed at increasing girls' and women's sport participation in the United Kingdom. In partnership with Sport England, it works directly with schools, colleges, and universities to increase opportunities for sport participation. It lends operational support to current best practices for working with girls in sport. In order to create new practices, Women in Sport involves girls and young women in the process of creating sport environments that allow them to thrive. As an organization that conducts original research, it shares insights with all school programs. It reaches marginalized girls and women through its specific work with organizations who work specialize in disability sport.

Women in Sport provides support for women's leadership and careers in sport. Getting more women on boards of sport organizations in the United Kingdom is a primary goal of the organization. Since 2004, Women in Sport has collected data about the gender representation on boards of sport organizations. For almost half of all the United Kingdom's national governing bodies funded by Sport England, less than 25 percent of board members are women. As of 2016, Women in Sport has expanded its efforts to work with boards in more sectors. The goal is to achieve at least 30 percent of women on sport organization boards. To achieve this aim, Women in Sport shares insights about the benefits of a gender-balanced board and best practices in supporting women in those roles. Support for women entering and advancing in sport careers is enhanced through the providing membership networking advantages and showcasing the different careers possible. Bringing current statistics to the conversation helps increase the urgency of taking proactive action. For example, in the United Kingdom, women make up only 18 percent of qualified coaches and 9 percent of senior coaches. Over 15 percent of men volunteer in sport while less than 10 percent of sport volunteers are women.

Another area of advocacy is promoting more media coverage of women's sport through information sharing and shaping policies that improve gender sport equality. One approach the organization takes is linking the business case for investing in women's sport and highlighting the current barriers. It has published three reports on the commercial investment in women's sports. The data show limited attention to making women's sport a highlight in various media outlets. Understanding different policies and the extent to which policies can have an impact on improving the visibility of female athletes and women's sport. Women in Sport lobbies sport policy makers to consider women's sport a priority. The group lobbies for policy changes about differences in sport opportunities such as working for inclusion of women in the decathlon. Another gender equality effort is making the case that women should play the same number of sets in tennis Grand Slam tournaments as the men. Helping shape policies so that more girls and women see the benefit and have positive experiences in sport is a key aim. The organization's research shows that girls and women who participate in sport are more confident, tend to pursue higher education, and bring unique leadership skills to the workplace.

Women in Sports and Events

Women in Sports and Events (WISE) is a nonprofit organization that brings together professional women working in sport business, functioning as both a "voice" and a resource to women. Through meetings, special events, and mentoring programs, WISE helps women connect and grow in their careers. The organization has 11 chapters in different cities throughout the United States. The programs they create and support help women learn about sport business, specific challenges, and opportunities for women at all levels of their careers. WISE was founded in 1993 as a 501(c)3 public charity, headquartered in New York City. The national organization has chapters in Atlanta, Boston, Chicago, Cleveland, Houston, Los Angeles, NYC Metro, Pittsburgh, San Diego, San Francisco/Bay Area, South Florida, and Washington D.C. The New York office is governed by a national board of directors, which leads the overarching direction and establishes strategies. Each WISE chapter elects its own board, carrying out the work and aims at the local level.

Each of the WISE chapters meets on a regular basis. One function is to host speakers and panelists who come from a wide array of sport industry sectors: individuals from ESPN, the NFL, Madison Square Garden, and more general companies such as USA Today. Topics include negotiation skills, philan-thropy and sports, building one's career, networking, and bal-ancing work and life. The largest event hosted by WISE in New York is the annual WISE Women of the Year Luncheon. At this event, three women are honored each year for their leadership in being a resource and a voice for women in sport business.

WISE has multiple resources for all members. CareerWise is a resource center that serves all members. WISE Insider showcases stories and perspectives from women working in sports business. WISE Insights helps connect early career women with experts to answer career-related questions. Sto-ries about challenges women are facing are also featured. In WISE Inspires, industry leaders talk about lessons they have learned along the way. WISE Reader is an online list of current books and readings of members. In WISE Training, specific live webinars about skills such as networking and interview-ing are offered. In 2014, WISE launched a new event called the WISE/R Symposium. The event is focused entirely on the personal and professional development for women in sports business. The larger sessions present the issues and challenges women face in the sports industry. The smaller breakout ses-sion focus on the skills and tools to help navigate and overcome many of the challenges.

Women Leaders in College Sports

In February 2017, the National Association of Collegiate Women Athletics Administrators changed its name to Women Leaders in College Sports. The organization has existed since 1979, but under this new name seeks to be more clearly focused on advancing women's leadership and development in intercol-legiate athletics. As a 501(c)3 organization, Women Leaders in College Sports offers a wide array of programs and support to all women working in or affiliated with college athletics. The organization decided it needed a new name as it grew in mem-bership, and the complexity of the various roles, departments, and responsibilities within collegiate athletics increased as well. Along with this growth is the concomitant growing need to support women in collegiate athletics leadership.

Women Leaders in College Sports (Women Leaders) has helped many women attain higher-level positions in athletic departments through their development programs, support, and job boards. In 2012, there were 19 women who were hired into higher-level positions such as athletic directors and conference commissioners. With concerted efforts, there were 37 women in 2016 who advanced in leadership roles. Seven women of color were among those 2016 hires. Spotlight female athletic directors such as Jennifer Cohen at the University of Washington, Sandy Barbour at Penn State, and Kathy Beauregard at Western Michigan all led highly successful athletic departments with top football programs.

Women Leaders has over 3,500 members from over 600 institutions and offers many programs and membership benefits. It partners with the NCAA as well as conducts its own programs in several areas of leadership development workshops and initiatives. Leadership development programs include the Women's Leadership Symposium, Institute for Administrative Advancement, Leadership Enhancement Institute, and Executive Institute workshops. It also hosts the Women Leaders National Convention annually. Other initiatives for the advancement of women's intercollegiate leadership are the Women of Color Initiative, which focuses on bringing to light the barriers for women of color to access leadership and organizations abilities to retain and advance women of color. Women Leaders also supports a job board and hires two interns annually to support its work.

In addition, Women Leaders serves as an information exchange organization. One of the programs through which it connects members is called Women Leaders Circle. These groups gather women who work similar jobs, have common interests, or share a specialization within collegiate athletics. Circle groups include academic development, athletic communication, coaches transitioning to administration, directors of operations, faculty and campus integration with athletics, legislation and governance, marketing and sales, athletes' mental health, strength and conditioning coaches, and Title IX compliance. Facilitators coordinate the activities and conversations around these special topics of interest. Another opportunity to share interests and best practices is through the Happy Hour program, informal gatherings hosted in various cities throughout the United States by current members.

For other programs and support, Women Leaders offers the Rising Stars program and scholarships. The Rising Stars program provides access to individuals who have influenced collegiate sport consistently over time. The format includes being able to ask questions directly and follow up emails with the highlights of the session. Learning valuable leadership lessons and perspectives from key people serves as a catalyst to growth and advancement. Key advice in this program is to be intentional about your own career by being "visibly" the best at what you do, develop authentic relationships with others based on real desires to learn, be consistently positive communication, and help other women advance. Several awards are given annually to women at various stages in their career. The awards include the Rising Star Award, Commitment Award, Administrator of the Year Award, the Nell Jackson Administrator of the Year Award, Lifetime Achievement Award, Honor Award, Dr. Claire Van Ummersen Presidential Leadership Award, Legacy Award, and the Award of Distinction. Each award recognizes women who have made distinct contributions to women in sport either through their service or through their work. Such recognition highlights the many ways that women make a difference in collegiate athletics across the United States.

Women's Sports Foundation

In 1974, Billie Jean King founded the WSF to improve the lives of all girls and women through sport participation. Over the years, the WSF has been able to grow in its efforts to advocate for girls and women in sport, provide education, support athletes, and facilitate women's leadership. Through more comprehensive efforts aimed at research, educational outreach, and advocacy, the WSF has become the most prominent organization championing girls' and women's rights and benefits to women and society through sport and physical activity. Advocacy has been at the core of the WSF's efforts from the beginning. Early actions were aimed at putting pressure on sport organizations to make policy and rule changes that would eliminate discrimination in sport and open up more opportunities for girls and women to benefit from sport. Today, WSF provides easy access to rules and policies that shape sport experiences. It provides parent resources for understanding what to look for and how to help young girls get access to sport. WSF also publishes many public position statements in response to ongoing initiatives and challenges to gender equality in sport. Some recent topics include the value of coeducational play, sexual harassment in athletics, and benefits of sport participation and staying healthy through physical activity.

One of the main functions of the WSF is to commission research and create reports that are highly accessible to all types of organizations. WSF provides free access to these reports on its website. Recent reports include research about important health benefits of sport and physical activity, showing how chronic illnesses are reduced and overall mental health is improved through regular physical activity. In addition, WSF funded a research project titled "Gender Bias and Coaches of Women's College Sports." The study consisted of a national online survey asking male and female coaches of women's teams to describe their experiences and workplace environments. The data show that there is consistent gender bias in collegiate athletics. Female coaches perceive gender bias whereas their male counterparts are largely unaware of the same bias. Four out of five female coaches believe that head coaching positions are easier for men to attain. Collegiate athletics remains male-centric in that most female coaches fear they would lose their jobs and experience hostility and retaliation if they voiced Title IX concerns. Most women feel silenced with respect to their thoughts on women in sport outside of their own immediate responsibilities and feel less involved in decision making than their male counterparts. WSF makes policy recommendations on all their research. Other areas of research topics include athletes of color, disability, LGBT inclusion, equity, media, health, and interscholastic and collegiate athletics.

The WSF supports current athletes in their endeavors through several programs, grants, and awards. The Speaker's Bureau Service connects professional, Olympic, and world-class athletes with events and organizations seeking inspirational speakers. This allows for current athletes to make an impact and use athletics as a platform for making change. The Travel and Training Fund provides financial support to female athletes who show potential to become elite-level athletes. Criteria for funding is a demonstrated financial need, lack of other resources to meet that need, the role that the award would play in the athlete's ability to continue training and competing, overall impact that the grant would have on advancing women in sports, the contribution the award might make to increased visibility of women's sports, and a plan for how the athlete might give back to women's sports either financially or through advocacy. Another program designed to support individual athletes is the Athlete Leadership Connection program. The program began in 2015, and is a one-day event in New York City designed to help current athletes make the transition from sport to careers. The day features guest speakers, workshops, and competitions that give athletes practical experiences and advice to be better prepared for their careers beyond sport.

The WSF also focuses on widespread efforts to get more young girls involved and empowered through sport and physical activity. General grants are awarded annually to organizations that support girls in middle and high school sports. In addition to grants, the WSF founded the GoGirlGo!

educational and support program in 2001. GoGirlGo! works with organizations to help them identify resources in their own communities, provide quality curriculum support, award grants, and facilitate strong networks so that local programs can enhance their services to encourage girls to be physically active. As of 2017, GoGirlGo! has helped more than one million girls and provided more than $5.6 million in funding. Beginning in 2015, WSF partnered with ESPNW to create the Sports 4 Life Program, which specifically helps local, community programs grow participation for girls who are underrepresented in athletics.

Understanding the need to support girls and women in all kinds of sport endeavors beyond the opportunities in schools and community programs, the WSF has two platforms that bring together insights on the topics of body–mind connections, health, and being a body in motion. The Get Inspired project highlights stories and research that show how being physically active can be defined through a wide range of activities including activities such as walking, yoga, and dance. The Get Inspired webpage features research on the connections between body and mind, showcasing ways that women and enhance their athletic endeavors. In addition, the project highlights what health really means, and shows how girls and women can be healthy at every size and in multiple, diverse ways. Advice on how to stay injury free or recover from illnesses and setbacks is also part of the Get Inspired resources. More recently, the S.H.E. Network was established to enhance the Get Inspired work. S.H.E. Network stands for Sports, Health, Education, Network. The platform provides a space for athletes, activists, and researchers to talk directly to young girls and other women. Grassroots efforts and personal projects in all kinds of sports help bring attention to all the great work that is being done to work toward gender equality in sport.

In order to recognize all the efforts of individuals who bring visibility and support to girls and women in sport, the WSF has established several awards. There are currently six awards given out annually. The Sportswoman of the Year Award goes to a female athlete from either an individual sport or a team sport, whose performance over the past year was outstanding. The Wilma Rudolph Courage Award is given to the female athlete who demonstrates the ability to overcome significant challenges and adversity to achieve athletic success and make a significant contribution to sports. The Billie Jean King Contribution Award is presented to either an individual or a group who has significantly advanced women's sports and made a distinct contribution to the WSF. The International Women's Sports Hall of Fame recognizes individuals with notable achievements, innovations, and ongoing commitment to women's sports worldwide. The Yolanda L. Jackson Give Back Award is awarded to an athlete who serves as a role model, especially in the area of giving back. Finally, the Darlene A. Kluka Award acknowledges the outstanding performance of researchers whose work helps move the efforts of the WSF forward.

Babe Didrickson Zaharias (1911–1956)

Babe Didrikson Zaharias (Babe) was named "Woman Athlete of the Half Century" by the Associated Press and *Sports Illustrated* in 1950 for her athletic skills and accomplishments. She excelled at basketball, track and field, and golf and proved highly competent in numerous other sports. Zaharias is known as one of the greatest female golfers in its history. She won 17 successive tournaments in 1946–1947 and a total of 82 tournaments over 20 years from 1933 to 1953. She was voted Woman of the Year by the Associated Press five times in 1936, 1945, 1947, 1950, and 1957. Prior to her golf career, Zaharias was an All-American basketball player and a two-time Olympic track-and-field gold medalist. One of her legacies was being one of the 13 founding members of the Ladies Professional Golf Association (LPGA) in 1949. She was also the first woman to play against men in a Professional Golf Association (PGA) tour event and the first American to win the British Women's

Amateur Championship. The 1920s sports writer and novelist, Paul Gallico, commented that Zaharias was commonly praised for her natural talent for sport, her will to win, and her competitive spirit. However, he noted that Zaharias's real strength was her patience that led to her putting in the time as well as her persistent drive to improve. Zaharias was known to hit over 1,000 golf balls in one day in order to perfect her drive off the tee.

Babe Didrikson Zaharias was born Mildred Ella Didrikson on June 26, 1911. She was the daughter of Norwegian immigrants. Her mother had been an outstanding skier and skater, and her father was ship's carpenter and cabinetmaker. When Zaharias was three, the family moved to Beaumont, Texas. Zaharias's father believed in staying physically fit and built a weight-lifting apparatus out of a broomstick and some old weights. Zaharias grew up playing games and sports with all the boys. After hitting five home runs in one baseball game, Zaharias earned her nickname "Babe." Once in high school, Zaharias started on the girls basketball team at age 15. McCombs, coach of one of the best girls' basketball teams in the nation, noticed her talent and offered her a job with Employers Casualty Company of Dallas. Once an employee, Zaharias began playing immediately for the company-sponsored women's basketball team, the Golden Cyclones. The Golden Cyclones won the national championship the next three years, and Zaharias was All-American forward for two of those years.

Zaharias's participation in Amateur Athletic Union basketball facilitated other sporting interests. Zaharias began to participate in track-and-field events, also sponsored by the Employers Casualty Company of Dallas. In 1931, she won first place in eight events. In 1932, Zaharias participated in the amateur track-and-field championships. She was the only person on her team representing the Employers Casualty Insurance Company of Dallas. Zaharias had to run from event to event to make it to a total of nine events. She finished first in five events: broad jump, shot-put, javelin, 80-meter hurdles, and the baseball throw. She tied for first in a sixth event, the high jump. Zaharias qualified for three Olympic events and earned a total of 30 team points for Employers Casualty. The second-place team, the Illinois Women's Athletic Club, scored 22 points and had a total of 22 athletes. At the 1932 Olympic Games in Los Angeles, women were allowed to enter only three events. Zaharias won gold medals in the javelin throw and 80-meter hurdles. Zaharias technically tied for the gold in the high jump, but her jump was disallowed because of her jumping style in which her head crossed the bar before her body. While illegal at that time, Zaharias's style was similar to the "Fosbury Flop" that is the dominant style today.

Zaharias also began playing golf during her track-and-field years sometime during 1931–1932. By April 1935, Zaharias won the Texas State Women's Championship. In early 1938, she met George Zaharias, and they married in December of that same year. Having been out of the amateur golf scene of a few years, she was reinstated at the request of her husband and returned to amateur golf in 1943. She practiced and went on to win numerous tournaments. After helping establish the LPGA in 1950, Zaharias also worked hard to keep the association going. Her personality drew crowds as she was outspoken and forthright, and her drives could go as far as many male golfers.

Although she was an exceptional athlete and admired by many, her appearance and refusal to fit the stereotypical feminine attire and look caused controversy. Often labeled a freak, facing questions as to whether or not she was a man or a woman was part of Zaharias's every day. Given that she was paid well by Employers Casualty, earning more than many men at that time, Zaharias did not fit the stereotype of womanhood. Zaharias eventually decided to conform to a more feminine style. By the time she met George Zaharias, she was wearing fancier dresses and wearing makeup. With these changes and her exceptional ability in golf, Zaharias helped the fledgling LPGA gain traction. In 1950, Zaharias met Betty Dodd, a younger LPGA golfer. They became inseparable, and Dodd moved into the

Zaharias's home at the Tampa Golf and Country Club. According to a source from *Gay and Lesbian Biography*, Zaharias and Dodd were partners, but Zaharias kept that aspect of her life very private. In 1953, Zaharias was diagnosed with colon cancer. Three and a half months after surgery, Zaharias played in a tournament. The following year, she won the U.S. Women's Open by 12 strokes. She spoke openly about her cancer, and became a spokesperson for cancer awareness and research. The cancer returned in 1955, and Dodd became her caretaker. In the last few months of her life, she and her husband established the Babe Didrikson Zaharias Fund to support cancer clinics and treatment centers. She passed away in Galveston, Texas, on September 27, 1956.

Introduction

This chapter highlights key trends, issues, advocacy efforts, and solutions pertaining to sport participation of girls and women as well as leadership of sport organizations. This chapter consists of relevant data and documents addressing the above efforts. The data section provides an overview of various trends in sport participation, leadership in sport organizations, and mainstream media coverage of women's sports. The documents section includes excerpts and highlights of key legislation, policy guidelines, and call to action plans aimed at gender equality in sport. Both sections include information from U.S. and international perspectives.

Data

Table 5.1. Participation Numbers of High School Athletes by Gender

Since Title IX, high schools have been held accountable for proactively providing athletic opportunities to girls. The National Federation of State High Schools tracks high school sport participation by gender. Table 5.1 details the growth of high school girls participating in sports since 1977. Out of 10 high school athletes, 3 were girls in 1977. By 2014, 4 out of

Two young, female athletes practice with their school's basketball team. (Monkey Business Images/Dreamstime.com)

Table 5.1   Participation Numbers of High School Athletes by Gender

Top 10 Sports	1977		2000		2014	
	Girls	Boys	Girls	Boys	Girls	Boys
Basketball	132,299	645,670	451,600	541,130	433,344	541,054
Volleyball	17,952	63,544	382,765	NA	429,634	NA
Soccer	700	78,510	270,273	330,044	374,564	417,419
Cross-country	1,719	166,281	154,021	183,139	218,121	252,547
Softball	9,813	3,982	343,001	NA	364,297	NA
Tennis	26,010	91,279	159,740	138,507	184,080	160,545
Track and field	62,211	692,390	405,305	480,791	478,885	580,321
Golf	1,118	120,078	NA	165,857	NA	152,647
Swimming and diving	17,229	91,309	138,475	86,640	165,779	138,373
Lacrosse	450	3,520	NA	NA	81,969	NA
Total athletes, all sports	**2,083,040**	**4,367,442**	**2,784,154**	**3,921,069**	**3,267,664**	**4,527,994**

Source: National Federation of State High School Associations (NFHS). Participation Statistics, 1969–2014. (Table compiled from various tables.) http://www.nfhs.org/ParticipationStatics/PDF/Participation%20Survey%20History%20Book.pdf. Accessed on February 23, 2017.

10 high school athletes were girls. The largest growing sport for girls during this same time period was soccer, which had 535 times the number for girls competing in 2014 than it did in 1977.

Table 5.2. Collegiate Sports Offered in NCAA Schools

The growth in high school sport participation combined with Title IX legislation is one explanation for the subsequent growth in the number of women's teams offered by colleges and universities under the jurisdiction of the NCAA. The total number of women's teams in the NCAA, which includes Division I, II, and III schools, has grown 27.7 percent since 2000 while the average number of women's teams per member school has slightly increased from eight to nine teams. Thus, most of the

Table 5.2 Collegiate Sports Offered in NCAA Schools

Year	Total Number of Women's Teams	Average Number of Women's Teams per School
2014	9581	8.83
2012	9274	8.73
2010	9087	8.64
2008	9101	8.65
2006	8702	8.45
2004	8402	8.32
2002	8132	8.35
2000	7501	8.14

Source: Acosta, Vivian, and L. J. Carpenter. 2014. "Women in Intercollegiate Sport. A Longitudinal, National Study, Thirty Seven Year Update. 1977–2014." (Table compiled from data in report.) www.acostacarpenter.org. Accessed on November 29, 2016.

growth in women's teams offered at the collegiate level occurred in the years prior to 2000. The data indicate that colleges and universities that may have had relatively few women's teams have added them in recent years. NCAA schools offer a total average of 19 teams, meaning that nearly 50 percent of NCAA collegiate teams are women's teams. Table 5.2 indicates the total number of women's teams combined for NCAA schools and the average number of teams per school.

Table 5.3. Percentage of Women's Varsity Teams in Intercollegiate Athletics for the Academic Year 2013–2014

In addition, the NCAA keeps records of participation by gender and race. Table 5.3 provides a list of sports offered for women at all three divisions within the NCAA for the academic year 2013–2014. They are ranked in order of total percentage of NCAA schools that offer each sport. For instance, 100 percent of all Division I schools offer women's basketball. However, not all schools at the Division I and II levels offer women's basketball. Thus, 99.1 percent of all NCAA colleges and universities offer women's basketball.

Table 5.3   Percentage of Women's Varsity Teams in Intercollegiate Athletics

Sport	Division I	Division II	Division III	Overall
Basketball	100.0	99.9	98.3	99.1
Cross-country	96.5	91.0	92.6	93.3
Volleyball	95.9	96.8	97.0	96.6
Track and field	92.9	66.5	68.4	75.4
Soccer	92.5	86.5	98.3	93.3
Tennis	90.6	75.5	85.3	84.2
Softball	82.4	94.8	90.5	89.2
Golf	71.8	60.6	45.5	57.7
Swimming and diving	64.1	25.8	62.3	52.7
Lacrosse	30.6	25.8	61.9	42.3
Field hockey	30.0	9.7	39.8	28.4
Crew	28.8	6.5	13.4	16.2
Gymnastics	21.2	1.9	4.8	9.0
Ice hockey	11.2	3.2	13.4	9.9
Bowling	9.4	6.5	1.7	5.4
Water polo	8.8	3.2	6.1	6.1
Fencing	8.8	1.3	3.0	4.3
Squash	4.7	0.0	7.4	4.5
Sailing	4.7	0.6	3.9	3.2
Riflery	4.1	1.3	0.9	2.0
Skiing	3.5	2.6	3.9	3.4
Riding and equestrian	3.5	1.9	7.4	4.7
Synchronized swimming	1.2	0.7	0.4	0.5
Badminton	0.0	0.7	0.4	0.2

Source: Acosta, Vivian, and L. J. Carpenter. 2014. "Women in Intercollegiate Sport. A Longitudinal, National Study, Thirty Seven Year Update. 1977–2014." (Table compiled from data in report.) www.acostacarpenter.org. Accessed on November 29, 2016.

Table 5.4. Top 10 Coaching Behaviors Desired by Collegiate Female Athletes

While there has been consistent growth in the number of girls and women participating in interscholastic and intercollegiate sport, the quality of the experience matters as well. Many girls

Table 5.4 Top 10 Coaching Behaviors Desired by Collegiate Female Athletes

1. Ability to teach	Female athletes valued strong communication skills that helped them feel valued as athletes and people. The ability for the coach to behave with their personal growth at all levels was the most important and effective coaching behavior.
2. Being fair and honest with players	Complementary to the ability to teach was that all processes and communications were perceived as fair, open, and honest.
3. Knowledge of the skills of the sport coached	This aspect was critical in that female athletes expected that learning new skills, tactics, and strategies would be part of their athletic experience. Coaches without this relevant knowledge were viewed as less competent.
4. Commitment to the development of sportsmanship in players	Tied to the aspect of fairness, female athletes valued overt reinforcement of fairness and respect.
5. The enjoyment of the players of their sport	A positive coaching style resulted in female athletes enjoying their sport more, which led to their desire to work harder and improve.
6. The preparation of athletes to play at a higher level	All female athletes reported valuing competition and winning, but not to the extent that it was emphasized over the above-mentioned values.
7. Knowledge of the rules of the sport coached	While a basic requirement, this aspect was not relatively important.
8. The prevention and care of injuries	This aspect was rated low due to the fact that athletic trainers with this expertise could be trusted to attend to injuries.
9. Individual commitment to winning	Consistently ranked low among the other values due to the external emphasis. It was not that female athletes were not competitive, but they believed that too much focus here worked against their growth as players and people.
10. Experience as a player in the sport coached	The ability to teach was significantly more important than whether the coach has prior experience playing the sport.

Source: Stewart, C. 2016. "Female Athletes' Rankings of Coaching Behavior: A Longitudinal Report." *Physical Educator, 73*(3): 417. (Table compiled from data.)

continue playing at the collegiate level because they desire a holistic education. In ongoing efforts to identify what a holistic education means to female college athletes, sport scholars have conducted studies about their experiences. Coaches are integral to the student-athlete's experience. Table 5.4 details the top 10 preferred coaching behaviors of female collegiate athletes. The data are based on the results of a 14-year study in which female student-athletes ranked a set of 10 coaching behaviors already known to be effective. The ability to teach the required skills and support athletes through transparent, equitable processes was most important to female athletes. Winning consistently ranked low on their list of priorities, whereas sport-specific playing time by the coach was the least important. Given that men coach over 56 percent of collegiate women's teams, it is likely that female athletes rank this low because it is common that men have not necessarily played the specific sport they coach. See Table 5.8 in this chapter for the percentages of head coaches in NCAA colleges and universities.

Table 5.5. Women's Participation in the Olympiad and Summer Olympic Games

Another area of significant growth has been the number of women participating in sport at the international level. The International Olympic Committee tracks the number of sports, events, and participants based on gender each Olympic year. Tables 5.5 and 5.6 present the actual numbers as well as overall percentages of women's events and participants in each Olympic Games. Since the first Olympiad in which women were allowed to compete, the number of female Olympians has grown from 22 in 1900 to over 4,700 in 2012. Table 5.5 displays the steady increase in number of Olympic sports available to female athletes. Beginning in 1900, women were allowed to compete in five sports: equestrian, croquet, golf, tennis, and sailing. The 2012 Olympic Games in London was the first time that at least one female represented every country and that women competed in all 26 sports.

Table 5.5 Women's Participation in the Olympiad and Summer Olympic Games

Year	Total Events	Percentage of Women's Events	Women Participants	Percentage of Women Participants
1900	95	2.1	22	2.2
1904	91	3.3	6	0.9
1908	110	3.6	37	1.8
1912	102	4.9	48	2
1920	154	5.2	63	2.4
1924	126	7.9	135	4.4
1928	109	12.8	277	9.6
1932	117	12	126	9
1936	129	11.6	331	8.3
1948	136	14	390	9.5
1952	149	16.8	519	10.5
1956	151	17.2	376	13.3
1960	150	19.3	611	11.4
1964	163	20.2	678	13.2
1968	172	22.7	781	14.2
1972	195	22.1	1,059	14.6
1976	198	24.7	1,260	20.7
1980	203	24.6	1,115	21.5
1984	221	28.1	1,566	23
1988	237	30.4	2,194	26.1
1992	257	33.5	2,704	28.8
1996	271	35.8	3,512	34
2000	300	40	4,069	38.2
2004	301	41.5	4,329	40.7
2008	302	42.1	4,637	42.4
2012	302	46.4	4,676	44.2
2016	306	47.4	~4700	~45

Source: International Olympic Committee. "Factsheet Women in the Olympic Movement update—June 2016." (Table omitted sport totals.) https://stillmed .olympic.org/media/Document%20Library/OlympicOrg/Factsheets-Reference- Documents/Women-in-the-Olympic-Movement/Factsheet-Women-in-the- Olympic-Movement-June-2016.pdf#_ga=1.252995658.234937761.1487175556. Accessed on February 22, 2017. Used by permission of the International Olympic Committee.

Table 5.6. Women's Participation in the Winter Olympic Games

Although the Winter Olympic Games is much smaller, Table 5.6 shows similar growth in opportunities for women to compete

Table 5.6   Women's Participation in the Winter Olympic Games

	Total Events	Percentage of Women's Events	Women Participants	Percentage of Women Participants
1924	16	12.5	11	4.3
1928	14	14.3	26	5.6
1932	14	14.3	21	8.3
1936	17	17.6	80	12
1948	22	22.7	77	11.5
1952	22	27.3	109	15.7
1956	24	29.2	134	17
1960	27	40.7	144	21.5
1964	34	41.2	199	18.3
1968	35	40	211	18.2
1972	35	40	205	20.5
1976	37	40.5	231	20.6
1980	38	39.5	232	21.7
1984	39	41	274	21.5
1988	46	41.3	301	21.2
1992	57	45.6	488	27.1
1994	61	45.9	522	30
1998	68	47.1	787	36.2
2002	78	47.4	886	36.9
2006	84	47.6	960	38.2
2010	86	47.7	1,044	40.7
2014	98	50	~1120	40.3

Source: International Olympic Committee. "Factsheet Women in the Olympic Movement update—June 2016." (Table omitted sport totals.) https://stillmed .olympic.org/media/Document%20Library/OlympicOrg/Factsheets-Reference-Documents/Women-in-the-Olympic-Movement/Factsheet-Women-in-the-Olympic-Movement-June-2016.pdf#_ga=1.252995658.234937761.1487175556. Accessed on February 22, 2017. Used by permission of the International Olympic Committee.

at the Olympic level in winter sports. There were 100 times more female winter Olympians at the 2014 Sochi Olympics than there were in the first Winter Olympics in 1924. As of 2014, women's events count for nearly half of all Winter Olympic events. Nordic Combined, in which athletes compete in ski jumping and cross-country skiing, remains the last winter sport for men only.

Table 5.7. Selected List of Professional Women's Sports and Most Common Methods of Compensation

At the professional level, women have the opportunity to compete in almost all of the same sports as men. There are a myriad of ways that women can become professional athletes. While many of the major team sports that are organized by leagues offer salaries to female athletes, the compensation is a fraction of what men are able to earn. For this reason, many women in lesser-known sports typically have to have outside support and additional endorsement, or work to be able to balance earning a living and competing at the highest levels. Additionally, opportunities for earning money are unevenly distributed across sports as well as global regions. For instance, indoor female volleyball players have few lucrative opportunities in the United States, but many more in Europe and South America because of the increased number of spectators. Table 5.7 (page 220) is a compilation of data from a variety of websites and highlights 15 sports and the various ways that female professional athletes earn money through their sport. The table includes the most popular women's professional sports along with a variety of the more recent additions to professional status for women such as cricket and lacrosse.

Figure 5.1. Relative Percentages of Female Participation in Team Sports, Outdoor Sports, and Indoor Activities for 2016

Aside from organized sport, women are increasingly becoming physically active and enjoying a range of outdoor and indoor recreational activities and sports. In 2016, 57 million people

Table 5.7   Selected List of Professional Women's Sports and Most
Common Methods of Compensation

Sport	Common Methods of Compensation	Average Salary in U.S. Dollars
Basketball	Salary, endorsements	72,000
Beach volleyball	Prize money, team sponsorship, endorsements	NA
Cricket*	Salary, endorsements, match fees, performance bonuses	49,000
Cycling (road)	Salary, performance bonuses, team sponsorship, prize money, part-time job	12,000
Golf	Prize money, endorsements	NA
Horse racing	Per ride wage, percentage of winnings for top three places	NA
Ice hockey	Salary, performance bonuses	15,000
Lacrosse	Salary, compensation for positive community involvement	0
Motorsport	Percentage of winnings, merchandise sales, sponsorship, endorsements	NA
Snowboarding and skiing	Prize money, endorsements	NA
Soccer	Salary, sponsorship, endorsements, part-time job	38,000
Softball	Salary, endorsements, bonuses based on attendance	5,500
Surfing	Prize money, endorsements	NA
Tennis	Prize money, endorsements	NA
Volleyball (rookie)	Salary, performance bonuses, endorsements, public appearances	8,000

Source: Table compiled from National Governing Bodies and sport associations.

* The average is calculated using data from England and Australia, two countries in which women's professional cricket is well developed and significant efforts toward pay equity have occurred in recent years.

participated in recreational activities. Girls and women made up 46 percent, or over 28 million, of all participants. Indoor sports included many activities found at local gyms such as yoga, lifting weights, treadmill running, aerobics, pool/billiards, and

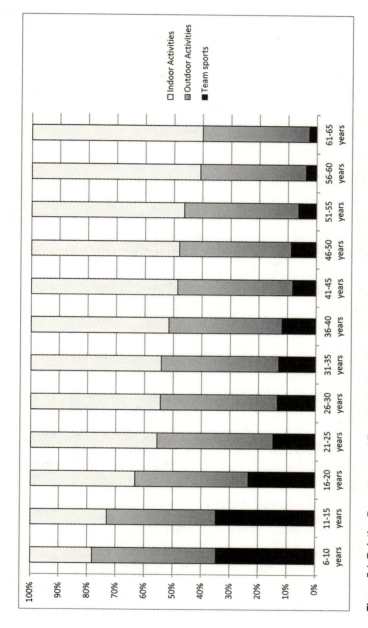

Figure 5.1 Relative Percentages of Female Participation in Team Sports, Outdoor Sports, and Indoor Activities for 2016

Source: The Outdoor Foundation. "2016 Outdoor Recreation Participation Report." (Chart created from selected data.) http://www .outdoorfoundation.org/research.participation.2016.html. Accessed on March 17, 2017.

table tennis. Outdoor activities included camping, canoeing, kayaking, backpacking, hiking, mountain biking, fly fishing, climbing, train running, skiing, snowboarding, scuba diving, skateboarding, surfing triathlon, wakeboarding, and wildlife watching. Running, jogging, and trail running top the list while walking is the most popular crossover activity among indoor and outdoor female participants. The Outdoor Industry Association sends annual surveys to gauge participation rates and assess them along the lines of gender and ethnicity. The data in Figure 5.1 (page 221) show the relative percentages of girls' and women's participation in team sports, outdoor activities, and indoor activities for 2016. The data indicate how participation in teams sports and outdoor activities decline for women over their lifetimes. The decline in team sports occurs primarily during the late teenage years, while women remain relatively active in the outdoors through their early forties. The trends show that beginning in their early twenties, women begin to spend more time in indoor activities, accounting for 45 percent of women's participation by their early sixties.

Figure 5.2. Comparison of Female and Male Outdoor Activity Participation Percentages for 2016

Looking specifically at women's participation compared to men for outdoor activities, Figure 5.2 (page 223) shows that from age 6 to 40, five out of every ten outdoor participants are girls and women. While boys and men participate at slightly higher rates, the difference is not more than 10 percent. By their early sixties, 28 percent of women participate in outdoor activities compared to 43 percent of men.

Table 5.8. Percentages of Women in Leadership Positions in NCAA Schools

Despite increased participation in sport and physical activity of girls and women, there are relatively few women in leadership positions across all types of sport organizations. In this section, women's leadership data are presented.

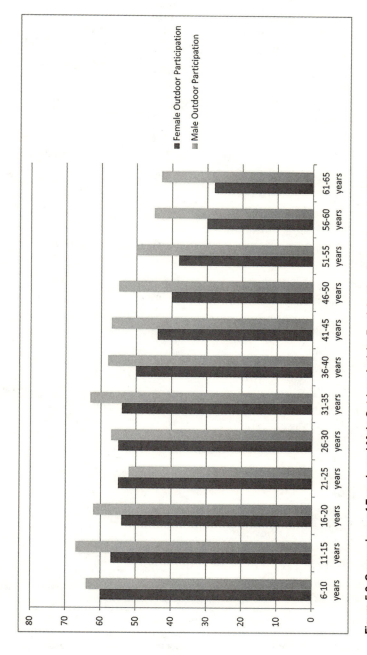

Figure 5.2 Comparison of Female and Male Outdoor Activity Participation Percentages for 2016

Source: The Outdoor Foundation. "2016 Outdoor Recreation Participation Report." (Chart created from selected data.) http://www .outdoorfoundation.org/research.participation.2016.html. Accessed on March 17, 2017.

Table 5.8 Percentages of Women in Leadership Positions in NCAA Schools

Year	Female Head Coaches	Female Paid Assistant Coaches	Female Athletic Directors	Athletic Programs with No Female Administrators
2014	43.4%	56.8%	22.3%	18.2%
2012	42.9%	57.1%	20.3%	15.6%
2010	42.6%	57.6%	19.3%	16.5%
2008	42.8%	57.1%	21.3%	12.6%
2006	42.4%	56.7%	18.6%	17.0%
2004	44.1%	57.2%	18.5%	18.8%
2002	44.0%	56.5%	N/A	20.6%
2001	44.7%	55.5%	17.9%	22.4%
2000	45.6%	55.3%	17.8%	23.8%
1999	46.3%	58.1%	19.4%	27.5%
1998	47.4%	57.7%	18.5%	21.5%
1997	47.4%	59.8%	21.0%	31.9%
1996	47.7%	60.5%	16.8%	32.8%
1995	48.3%		15.9%	37.0%
1994	49.4%		16.1%	38.3%
1993	48.1%		15.2%	36.9%
1992	48.3%		17.0%	
1991	47.7%		N/A	
1990	47.3%		20.0%	
1989	47.7%			
1988	48.3%			
1987	48.8%			
1986	50.6%			
1985	50.7%			
1984	53.8%			
1983	56.2%			
1982	52.4%			
1981	54.6%			
1980	54.2%			
1979	56.1%			
1978	58.2%			
1972	.90+			

Source: Acosta, Vivian, and L. J. Carpenter. 2014. "Women in Intercollegiate Sport. A Longitudinal, National Study, Thirty Seven Year Update. 1977–2014." (Table compiled from data in report.) www.acostacarpenter.org. Accessed on November 29, 2016.

For over 37 years, professors R. Vivian Acosta and Linda Jean Carpenter have sent out questionnaires to NCAA senior women administrators in the fall annually prior to 2006 and every other year since 2006. The surveys ask for the number of women participating, in administration, coaching, and more recently holding athletic trainer positions. The report, Women in Intercollegiate Sport, is then compiled from the primary data they collect. Table 5.8 (page 224) displays the percentage of women on key leadership positions in NCAA schools. Post Title IX, the number of female coaches has significantly decreased. Although the total number of head coaching positions has significantly increased with increased female student-athlete participation, men are being hired the majority of the time since the late 1980s. Instead, more women are hired into assistant coaching positions. Approximately four out of five athletic directors are male. While nine out of ten athletic departments have at least one female on the administration staff in 2014, 18 percent of NCAA member schools had no female on staff. Not represented in the table due to data being collected only since 2012 is information about sport information directors and strength and conditioning coaches. In 2014, approximately 88 percent of sports information directors, who are responsible for all social media, press releases, and website updates, were male. Also, almost 70 percent of NCAA schools have strength and conditioning staff. Of those schools with a salaried staff, 28.6 percent of them have at least one female strength and conditioning coach.

Table 5.9. Summary of Efforts toward Gender Equality in Professional Sport Leadership

For over 20 years, Dr. Richard Lapchick has led the Institute for Diversity and Ethics in Sport. The institute collects data on leadership positions in the following five professional sports within the United States: Women's National Basketball Association (WNBA), Major League Soccer (MLS), Major League Baseball (MLB), the National Football League (NFL), and the National Basketball Association (NBA). Initially, the institute

Table 5.9   Summary of Efforts toward Gender Equality in Professional Sport Leadership

	Hiring Practices	Coaching	Front Office	Overall Grade
WNBA	A+	54.50%	40.25%	A+
MLS	A–	none	13.90%	B
MLB	B+/A–	none	17%	C+
NFL	C+	none	15.50%	C
NBA	A	none	18.75%	B+

Source: The Institute for Diversity and Ethics in Sport. "The Complete Racial and Gender Report Card." (Table compiled from data in the report.) http://www .tidesport.org/reports.html. Accessed on March 5, 2017.

collected data on race, but beginning in 1998, data were collected regarding gender profiles of key leadership positions. Table 5.9 shows data from 2013, the latest report that includes all five professional sports. The table reports data in two different formats. First, each organization's hiring practices and overall grade are given alpha values. The institute systematically determines both hiring practices and overall grade based on relative importance of the positions being hired for and positions held at the end of the season. The overall grade scale aligns with the following percentages of women across the entire organizations: A indicates about 40 percent, B equals 32 percent, C equals 27 percent. The coaching staff and front office staff data show the percentages of women in those roles in 2013. The coaching category includes the average of head and assistant coaches. The front office percentages are the average of team manager, vice presidents, senior administrators, and professional administration.

Figure 5.3. Mainstream Media Coverage of Women's Sports

Sports media has proliferated in the recent decades. Special programming on television, social media, and numerous websites have emerged to showcase the many sports in which both men and women participate. While these alternative media avenues

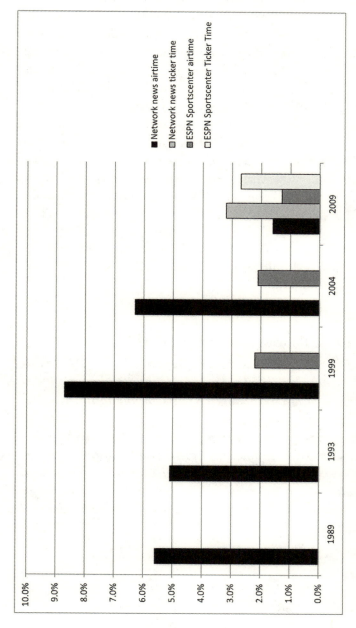

Figure 5.3 Mainstream Media Coverage of Women's Sports

Source: Cooky, Cheryl, Michael A. Messner, and Robin H. Hextrum. 2013. "Women Play Sport, but Not on TV: A Longitudinal Study of Televised News Media." http://www.michaelmessner.org/wp-content/uploads/2014/05/cooky_Messner.pdf. Accessed on March 3, 2017.

often highlight women's sports, mainstream media coverage of women's sports has remained almost nonexistent for nearly 20 years. Since 1989, professors Michael Messner and Cheryl Cooky have kept track of mainstream sport media stories in the Los Angeles area. Figure 5.3 shows the number of news stories on both local and ESPN Sportscenter in which female athletes are featured. In 1999, the U.S. Women's National Soccer Team competed in and won the World Cup. In that year, mainstream media dedicated 8.7 percent of their total airtime to women's sports. This percentage represented a spike in both airtime and ticker time. However, in 2009, women's sport media coverage dropped to all-time lows of 1.6 percent of airtime on TV and 1.3 percent of airtime on ESPN Sportscenter. While ticker times were slightly better at 3.2 percent and 2.7 percent, respectively, in 2009, the data clearly show that male athletes and men's sports dominate mainstream media.

Documents

Title IX of the Education Amendments (1972)

Title IX is a comprehensive federal law passed in 1972 regarding sex discrimination legislation. It protects individuals from discrimination and discriminatory practices in any institution that receives federal funding for any educational program or activity. Although secondary and elementary schools as well as colleges and universities comprise the majority of educational institutions, any training program run by an organization that receives federal funds is also held accountable to Title IX legislation. The major points of Section 1681 pertaining directly to sex discrimination within Title IX are as follows:

Sec. 1681. Sex

(a) Prohibition against discrimination; exceptions

No person in the United States shall, on the basis of sex, be excluded from participation in, be denied the benefits of, or be subjected to discrimination under any education program or activity receiving Federal financial assistance, except that:

(1) Classes of educational institutions subject to prohibition in regard to admissions to educational institutions, this section shall apply only to institutions of vocational education, professional education, and graduate higher education, and to public institutions of undergraduate higher education;

. . .

(3) Educational institutions of religious organizations with contrary religious tenets this section shall not apply to an educational institution which is controlled by a religious organization if the application of this subsection would not be consistent with the religious tenets of such organization;

. . .

(5) Public educational institutions with traditional and continuing admissions policy in regard to admissions this section shall not apply to any public institution of undergraduate higher education which is an institution that traditionally and continually from its establishment has had a policy of admitting only students of one sex;

(6) Social fraternities or sororities; voluntary youth service organizations

. . .

(c) "Educational institution" defined

For purposes of this chapter an educational institution means any public or private preschool, elementary, or secondary school, or any institution of vocational, professional, or higher education, except that in the case of an educational institution composed of more than one school, college, or department which are administratively separate units, such term means each such school, college, or department.

Source: The U.S. Department of Justice. Overview of Title IX of the Education Amendments of 1972, 20 U.S.C. A§ 1681 Et. Seq. https://www.justice.gov/crt/overview-title-ix-education-amendments-1972–20-usc-1681-et-seq. Accessed on January 12, 2017.

Intercollegiate Athletics Policy: Three-Part Test (1973)

While Title IX was intended to give women equal opportunities to higher education, women who played club sports at colleges realized how it should also apply to athletics. Its application to athletics was a complicated and difficult path, but today, Title IX is most associated with equal opportunity for women in sports. In 1979, the U.S. Department of Education drafted an "Intercollegiate Athletics Policy Interpretation." In order to determine fair and equal opportunities in athletics, the "three-part test" is a cornerstone of determining compliance with Title IX. The U. S Department of Education provides easy-to-understand overviews of all aspects of Title IX legislation. The Office for Civil Rights (OCR) is a sub-agency of the U.S. Department of Education and is responsible for enforcing Title IX. The main features of the three-part test are described below:

What is the three-part test?

Answer: The regulation implementing Title IX requires institutions to provide equal athletic opportunities for members of both sexes and to effectively accommodate students' athletic interests and abilities. The Department's 1979 "Intercollegiate Athletics Policy Interpretation" (1979 Policy Interpretation), published on December 11, 1979, sets out a three-part test that OCR uses as part of determining whether an institution is meeting its Title IX obligations. An institution is in compliance with the three-part test if it meets any one of the following parts of the test:

(1) The number of male and female athletes is substantially proportionate to their respective enrollments; or

(2) The institution has a history and continuing practice of expanding participation opportunities responsive to the developing interests and abilities of the underrepresented sex; or

(3) The institution is fully and effectively accommodating the interests and abilities of the underrepresented sex.

. . .

What is required for an institution to comply with Part Three?

Answer: As stated in the 1996 Clarification and as discussed in the Dear Colleague letter, OCR considers a multitude of indicators in the context of evaluating the following three questions to determine whether an institution is in compliance with Part Three.

(1) Is there unmet interest in a particular sport?

(2) Is there sufficient ability to sustain a team in the sport?

(3) Is there a reasonable expectation of competition for the team?

If the answer to all three questions is "Yes," OCR will find that an institution is *not* fully and effectively accommodating the interests and abilities of the underrepresented sex and therefore is *not* in compliance with Part Three

. . . .

An institution is not required to administer a survey to be in compliance with Part Three, nor does OCR evaluate a survey alone in order to determine compliance with Part Three. A survey is only one indicator that may be used as part of an overall assessment of interests and abilities of the underrepresented sex. In addition to the survey, OCR will evaluate the other indicators of interest and ability discussed in the Dear Colleague letter.

Source: U.S. Department of Education. Office for Civil Rights. "Intercollegiate Athletics Policy: Three-Part Test—Part Three."

https://www2.ed.gov/about/offices/list/ocr/docs/title9-qa-201 00420.html. Accessed on November 12, 2016.

Brighton Plus Helsinki Declaration on Women and Sport (2014)

In 1994, the first international conference on women and sport was held in Brighton, United Kingdom. A joint venture between the British Sports Council and the International Olympic Committee, the conference in Brighton addressed the inequities facing women involved in sport. The Brighton Declaration emerged from that meeting of 280 delegates from 82 countries, in which explicit aims were set forth to increase women's participation at all levels and in all roles globally. To enforce the declaration, the International Working Group (IWG) on Women and Sport was formed. Twenty years later, the IWG undated the Brighton Declaration in order to include physical activity in addition to organized sport. The conference host organization, International University Sports Federation, summarized the Brighton Plus Helsinki 2014 Declaration on Women and Sport as follows:

June 12–15, 2014, more than 800 delegates from close to 100 countries attended the 6th IWG World Conference on Women and Sport, in Helsinki "Lead the Change, Be the Change." Reaffirming the Brighton Declaration, the Conference also approved an updated version "Brighton Plus Helsinki 2014 Declaration on Women and Sport," which embraces physical activity as an essential extension of organised sport, especially for girls and women. Hence, the Declaration includes reference to physical activity as well as sport, throughout.

The IWG World Conferences on Women and Sport are milestone events, which every four years focus global attention on specific goals and action steps aimed at offering men and women equal opportunities in the sport arena.

. . .

The Brighton Declaration on Women and Sport is a legacy of the first World Conference on Women and Sport organised in 1994 in Brighton, United Kingdom of Great Britain and Northern Ireland. It is addressed to all those governments, public authorities, organisations, businesses, educational and research establishments, women's organisations and individuals who are responsible for, or who directly or indirectly influence, the conduct, development or promotion of sport or who are in any way involved in the employment, education, management, training, development or care of women in sport.

. . .

On 14 June 2014 the participants of the 6th IWG World Conference on Women and Sport unanimously adopted the updated Brighton Plus Helsinki 2014 Declaration on Women and Sport as part of the conference legacy document *Helsinki calls the world of sport to "Lead the Change, Be the Change."* The legacy document also includes the second annex *Conclusions and Recommendations of the 6th IWG World Conference on Women and Sport "Lead the Change, Be the Change."*

The following excerpts from the Brighton Plus Helsinki 2014 Declaration on Women and Sport highlight the specific aims and recommendations:

The overriding aim is to develop a sporting culture that enables and values the full involvement of women in every aspect of sport and physical activity.

. . .

It is in the interests of equality, development and peace that commitment be made by governmental, non-governmental organisations and all those institutions involved in sport, physical education and physical activity to apply the Principles and Recommendations set out in this Declaration by developing appropriate policies, structures and mechanisms which:

- mainstream the values and principles of equity and diversity into all international, regional, national and local strategies for sport and physical activity;

- ensure that all women and girls have opportunity to participate in sport and physical activity in a safe and supportive
environment which preserves the rights, dignity and respect
of the individual;

- recognise the diversity of women's and girls' needs, especially those with disabilities through delivery of Article 30
of the 2006 UN Convention on the Rights of Persons with
Disabilities; and those living and working in cultures and
contexts which may be hostile to female participation and
performance;

- increase and support the involvement of women in sport
and physical activity, at all levels and in all functions and
roles;

- ensure that the knowledge, experiences and values of women
contribute to the development of sport and physical activity;

- promote the recognition of women's and girls' involvement
in sport and physical activity as a contribution to public life,
community development and in building healthy nations;

- promote the recognition by women of the intrinsic value of
sport and physical activity and its contributions to personal
development and healthy lifestyles.

- increase cooperation between women and men and ensure
support of men in order to promote gender equality in sport
and physical activity.

. . . .

We recommend that,

1. Governments, sport and sport-related organisations adopt
policies that support health-enhancing physical activity
for women and girls during their whole life span and take
action to implement these policies effectively.

2. Sport organisations adopt policies and take actions to
protect women and girls from being adversely affected by

issues related to sport and physical activity such as eating disorders and sport injuries.

3. Health-enhancing physical activity that meets the special needs of women and girls be included in all policies such as sport, health, education and environment.

Source: International University Sports Federation. 2014. "Brighton Plus Helsinki 2014 Declaration on Women and Sport." http://www.fisu.net/events/educational-services/gender-equality/brighton-declaration. Accessed on February 3, 2017. Used by permission of the International University Sports Federation.

Los Angeles Declaration (2012)

The International Olympic Committee formed its own specific group, Women and Sport Working Group, in 1995 just after the Brighton Declaration to organize efforts around gender equality specific to the Olympic movement. The group meets every four years to assess progress regarding women and sport at all levels in International Federations and National Olympic Committees. At the 5th World Conference on Women and Sport, over 800 attendees approved the Los Angeles Declaration, which not only reinforced a commitment to gender equality in sport participation, but also set forth aims to improve the quality of life for all women through sport participation. The primary directives are as follows:

ii. That the IOC should revisit and review the minimum number of women to be included in leadership roles which it set for its constituents, and set up a mechanism to monitor and ensure that this minimum number is being respected. Recognising the importance of gender equality in sport, each International Federation should review its programmes for the Olympic Games and ensure that equality in participation is achieved;

iii. That the IOC and all the constituents of the Olympic Movement, especially the NOCs, International Federations and national federations, should ensure that, for the 2012/13 and all future election cycles, they achieve a more equitable representation on their Executive Committees;

iv. Recognising that for these initiatives to be successful, the support of men and women is required, the IOC's decision to link gender equality to good governance within the Olympic Movement should be adopted as policy by sports organisations and widely publicised;

v. That there should be greater collaboration and cooperation between all organisations and institutions which support the promotion, rights and welfare of women and girls;

vi. That the promotion of women's participation in sports activities, management and administration should, and must, serve the wider goal of supporting the international agenda of gender equality and the empowerment of women and girls;

vii. That the IOC must leverage its historic achievement of Permanent Observer status to the United Nations to contribute to the achievement of the Millennium Development Goals, especially as they relate to gender development and the empowerment of women;

viii. That the IOC should establish closer working partnerships with the UN and its agencies, especially UN Women, and share in the work of the UN Committee on the Status of Women in order to foster its own gender equality agenda. Similar partnerships should be established at local levels between national sports organisations, UN country teams and civil society;

ix. That the IOC and other international organisations dedicated to the cause should interact more closely with the Inter-Parliamentary Union in order for their message to reach, and be acted upon by, governments;

x. That the IOC should take the lead in establishing a platform for networking, thereby creating a place for exchanging and sharing ideas and good practices in the area of women and sport.

Source: International Olympic Committee. 2012. 5th IOC World Conference on Women and Sport. "The Los Angeles Declaration." https://stillmed.olympic.org/Documents/Commissions_PDFfiles/women_and_sport/Los-Angeles-Declaration-2012.pdf. Accessed on March 1, 2017. Used by permission of the International Olympic Committee.

NCAA Gender Equity Planning: Best Practices (2016)

The NCAA publishes principles and guidelines intended to aid colleges and universities understand gender equity and promote it within the intercollegiate context. Following are the principles and guidelines from the 2016 booklet.

The NCAA Constitution includes the following principles:

2.3.1 Compliance with Federal and State Legislation. It is the responsibility of each member institution to comply with federal and state laws regarding gender equity.

. . .

2.6 The Principle of Nondiscrimination. The Association shall promote an atmosphere of respect for and sensitivity to the dignity of every person. It is the policy of the Association to refrain from discrimination with respect to its governance, policies, educational programs, activities and employment policies including on the basis of age, color, disability, gender, national origin, race, religion, creed or sexual orientation. It is the responsibility of each institution to determine independently its own policy regarding nondiscrimination.

. . .

While the NCAA does not enforce Title IX, the NCAA membership expects all schools to have an active gender equity plan. The plan is meant to guide the institution in evaluating, monitoring and improving its gender equity performance. The membership, in addition to federal reporting requirements, participates in an annual financial and demographics reporting system that includes gender equity data.

. . .

Keys to a Positive Outcome

The keys to having a positive equity outcome are education, communication and commitment. There are various steps that an institution can take to facilitate achieving gender equity:

1. Include gender equity in the institutional mission statement.

2. Help people to understand gender equity and Title IX. Educating for understanding will result in better buy-in and commitment to achieving equity.

3. Include Title IX and gender equity information in department and university speakers forums that are available to student-athletes, coaches, administrators and faculty.

    There are many speakers nationally who can enhance your educational efforts.

4. Discuss with staff, administration, board and community members the importance of gender equity in athletics, including Title IX.

5. Evaluate the program objectively for equity, and on an ongoing basis. The process should be a continuous one of action and progress.

6. Obtain a commitment from the department and university administrators to correct any inequities in a timely manner. Support from key decision-makers is critical to achieving equity.

7. Identify ways to implement changes in a constructive manner. Involve staff in identifying solutions. It is easier to make changes when those affected are a part of the process.

8. Be open and honest in communicating any changes.

9. Establish a gender equity committee with diverse representation. The committee should include men and women from various campus departments and disciplines and of diverse races and ethnicities. Different perspectives and experiences will allow for a thorough evaluation of men's and women's programs and expansive exploration of solutions where disparities exist. The committee should be a standing committee, so it is available not only to develop the plan, but also to help monitor progress on goals, adjust the plan over time and communicate with campus and community constituents about the efforts.

Source: National Collegiate Athletics Association. "Gender Equity Planning: Best Practices." http://www.ncaa.org/sites/default/files/Final%2Bonline%2Bversion.pdf. Accessed on March 15, 2017. Used by permission of the NCAA.

NCAA Inclusion of Transgender Student-Athletes (2011)

At the collegiate level, transgender student-athlete participation requires more than identification with a specific gender. The NCAA has different policies, depending on the status of hormone treatment and birth sex. The policies are as follows:

The following policies clarify participation of transgender student-athletes **undergoing hormonal treatment for gender transition**:

1. A trans male (FTM) student-athlete who has received a medical exception for treatment with testosterone for diagnosed Gender Identity Disorder or gender dysphoria and/or Transsexualism, for purposes of NCAA competition may compete on a men's team, but is no longer eligible to compete on a women's team without changing that team status to a mixed team.

2. A trans female (MTF) student-athlete being treated with testosterone suppression medication for Gender Identity Disorder or gender dysphoria and/or Transsexualism, for the purposes of NCAA competition may continue to compete on a men's team but may not compete on a women's team without changing it to a mixed team status until completing one calendar year of testosterone suppression treatment.

Any transgender student-athlete who is **not taking hormone treatment** related to gender transition may participate in sex-separated sports activities in accordance with his or her assigned birth gender.

- A trans male (FTM) student-athlete who is not taking testosterone related to gender transition may participate on a men's or women's team.
- A trans female (MTF) transgender student-athlete who is not taking hormone treatments related to gender transition may not compete on a women's team.

Source: National Collegiate Athletics Association. "NCAA Inclusion of Transgender Student-Athletes." http://www.ncaapublications.com/p-4335-ncaa-inclusion-of-transgender-student-athletes.aspx. Accessed on March 12, 2017. Used by permission of the NCAA.

Los Angeles Policy Transgender Students—Ensuring Equity and Nondiscrimination BUL-6224.0 (2014)

On February 7, 2014, the Office of General Counsel for the Los Angeles Unified School District finalized the district's policy (BUL-6224.0) on transgender students, including specific policies on transgender athletes. The policy is regarded as a model policy for school districts. Following are excerpts from the policy.

This policy reflects the reality that transgender and gender nonconforming students are enrolled in the District. Its purpose is to advise District staff regarding issues relating to transgender students in order to create and maintain a safe learning environment for all students.

. . .

California Education Code §210.7 states that "gender means sex," and includes a person's gender identity and gender related appearance and behavior whether or not stereotypically associated with the person's assigned sex at birth.

California Education Code §220 and District policy require that all educational programs and activities should be conducted without discrimination based on actual or perceived sex, sexual orientation, or gender identity and expression.

California Education Code §201 provides that public schools have an affirmative obligation to combat sexism and other forms of bias, and a responsibility to provide an equal educational opportunity to all students.

Title IX of the Education Amendments of 1972 states, "No person . . . shall, on the basis of sex, be excluded from participation in, be denied the benefits of, or be subjected to discrimination under any education program or activity receiving federal financial assistance."

. . .

II. Guidelines

The school shall accept the gender identity that each student asserts. There is no medical or mental health diagnosis or treatment threshold that students must meet in order to have their gender identity recognized and respected. The assertion may be evidenced by an expressed desire to be consistently recognized by their gender identity. Students ready to socially transition may initiate a process to change their name, pronoun, attire, and access to preferred activities and facilities. Each student has a unique process for transitioning. The school shall customize support to optimize each student's integration.

A. Privacy and Confidentiality

1. All persons, including students, have a right to privacy. This includes keeping a student's actual or perceived gender identity and expression private. Such private information shall be shared only on a need to know basis.

2. Students have the right to openly discuss and express their gender identity and expression, and to decide when, with whom, and how much information to share.

. . .

D. Names/Pronouns

1. Students shall be addressed by the name and pronoun that corresponds to their gender identity asserted at school without obtaining a court order, changing their official records or obtaining parent/legal guardian permission.

. . .

F. Locker Room Accessibility

1. Schools may maintain separate locker room facilities for male and female students. Students shall have access to the locker room facility that corresponds to their gender identity asserted at school.

2. If there is a request for increased privacy, any student shall be provided access to a reasonable accommodation such as:

    a. Assignment of a student locker in near proximity to the coaches' office or a supportive peer group.

    b. Use of a private area within the public area of the locker room facility (e.g. nearby restroom stall with a door or an area separated by a curtain).

    c. Use of a nearby private area (e.g. nearby restroom or a health office restroom).

    d. A separate changing schedule.

. . .

G. Sports, Athletics, and Physical Education

1. Physical education classes are typically co-gender. In the event that the classes or activities are sex-segregated, transgender students shall participate in physical education by their gender identity asserted at school.

2. When conducting physical education classes and fitness evaluations, the teacher will address and evaluate the student by their gender of identity. Performance on the state physical fitness test (Fitnessgram) is evaluated by the State of California in accordance with the sex reported on the student's initial enrollment, even when the student identifies as transgender. In these events, the physical education teacher shall make every effort to maintain confidentiality of student information.

3. Participation in competitive athletics, intramural sports, athletic teams, competitions, and contact sports shall be facilitated in a manner consistent with the student's gender identity asserted at school and in accordance with the California Interscholastic

   Federation bylaws (Gender Identity Participation, 300.D, page 56).

Source: Los Angeles Unified School District. BUL-6224.0. http://notebook.lausd.net/pls/ptl/docs/PAGE/CA_LAUSD/ FLDR_ORGANIZATIONS/FLDR_GENERAL_COUN SEL/BUL-6224.1%20TRANSGENDER%20POLICY,%20 08-15-14%20-%20ADDED%20ED%20CODE%20 221%205.PDF. Accessed on March 22, 2017. Used by permission of the Los Angeles Unified School District.

Sport for Success: The Socio-Economic Benefits of Women Playing Sport (2014)

Women in Sport is an advocacy organization based in London, United Kingdom. It has been conducting research on women in

sport for over 30 years. Its mission is to transform sport at every level to make sport a great place for women. It believes that the world becomes a better place when women can enjoy sport. In 2014, Women in Sport partnered with a research organization to learn more about how sport participation has positive outcomes for women in their professional careers. Selected findings from the report, Sport for Success: The Socio-Economic Benefits of Women Playing Sport, *follow:*

Of women who play sport, almost half (45%) are in management roles; amongst women who do not play sport, not even a third (30%) of this group are managers. A significant majority (77%) of managers play sport to some extent compared with almost four in ten women who work in semi-routine/routine roles or who have never worked, who do not participate in sport at all.

. . .

Women who play regular sport showed higher levels of confidence. A quarter of women who play sport three times a week or more, said that the statement "I am confident that I could deal efficiently with unexpected events" was exactly true for them, compared to just 19% of women who do not do any sport at all.

. . .

All women acknowledged that once playing, sport had brought them many benefits. It was a source of great enjoyment and satisfaction in its own right. But participation in sport had also helped to form their character and their outlook, giving them skills and attitudes which improved their ability to respond to the challenges around them and make the most of the opportunities they encountered, both in and outside the workspace

. . .

A critical dimension to confidence and success for women in business is being ready to engage in learning—it shows the individual has belief that they can improve. We found that making progress is an important part of sport: participants often need to cast a critical eye over their performance and evaluate what needs to be changed to improve. This needs to happen at work too.

. . .

Working in a team has always been an important part of the workplace, but the emphasis on teamwork is accelerating. Companies are changing the way they are organised, often abandoning functional silos and instead bringing employees into cross-disciplinary teams that focus on specific customers, products or problems. As a result, teams may now be more fluid, global and virtual, making it important to know how to quickly and effectively work with others and be able to make the most of their contribution and one's own in different contexts and for a wide variety of activities.

. . .

Interviewees found that playing sport requires them to be themselves and have integrity both on and off the field. When participating, an individual has to be authentic. It is not possible to pretend, in particular about something you are not capable of. This personal integrity is fundamental both for being part of a team and also a leader of others.

. . .

Working in a team can mean interacting with people from different backgrounds and disciplines. Regardless of this diversity, the team needs to be able to come together to successfully deliver on their task.

. . .

Underpinning these aspects to team work is effective communication. In our interviews, many of the individuals we spoke to referred to this skill both implicitly and explicitly. It was acknowledged that the experience of playing sport can help one get better at expressing and receiving opinions in different types of situations.

. . .

It is about more than just benefits at the level of the individual; the workplace can gain too from the increased effectiveness of their female staff. This has further implications at a macro level: with higher performing organisations, the wider economy also benefits.

For these positive outcomes to be realised, more opportunities for women and girls to be active are needed. This requires support at all different levels, ranging from increased sponsorship of female sports professionals to ensure greater visibility of role models, down to permission to be active during the working day within organisations. It is time to move from barriers to benefits.

Source: Women in Sport. London, UK. "Sport for Success: The Socio-Economic Benefits of Women Playing Sport." https://www.womeninsport.org/wp-content/uploads/2016/07/Sport-For-Success.pdf?938151. Accessed on March 5, 2017. Used by permission of Women in Sport.

Introduction

Women and sport has been the focus of numerous research articles, popular articles, and gender equality in sport efforts. The items in this chapter represent a very small but representative array of the materials available about women and girls in sport. General topics include history of participation, Title IX, bodies and body image, sport injuries, sport cultures, coaching, sport leadership, eating disorders, media, LGBT advocacy, and fandom. The resources are divided by the following categories: books, articles, reports, and Internet resources.

Books

Birrell, Susan, and Cheryl L. Cole, eds. 1994. *Women, Sport and Culture*. Champaign, IL: Human Kinetics.

> This collection of 24 essays provides a range of feminist perspectives on women in sport. The book is organized in five major sections consisting of an overview of feminist theories, the ways gender shapes sport organizations, key practices in sport that marginalize women, sport media, and the impact of heterosexism.

A lineout during a women's collegiate rugby match between Navy and Brigham Young University in the NCAA Division I College Championship quarterfinals in Blaine, MN, on April 30, 2011. (Mark Herreid/Dreamstime.com)

Bonnette, Valerie McMurtie, and Mary Von Euler. 2004. *Title IX and Intercollegiate Athletics: How It All Works—In Plain English*. San Diego, CA: Good Sports.

> A workbook for colleges and universities to self-evaluate how well they are Title IX–compliant. Checklists for coaching, recruiting, participation, scholarships, and the "laundry list" are included. Guidelines for identifying and ameliorating issues are offered.

Boutilier, Mary A., and Lucinda SanGiovanni, eds. 1983. *The Sporting Woman*. Champaign, IL: Human Kinetics Publishers, Inc.

> Pioneering female sport scholars are featured in this collection of early research on women and sport. Topics include psychological aspects of sport participation, family support, sociological perspectives, media, educational environment, and government policies.

Brackenridge, Celia. 2001. *Spoilsports: Understanding and Preventing Sexual Exploitation in Sport*. London: Routledge.

> A book based on 15 years of research about sexual exploitation and abuse of athletes. The book contains personal stories of abuse as well as provides advice for coaches, policy makers, and leaders in sport organizations.

Brake, Deborah L. 2010. *Getting in the Game: Title IX and the Women's Sports Revolution*. New York: New York University Press.

> The author analyzes the successes and shortcomings of Title IX from a legal perspective.

Bruce, Toni. 2016. *Terra Ludus: A Novel about Media, Gender and Sport*. Boston: Sense Publishers.

> Written by a sports sociologist and media scholar, this novel is a fictional tale of what professional women's sports could look like in the future.

Cahn, Susan K. 2015. *Coming on Strong: Gender and Sexuality in Twentieth-Century Women's Sport*. Urbana: University of Illinois Press.

This book is an updated edition of the most-cited comprehensive history of women in sport. It is organized around the issues of gender, race, sexuality, social class, and official policies that have shaped women's participation in sport. In this version of the original book published in 1994, the author includes a history of the impact of Title IX.

Carpenter, Linda Jean, and R. Vivian Acosta. 2005. *Title IX*. Champaign, IL: Human Kinetics.

The authors present the main tenets of Title IX and explain how the law applies to sport, recreation, physical education programs, and intramurals. The book presents a clear overview of the law and implications for all athletic programs.

Caudwell, Jayne, ed. 2007. *Sport, Sexualities and Queer/Theory*. London: Routledge.

Respected sport scholars present a wide variety of queer theoretical analyses regarding the intersections of sexuality, gender, and sport. This highly academic book is a solid introduction to the use of queer theory in understanding sport contexts and experiences.

Choi, Precilla YL. 2005. *Femininity and the Physically Active Woman*. London: Routledge.

This short book is a psychological examination of the tensions physically active women experience between their muscular athletic bodies and societal expectations of femininity.

Creedon, Pamela J. ed. 1994. *Women, Media and Sport: Challenging Gender Values*. New York: Sage publications.

This book is the first collection of essays that employs media theory in the discussion of women in sport media. Authors present both theoretical and practical aspects of sports reporting, gendered media coverage, and ways to improve sports journalism.

Daniels, Dayna B. 2009. *Polygendered and Ponytailed: The Dilemma of Femininity and the Female Athlete*. Toronto, Ontario, Canada: Women's Press.

The author takes a detailed look at the ways female athletes experience gender in sport. The argument is that the gender binary of masculine–feminine is problematic. She argues for a polygendered approach to thinking about female athletic identities.

Davis, Paul, and Charlene Weaving, eds. 2009. *Philosophical Perspectives on Gender in Sport and Physical Activity*. New York: Routledge.

The editors have compiled a wide array of perspectives on gender and sport. The essays are organized into four main sections: how "female" is constructed in sport, objectification of the female body, exploration of sex at its boundaries inclusive of the ambiguities, and homophobia. Both philosophical and sociological perspectives are included. Of note is the inclusion of Iris Marion Young's seminal essay on how women are excluded in sport.

Demers, Guylaine, Lorraine Greaves, Sandra Kirby, and Marion Lay, eds. 2014. *Playing It Forward: 50 Years of Women and Sport in Canada*. Toronto, Canada: Second Story Press.

This book is a collection of stories by activists, athletes, coaches, and educators who shaped the landscape of women in sport in Canada. The accounts are personal, detailing specific moments of discrimination and marginalization and moments of joy in being physically active and competing in sport.

Dowling, Colette. 2001. *The Frailty Myth: Redefining the Physical Potential of Women and Girls*. New York: Random House.

An insightful discussion of how girls and women have been socialized to be much less physically active than men. The author shows how these practices lead to weaker bodies and perpetuate the view that women are weaker than men. Based on research about female athletes, she argues that the strength gap between women and men is much less than previously thought. The implications for women's equality are discussed.

Festle, Mary Jo. 1996. *Playing Nice: Politics and Apologies in Women's Sports*. New York: Columbia University Press.

The author details the history of policies governing women's involvement in basketball, tennis, and collegiate sports since the 1950s. More importantly, the policies are examined in relation to larger social movements and historical events.

Fields, Sarah K. *Female Gladiators: Gender, Law, and Contact Sport in America*. Urbana: University of Illinois Press, 2004.

This book captures the history of women's rights to play contact sports from social and legal perspectives. These accounts feature the legal battles for women to play on men's teams as well as play sports traditionally only available to boys. Sports covered are baseball, football, basketball, soccer, wrestling, and boxing. The legal cases made for boys to be able to compete on girls lacrosse teams provide another view regarding the impact of Title IX. One of the appendices provides a timeline of major laws and cases.

Fuller, Linda K. 2006. *Sport, Rhetoric, and Gender: Historical Perspectives and Media Representations*. New York: Palgrave Macmillan.

This edited book captures a range of unique perspectives about how the language, imagery, and symbolic representations of sport permeate everyday life. Featuring 22 chapters by respected scholars, the connections between sport discourse and the way we think about leadership, teamwork, and achieving goals are thoroughly discussed.

Griffin, Pat. 1998. *Strong Women, Deep Closets: Lesbians and Homophobia in Sport*. Champaign, IL: Human Kinetics Publishers.

Written in an accessible style, this frequently cited book draws on experiences of lesbian coaches, athletes, and administrators to highlight the ways that homophobia operates in sport settings. It offers insights into lesbians in sport and works to counteract the fear of lesbians in sport.

Guthrie, Sharon, Michelle Magyar, and Alison Wrynn, 2008. *Women, Sport and Physical Activity: Challenges and Triumphs.* Dubuque, IA: Kendall/Hunt Publishing Company.

This book contains 18 chapters divided into four major sections focused on historical, sociological, psychological, and biomedical perspectives. Topics include the control of women in sport in the early 1900s, why women fear feminism, physicality and self-esteem, and health issues specific to sport participation. There are activity sheets at the end of each section that allow readers to think about the content from their own perspectives.

Hall, M. Ann. 1996. *Feminism and Sporting Bodies: Essays on Theory and Practice.* Champaign, IL: Human Kinetics.

In one of the most-cited books in women and sport literature, the author traces her own development as a feminist sport scholar through various stages of feminism. The book is relatively short and offers an excellent overview of how to think about sport from feminist perspectives.

Hall, M. Ann. 2016. *The Girl and the Game: A History of Women's Sport in Canada.* 2nd ed. Toronto: University of Toronto Press.

A very well-written and researched history of Canadian women in sport. This edition begins with a chapter on aboriginal women and concludes with present day ongoing issues and successes as athletes, coaches, and leaders for gender equality in sport.

Hargraeves, Jennifer. 1994. *Sporting Females: Critical Issues in the History and Sociology of Women's Sports.* New York: Routledge.

Containing 11 chapters, this comprehensive book high-lights key historical understandings about women in sport, frames sport as a masculine domain, highlights issues for female athletes centered on considerations of their bodies, and proposes that viewing sport as physically empowering and pleasurable for all girls and women will move us toward gender equality in sport.

Hargreaves, Jennifer, and Eric Anderson, eds. 2014. *Routledge Handbook of Sport, Gender and Sexuality*. London: Routledge.

This is the most comprehensive collection of essays writ-ten by over 60 international sport scholars who discuss a wide array of topics at the intersections of sport, gender, and sexuality. While both women and men are discussed, the essays provide valuable insights into the ways in which women experience sport. The essays are grouped into eight sections: historical perspectives, international issues, division in sports due to diversity, gender conformity, homosexuality, transgender athletes, power and control of sport, and media.

Hartmann-Tews, Ilse, and Gertrud Pfister. 2003. *Sport and Women: Social issues in International Perspective*. London: Routledge.

The authors present what sport is like for women in 16 countries from North and South America, Asia, Eastern and Western Europe, and Africa. They discuss both the barriers to sport and the success of political efforts to improve sport for women.

Heywood, Leslie, and Shari L. Dworkin. (2003). *Built to Win: The Female Athlete as Cultural Icon*. Minneapolis, MN: University of Minneapolis Press.

The authors were the first to acknowledge a shift in the ways female athletes embraced their athleticism and strength for personal empowerment and, in some instances, monetary gain. This book provides an excellent overview of the shift from second-wave to third-wave feminism.

Ikard, Robert W. 2005. *Just for Fun: The Story of AAU Women's Basketball.* Little Rock: University of Arkansas Press.
A well-written and thoroughly researched history of women's basketball in the United States from the 1920s to the late 1970s.

Jinxia, Dong. 2003. *Women, Sport, and Society in Modern China: Holding up More Than Half the Sky.* London: Psychology Press.
The author details the rise of Chinese female athletes from the 1950s, through the cultural revolution and market economy. Topics include Olympic success, drug violations, the sacrifices and rewards of Chinese female athletes, and life after sport.

LaVoi, Nicole M. 2016. *Women in Sports Coaching.* Routledge Research in Sports Coaching. New York: Routledge.
This edited book explores the phenomenon of female coaches. Chapters address theoretical perspectives for understanding the lack of female coaches as well as explore issues specific to female coaches such as motherhood, coaching men, sexuality, race, and leadership. Suggestions for how to understand more fully and foster supportive environments for female coaches are discussed.

LeBlanc, Diane, and Allys Swanson. 2016. *Playing for Equality: Oral Histories of Women Leaders in the Early Years of Title IX.* Jefferson, NC: McFarland & Company.
The authors capture personal stories and accounts of eight women who played key roles in bringing equality for girls and women in sport and physical activity. The chapters highlight the life and important work of Catharine Allen, Ruth Shellberg, Celeste Ulrich, Fay Biles, Dorothy McIntyre, Willye White, and Anita DeFrance.

Markula, Pirkko. ed. 2009. *Olympic Women and the Media: International Perspectives*. New York: Springer.

> Sport scholars highlight the ways in which female Olympians from 11 different countries from Asia, Europe, North America, and the South Pacific are featured in Olympic media coverage. Intersections among gender, sexuality, and nationalism constitute the framework for the analyses.

McCrone, Kathleen. 2014. *Sport and the Physical Emancipation of English Women (RLE Sports Studies): 1870–1914*. London: Routledge.

> While British sport flourished at the turn of the century, this book is dedicated to programs for girls and women in British history. The author highlights sport for girls and women in colleges, public schools, and physical recreation programs.

McDonagh, Eileen, and Laura Pappano. 2007. *Playing with the Boys: Why Separate Is Not Equal in Sports*. New York: Oxford University Press.

> The authors present a well-developed argument that sex segregated sport does not serve women well and actively keeps women subordinated not only in sport but also in society at large.

Messner, Michael. 2002. *Taking the Field: Women, Men, and Sports*. Minneapolis: University of Minnesota Press.

> This book takes a three-pronged approach to making sense of how highly visible sports such as football, basketball, and baseball perpetuate a narrow view of sport values. Through social interactions, sport organization practices, and cultural symbols, the author argues that popular sports perpetuate a narrow form of masculinity, which marginalizes women and other men, and even constrains the way men who participate in these sports act.

Milner, Adrienne. N., and Jo Mills Braddock II. 2016. *Sex Segregation in Sports: Why Separate Is Not Equal*. Santa Barbara: ABC-CLIO.

> In this book, the authors argue that sex segregation continues to subordinate women's sport and women's experiences in sport. They explore why sex segregation in sport seems so normal when most other endeavors such as working and going to school are integrated. The final chapter offers potential benefits to women and society when sex categories are abandoned.

Oliver, Kimberly L., and David Kirk. 2015. *Girls, Gender and Physical Education: An Activist Approach*. New York: Routledge.

> This book critiques current physical education pedagogy and offers alternative ways of positively engaging young girls in physical education.

O'Reilly, Jean, and Susan K. Cahn. 2007. *Women and Sports in the United States: A Documentary Reader*. Boston: Northeastern University Press.

> This collection of 53 essays provides a balanced perspective of the history of women in sport in the United States. It is divided into seven major sections covering early history, the masculinity–femininity tension, biological aspects, institutionalized inequality, sexuality, sports media, and Title IX.

Osborne, Anne Cunningham, and Danielle Sarver Coombs. 2015. *Female Fans of the NFL: Taking Their Place in the Stands*. New York: Routledge.

> The book is a detailed account of the changing nature of female NFL football fans. It highlights the ways that these women experience fandom in a male-dominated sport.

Pieper, Lindsay Parks. 2016. *Sex Testing: Gender Policing in Women's Sports*. Urbana: University of Illinois Press.

The most comprehensive account of sex testing of women in the Olympic Games beginning in the 1930s. Well-researched chapters not only recount the details of sex testing and gender verification, but also point out the larger societal implications of how women are perceived in society.

Roper, Emily A., ed. 2014. *Gender Relations in Sport*. New York: Springer Science & Business Media.
This edited volume provides a solid overview of the current state of women in sport. It is designed to be an undergraduate textbook.

Ryan, Joan. 2013. *Little Girls in Pretty Boxes*. New York: Doubleday.
A critical account of the intense and often abusive world of women's gymnastics and figure skating.

Shephard, Sarah, and Chrissie Wellington. 2016. *Kicking off: How Women in Sport Are Changing the Game*. London: Bloomsbury.
In this book, the authors showcase several personal stories from highly successful female athletes. Questions as to why women remain subordinate to men in sport are reviewed and discussed candidly.

Sokolove, Michael. 2008. *Warrior Girls: Protecting Our Daughters against the Injury Epidemic in Women's Sports*. New York: Simon and Schuster.
The author exposes the rate at which female athletes suffer concussions and knee injuries among other rapidly rising injury rates for young girls and women. The author concludes with solutions about how to approach well-being and injury prevention for girls.

Summit, Pat, and Sally Jenkins. 2013. *Sum It Up: A Thousand and Ninety-Eight Victories, a Couple of Irrelevant Losses, and a Life in Perspective*. New York: Random House.

This book is an autobiographical account of Pat Summit's resilience and life when diagnosed with early-onset
Alzheimer's disease. Pat Summit is the all-time winningest
coach in NCAA basketball, inclusive of men.

Thompson, Ron A., and Roberta Trattner Sherman. 2011. *Eating
Disorders in Sport*. New York: Routledge.
This book describes eating disorders, the risks involved,
how to identify symptoms, and treatment for physically
active women. It also contains an extensive list of resources
about eating disorders and athletes.

Wellard, Ian, ed. 2007. *Rethinking Gender and Youth Sport*. New
York: Routledge.
This edited collection of essays provides solid starting
points for thinking more broadly about youth sport and
the implications of the social constructions of gender.
Topics include the body, competence, sport culture, gendered sport spaces, and human rights.

Wheaton, Belinda, ed. 2004. *Understanding Lifestyle Sport:
Consumption, Identity and Difference*. London: Routledge.
An extensive collection of essays about lifestyle sports
such as windsurfing, surfing, snowboarding, and skateboarding. The contributors analyze these sports through
the lens of gender and commercialization.

Articles

Allison, Rachel. 2016. "Business or Cause? Gendered Institutional
Logics in Women's Professional Soccer." *Journal of Sport and
Social Issues*, 40(3): 237–262.
Based on ethnographic data of U.S. women's professional soccer, the author points out the paradoxical goals
of women's sport organizations. The author suggests that
the masculine model of success and the feminized model

of empowerment create divergent goals within women's sport organizations.

Arnold, Tara, Steve Chen, and William Hey. 2015. "The Rise of Women Sportscasters: A Struggle from Sideline to the Centerfield." *Missouri Journal of Health, Physical Education, Recreation & Dance*, 25: 36–43.
   The authors detail the ways in which female sports broadcasters experienced bias, sexism, and unfriendly workplaces.

Bandy, Susan J. 2016. "Gender and the 'Cultural Turn' in the Study of Sport and Physical Cultures." *Sport in Society*, 19(5): 726–735.
   The author points out the progression of the study of gender and sport to embracing physical culture, which includes all ways in which women are physically active and embrace movement.

Barreira, Júlia, and Carlos Da Silva. 2016. "National Teams in Women's Soccer World Cup from 1991 to 2015: Participation, Performance and Competitiveness." *Journal of Physical Education and Sport*, 16(3): 795–799.
   This study is an analysis of the performance and competitiveness of national teams in Women's World Cup from 1991 to 2015. They conclude that women's soccer increased in competitiveness over the time period and that the United States, Germany, and Norway support their national teams consistently well.

Beaver, Travis. 2012. ""By the Skaters, for the Skaters": The DIY Ethos of the Roller Derby Revival." *Journal of Sport and Social Issues*, 36(1): 25.
   The author argues that the do-it-yourself ethic within roller derby is grounded in a collective sense of ownership of the sport and each organization. The article highlights

how roller derby reemerged as a sport for women and organized by women.

Bruening, Jennifer E., Ketra L. Armstrong, and Donna L. Pastore. "Listening to the Voices: The Experiences of African American Female Student Athletes." *Research Quarterly for Exercise and Sport*, 76(1): 82–100.

This qualitative study details the experiences of 12 female African American athletes at the collegiate level with respect to being silenced about their experiences as student-athletes.

Clavio, Galen, and Andrea N. Eagleman. 2011. "Gender and Sexually Suggestive Images in Sports Blogs." *Journal of Sport Management*, 25(4): 295–304.

In this quantitative study, the authors show that sports blogs reproduce mainstream sports media's portrayal of women. Findings show that women receive far less coverage and are significantly more likely to be portrayed in a sexually suggestive manner.

Cooky, Cheryl, Michael A. Messner, and Michela Musto. 2015. "'It's Dude Time!': A Quarter Century of Excluding Women's Sports in Televised News and Highlight Shows." *Communication & Sport*, 1–27.

The authors report on the absence of women's sports from mainstream media. They note the persistent lack of coverage and detail the ways in which the quality of coverage is less overtly sexist but remains trivialized.

Cooky, Cheryl, Ranissa Dycus, and Shari Dworkin. 2013. "'What Makes a Woman a Woman?' versus 'Our First Lady of Sport': A Comparative Analysis of the United States and the South African Media Coverage of Caster Semenya." *Journal of Sport and Social Issues*, 37(1): 31–56.

The authors show how the United States framed the sex testing of Semenya as a fairness issue while South African coverage focused on racism and human rights. Implications for sex testing are discussed.

Daniels, Elizabeth. 2012. "Sexy versus Strong: What Girls and Women Think of Female Athletes." *Journal of Applied Developmental Psychology*, 33(2): 79–90.
> In this study, the author shows that girls and women aged 13–22 had positive views of female athletes when they were shown being physically active. When shown imagery of sexualized female athletes, participants interpreted the imagery as objectification of women.

DiCarlo, Danielle. 2016. "Playing Like a Girl? The Negotiation of Gender and Sexual Identity among Female Ice Hockey Athletes on Male Teams." *Sport in Society*. 9(8/9): 1363–1373.
> In this qualitative study of seven women who played hockey with men, the author describes that ways in which these women were constrained by dominant notions of femininity and heteronormativity.

Duncan, Margaret, and Lori Klos. 2014. "Paradoxes of the Flesh: Emotion and Contradiction in Fitness/Beauty Magazine Discourse." *Journal of Sport and Social Issues*, 38(3): 245–256.
> The authors present a textual analysis of the ways in which dieting, weight loss, health, and beauty are talked about in fitness magazines. They present numerous examples of the contradictory language to which women are subject.

Edwards, Lisa, Paul Davis, and Alison Forbes. 2015. "Challenging Sex Segregation: A Philosophical Evaluation of the Football Association's Rules on Mixed Football." *Sport, Ethics & Philosophy*, 9(4): 389–400.
> The authors discuss the early actions taken since 1978 to allow girls to play football with boys. While they applaud the recent increases of the age limits to 18, they argue that the age limit in mixed football should be removed altogether.

Fink, Janet S. 2015. "Female Athletes, Women's Sport, and the Sport Media Commercial Complex: Have We Really 'Come a Long Way, Baby'?" *Sport Management Review*, 18(3): 331–342.

    The author provides an insightful review of the quantitative and qualitative literature regarding lack of coverage of women's sports by mainstream media.

Fink, Janet S., Laura Burton, Annemarie Farrell, and Heidi Parker. 2012. "Playing It out." *Journal for the Study of Sports and Athletes in Education*, 6(1): 83–106.

    In this qualitative study, the authors find that coming out in collegiate sports is dependent upon the presence of trailblazers and allies within the athletic department. Notably, they discuss the lack of consistent policies and attitudes across athletic departments in terms of creating safe spaces.

Gaines, Stacey, and Taylor Burnett. 2014. "Perceptions of Eating Behaviors, Body Image, and Social Pressures in Female Division II College Athletes and Non-Athletes." *Journal of Sport Behavior*, 37(4): 351–369.

    The authors show that female athletes feel better about their bodies and report lower disordered eating behaviors than nonathletes. Those athletes who reported eating disorders did not report improved self-esteem due to being an athlete. Peer pressure was determined to be the most influential for female athletes with respect to body image perceptions, disordered eating behaviors, and self-esteem.

Hively, Kimberly, and Amani El-Alayli. 2014. "'You Throw Like a Girl': The Effect of Stereotype Threat on Women's Athletic Performance and Gender Stereotypes." *Psychology of Sport & Exercise*, 15(1): 48–55.

    The authors present their findings that female college basketball players are subject to stereotype threat, performing worse on difficult athletic tasks when told that women typically perform less well than men on that task. When stereotype threat was absent, the women performed as well as the men. Implications for practice are discussed.

Jones, Amy, and Jennifer Greer. 2011. "You Don't Look Like an Athlete: The Effects of Feminine Appearance on Audience Perceptions of Female Athletes and Women's Sports." *Journal of Sport Behavior*, 34(4): 358–377.
  Based on their experimental study, the authors conclude that men prefer sport media of female athletes in feminine sports such as volleyball. Women preferred sport media of female athletes of any sport as long as they were depicted in more masculine ways. Female participants felt that the latter depiction represented empowerment.

Kane, Mary Jo, and Heather D. Maxwell. 2011. "Expanding the Boundaries of Sport Media Research: Using Critical Theory to Explore Consumer Responses to Representations of Women's Sports." *Journal of Sport Management*, 25(3): 202–216.
  Employing a critical feminist perspective, the authors show how consumers prefer to see female athletes as strong, competent athletes.

Keathley, Kristen, Melissa Himelein, and Grace Srigley. 2013. "Youth Soccer Participation and Withdrawal: Gender Similarities and Differences." *Journal of Sport Behavior*, 36(2): 171–188.
  This study explores the motivations behind young athletes' decision on whether or not to continue playing sports at a high level. The researchers discover that both high school boy and girl soccer players attribute the time demand associated with playing at a high level as the primary deterrent, while girls are more likely to make their decision based off of the relationships they do or do not form.

Kilty, Katie. 2006. "Women in Coaching." *Sport Psychologist*, 20(2): 222–234.

This article provides a comprehensive overview of the challenges female coaches consistently face, and then discusses ways in which the development of women coaches can be improved. The authors utilize perspectives from women who have attended USOC/NCAA Women in Coaching conferences.

Knapp, Bobbi. 2014. "Smash Mouth Football: Identity Development and Maintenance on a Women's Tackle Football Team." *Journal of Sport and Social Issues*, 38(1): 51–73.

The author utilizes a feminist interactionist framework to examine how female football players have created and maintained their identities as football players. They discover that female football players do this by playing the right way, recognizing their uniqueness, and demanding respect.

MacKay, Steph, and Christine Dallaire. 2014. "Skateboarding Women: Building Collective Identity in Cyberspace." *Journal of Sport and Social Issues*, 38(6): 548–566.

The authors hope to gain a better understanding of how young women who visit a female skateboarding blog interpret representations of female skateboarders and to what extent they engage in the movement promoting skateboarding among women after visiting the blog. They perform a discourse analysis of a blog produced by a group of female skateboarders and conduct interviews on the blog's users to gather information.

McDonald, Mary G. 2015. "Imagining Neoliberal Feminisms? Thinking Critically about the US Diplomacy Campaign, 'Empowering Women and Girls through Sports.'" *Sport in Society*, 18(8): 909–922.

This author takes a critical look at sport programs in developing countries aimed at empowering young girls. The primary argument is that these programs are often based on Western ideals and support individual empowerment. The author notes the drawbacks of such assumptions in being able to make substantive social change.

Moore, Mark E., Bonnie L. Parkhouse, and Alison M. Konrad. 2010. "Women in Sport Management: Advancing the Representation through HRM Structures." *Gender in Management: An International Journal,* 25(2): 104–118.

Utilizing a questionnaire sent to 500 collegiate and professional sport organizations, this study strives to examine how organizational characteristics, philosophical support, and substantive human resource management can promote gender equality in sport organizations.

Mullins, Nicole M. 2015. "Insidious Influence of Gender Socialization on Females' Physical Activity: Rethink Pink." *Physical Educator,* 72(1): 20–43.

This article studies the social influences that cause girls to be less active than boys at young ages. The author aims to raise awareness by effectively communicating these risks, in hope of promoting changes that positively impact physical activity for females.

Parmett, Helen. 2015. "'Shredding' the Love: A Feminist Political Economy Critique of Gendered Lifestyle Branding." *Journal of Sport and Social Issues,* 39(3): 202–224.

In 2008, Burton Snowboard Company released a snowboard series that featured mostly nude Playboy Playmates from the 1980s, which caused serious controversy. This article utilizes this example as a case study for understanding practices of gendered lifestyle branding in alternative sport.

Pope, Stacey. 2013. "'The Love of My Life': The Meaning and Importance of Sport for Female Fans." *Journal of Sport and Social Issues,* 37(2): 176–195.

The author utilizes a "grounded-theory" approach in order to fill the void in research on the importance of sports to female fans. She conducts 85 semi-structured interviews on females who are fans of either men's soccer or men's rugby and discovers diverse supporter styles. More research on the topic is necessary in order to discover a more comprehensive understanding of female sports fans.

Priyadharshini, Esther, and Amy Pressland. 2016. "Doing Femininities and Masculinities in a 'Feminized' Sporting Arena: The Case of Mixed-Sex Cheerleading." *Sport in Society*, 19(8/9): 1234–1248.

Inspired by the idea that mixed-gender sports have transformative potential to destabilize gender constructions, the authors explore the experiences of three college-aged participants in cheerleading. Findings suggest that individual understandings and experiences of gender tend toward progressive attitudes. However, the authors show that simply participating in a mixed-gender sport does not necessarily promote gender equality. They suggest that organizational aims toward these aims need to be explicit and supported by structural changes.

Sanderson, Jimmy, and Kelly Gramlich. 2016. " 'You Go Girl!': Twitter and Conversations about Sport Culture and Gender." *Sociology of Sport Journal*, 33(2): 113–123.

Through analyzing the content of 1,434 tweets following the historic hire of Becky Hammon by the San Antonio Spurs, the authors discover ways in which Twitter offers a unique avenue for cultivating discussions surrounding gender and sport. Through these discussions, the authors are able to see evidence that challenge society's current sport gender roles, as well as the resistances associated with these changes. Moving forward they believe Twitter will be a valuable platform for advocates to utilize as they continue to promote societal change.

Sherry, Mark, and Kristi Zeller. 2014. "Gender and Motivation: A Study of the Athletic and Academic Motivations of Division I Female College Basketball Players." *Women's Studies*, 43(1): 73–92.
    This article identifies different aspects that may affect academic motivation of student-athlete populations, by gaining perspectives of athletes, coaches, and athletic advisors associated with a Division I women's basketball team.

Soares, Jorge, Helio Antunnes, and Roland Van Den Tillaar. 2013. "A Comparison between Boys and Girls about the Motives for the Participation in School Sport." *Journal of Physical Education and Sport*, 13(3): 303–307.
    Utilizing a questionnaire taken by 722 boy and 595 girl participants, this research studies the effects of gender on motivation for participation in school sports. Three motivational themes were employed within the questionnaire: social motives, competition motives, and health motives. The research found boys were more likely to be motivated by competitive factors, while girls emphasize social and health aspects as reasons to participate.

Stewart, Craig. 2016, "Female Athletes' Rankings of Coaching Behavior: A Longitudinal Report." *Physical Educator*, 73(3): 417–432.
    The author presents 12 years of data on undergraduate female athletes who were asked to rank 10 characteristics of an ideal coach. The coaches' ability to teach, ability to be fair, and their commitment to the development of sportsmanship were consistently the top three traits prioritized for females throughout the study. These are important components to understand and research, as people continue to learn the unique nuances associated with coaching female athletes.

Surujlal, J., and S. Vyas-Doorgapersad. 2015. "The Glass Ceiling in Sport Coaching: Perceived Challenges of Female Coaches."

African Journal for Physical, Health Education, Recreation & Dance, 21(Supplement 1): 80–94.

> Using a qualitative method, the authors gain insight from female sport coaches on their perceived challenges in progressing within their careers. Gender discrimination, stereotyping, career path opportunities, and organizational support were four themes that emerged from the data. In order to level the playing field, it is critical for sport organizations to ensure both men and women have equal opportunities to progress.

Swanson, Lisa. 2016. "A Generational Divide within the Class-Based Production of Girls in American Youth Soccer." *Soccer & Society,* 17(6): 898–909.

> The author aims to gain an understanding on how middle-class American lifestyles may contribute to certain gender-based paths in youth sport, through engaging in ethnographic-style conversations with girl soccer players between 11 and 14 years old as well as the players' mothers.

Taylor, John. 2016. "Investing in the Development of Young Female Sport Leaders: An Evaluation of the 'Girls on the Move' Leadership Programme." *Managing Sport & Leisure,* 21(2): 75–90.

> "Girls on the Move" is a leadership program designed to develop young female sport leaders by providing opportunities for young women to participate in physical activity while teaching them invaluable leadership skills. This article aims to gain a better understanding of the impacts of this program by conducting surveys and interviews. Through this research, importance of investing in the development of young female leaders was illustrated.

Theune, F. 2016. "The Shrinking Presence of Black Female Student-Athletes at Historically Black Colleges and Universities." *Sociology of Sport Journal,* 33(1): 66–74.

Although Title IX has significantly increased female sports participation, black women have not seen the same degree of growth that white women have. Current Title IX discussions about inequalities in sport fail to acknowledge inequalities involved with being both black and female. This research utilizes NCAA data to examine the intersectionality of gender and race, and demonstrates the impact of Title IX on black female athletic participation at historically black colleges and universities.

Thorpe, Holly. 2009. "Bourdieu, Feminism and Female Physical Culture: Gender Reflexivity and the Habitus-Field Complex." *Sociology of Sport Journal*, 26(4): 491–516.
In this scholarly account, the author illustrates how Pierre Bourdieu's macro social theory can help uncover the various ways women are both empowered and constrained by sport. Using snowboarding and female snowboarders as a case study, specific ways these women experience freedom and limitations in snowboarding culture are discussed.

Thorpe, Holly. 2016. "Athletic Women's Experiences of Amenorrhea: Biomedical Technologies, Somatic Ethics and Embodied Subjectivities." *Sociology of Sport Journal*, 33(1): 1–13.
The author considers both the biological and social female body in this article about women's experiences of amenorrhea. This academic consideration explores the intersections of physical body experiences and sociological understandings of how these women respond to medical advice.

Travers, Ann, and Jillian Deri. 2010. "Transgender Inclusion and the Changing Face of Lesbian Softball Leagues." *International Review for the Sociology of Sport*, 46(4): 488–507.
The authors conduct participation observations and semi-structured interviews with transgendered individuals participating in North American lesbian softball

leagues to gain a better understanding of these leagues' non-sex-binary-based transinclusive policy models.

Reports

Donnelly, Peter, and Michele Donnelly. *The London 2012 Olympics: A Gender Equality Audit.* University of Toronto Centre for Sport Policy Studies, March 2013. http://www.playthegame.org/fileadmin/documents/Report_-_Olympic_Gender_Equality.pdf.

This report was produced to demonstrate the inaccurate assumptions that were seemingly made about female sport participation after the 2012 Olympic Games. The audit provides a detailed account of all the remaining differences in existence between the men's and women's Olympic sports.

Henry, Ian P., and Leigh Robinson. *Gender Equality and Leadership in Olympic Bodies: Women, Leadership and the Olympic Movement.* [Lausanne, Switzerland]: International Olympic Committee, April 2010. http://www.canoeicf.com/sites/default/files/gender-equity-and-leadership-in-olympic-bodies-2010.pdf.

This report was commissioned by the Department of International Cooperation and Development from the Centre for Olympic Studies and Research at Loughborough University in 2009. It seeks to gain insight on women's experiences submitting themselves as candidates for senior positions for National Olympic Committees and International Federations.

Messner, Michael A., and Cheryl Cooky. *Gender in Televised Sports: News and Highlights Shows, 1989–2009.* University of Southern California Center for Feminist Research, June 2010. http://dornsifecms.usc.edu/assets/sites/80/docs/tvsports.pdf.

This is a report comparing the quantity and quality of news coverage for female versus male athletic events. It builds off and uses methods used in previous studies so that change over time can be illustrated.

Internet

All-American Girls Professional Baseball League. https://www.aagpbl.org/. Accessed on February 5, 2017.

> The All-American Girls Professional Baseball league was a women's professional baseball league that existed from 1943 to 1954. This website provides a wonderfully detailed history of the league

Alsharif, Asma. "Saudi Women Push for the Right to Play Sports." http://www.reuters.com/article/us-saudi-women-sport-idUSTRE81S1BX20120229. Accessed on February 5, 2017.

> This Internet article accounts the implications of Saudi Arabia's law banning girls from playing sports, and the slow evolution toward female participation.

Athlete Ally. "Allies: Heather O'Reilly." https://www.athleteally.org/allies/heather-oreilly/. Accessed on February 5, 2017.

> Athlete Ally is a nonprofit organization that aims to raise public awareness and provide resources to foster inclusive sports communities. The organization utilizes high-level athletes as allies to help foster such athletic environments. Heather O'Reilly is on the U.S. Women's National Soccer Team and serves as one of these allies.

Blumenthal, Karen. "The Truth about Title IX." *The Daily Beast.* http://www.thedailybeast.com/articles/2012/06/22/the-truth-about-title-ix.html. Accessed on February 5, 2017.

> Title IX has been around for more than 40 years, yet its implications still remain misunderstood and controversial. This articles aims to detail the events that led to Title IX's passing and how its implementation came to be what it is today. Notably it captures the sentiments toward women's sport at the time Title IX was passed.

Brennan, C. "Finally: It's All about the Women at the London Olympics." *USA Today.* http://usatoday30.usatoday.com/

sports/story/2012-07-25/London-Olympics-Brennan-women/
56488526/1. Accessed on February 5, 2017.

> The 2012 London Olympic Games was notable for the
> United States in that it was the first time female Olym-
> pians outnumbered male Olympians. This article high-
> lights this milestone. Perspectives from high-profile
> female Olympians throughout the article present various
> viewpoints.

Burke, Martha. "The Men behind the Olympic Curtain."
Huffington Post. http://www.huffingtonpost.com/martha-burk/
the-men-behind-the-olympi_b_4725449.html. Accessed on
February 5, 2017.

> The article provides an interesting perspective on the lack
> of female representation at the Olympics in regard to
> female athlete participation and number of women work-
> ing for Olympic ruling bodies both in the United States
> and in outside countries. The author suggests that this
> misrepresentation may be causing the rampant sexism we
> still see today in Olympic sports.

Canadian Women's Hockey League. http://www.thecwhl.com/.
Accessed on February 5, 2017.

> The Canadian Women's Hockey League was founded
> in 2007 as a place for the highest level women's hockey
> players to compete while creating a future for the sport
> of women's hockey. The league currently has four teams
> competing from October to February each year.

Clift, Elayne. "Finishing Strong—Older Women Athletes Show
the Way." Women's Media Center. http://www.womensmedia
center.com/feature/entry/finishing-strongolder-women-athletes-
show-the-way. Accessed on February 5, 2017.

> The accounts of several older women through their pur-
> suits of continued athletic activities are detailed, displaying
> their amazing ability to garner high athletic achievements

even at an older age. Older women can sometimes be more athletically successful as they get older because they are not only smarter and more disciplined, but they also have higher levels of estrogen levels, which helps protect muscles from wear and tear as compared to men.

Committee for Equity in Women's Surfing. http://www.surf equity.org/#cews. Accessed on February 5, 2017.

The Committee for Equity in Women's Surfing aims to create a separate women's division for women's surfing in the 2017–2018 Mavericks Surf content in order to create a more equitable experience for female surfers.

Couch, Greg. "Serena's Court 2 Placement Raises Racism, Sexism Suspicions." *Sporting News*. http://www.sportingnews.com/sport-news/189949-serenas-court-2-placement-raises-racism-sexism-suspicions. Accessed on February 5, 2017.

In 2011, Serena Williams was scheduled to play her first Wimbledon match on Court #2, while the likes of Roger Federer, Rafael Nadal, and even Gisela Dulko, who had few credentials, all got to play their first matches on Centre Court or Court #1. This online article raises suspicions on the racial inequalities ingrained in tennis and Wimbledon, and the challenges faced by Serena Williams for not fitting the typical white tennis ideal.

Dooley, Jessica. "Young, Wild, and Female: Gendered Experiences at an Outdoor Adventure Camps." University of Wyoming. http://repository.uwyo.edu/cgi/viewcontent.cgi?article=1056 &context=honors_theses_15-16. Accessed on February 5, 2017.

This college undergraduate honors thesis explores the unique challenges women face when trying to get involved in outdoor activities, which have been historically dominated by men. It provides an account for what women may consistently deal with in this particular environment and how they may confront/overcome these challenges.

Eichelberger, Curtis. "Concussions among Women Exceed Men as Awareness Is Found Lacking." *Bloomberg Business*. https://www .bloomberg.com/news/articles/2013-07-17/concussions-among-women-exceed-men-as-awareness-is-found-lacking. Accessed on February 5, 2017.

As concussion awareness and education continue to rise, there has been little attention paid to female concussions specifically. Females can have a higher risk of sustaining a concussion and oftentimes take longer to heal from the injury, so it is imperative to understand the implications of concussions for all genders. This article aims to explain these implications in more detail.

Feldman, Kate. "Eight Women Breaking Barriers in Men's Sports as Coaches, Referees and Broadcasters." *New York Daily News*. http://www.nydailynews.com/sports/women-breaking-barriers-men-sports-article-1.2504642. Accessed on February 5, 2017.

Eight accounts of women working in men's sports are provided. The short list features brief descriptions of these female coaches, broadcasters, and referees. Some accounts mention career path highlights.

"Female Executives Say Participation in Sport Helps Accelerate Leadership and Career Potential." *PR Newswire*. http://www .prnewswire.com/news-releases/female-executives-say-participation-in-sport-helps-accelerate-leadership-and-career-potential-278614041.html. Accessed on February 5, 2017.

Ernst and Young's Women Athletes Business Network and espnW provide insight on the positive influence sports can have on accelerating women's leadership skills and career potential. The article provides statistical data to illustrate the benefits that playing sports can have for women in their careers.

"Female Physiology and Considerations for Coaching Practice." Women's Sport and Fitness Foundation. https://www.women insport.org/wp-content/uploads/2016/04/Physiology-and-considerations-for-female-athletes.pdf?938151. Accessed on February 5, 2017.

> This useful factsheet provided by the Women's Sport and Fitness Foundation offers insight for those who coach women. The factsheet summarizes information and challenges associated with puberty when coaching females.

Florio, Mike. "Aponte Could Be on Track to Become NFL's First Female G.M." *NBC Sports.* http://profootballtalk.nbcsports .com/2013/04/14/aponte-could-be-on-track-to-become-nfls-first-female-g-m/. Accessed on February 5, 2017.

> This online article discusses Dawn Aponte's significant responsibilities with the Miami Dolphins in 2013 and her potential of becoming the first female general manager in NFL history.

"Game Changers: Women in Sports Business." *Sports Business Daily.* http://www.sportsbusinessdaily.com/Journal/Issues/2011/ 10/10/Game-Changers/Intro.aspx?hl=The..&sc=0. Accessed on February 5, 2017.

> Sports Business Daily presents profiles on notable "Game Changing" women working in the business of sports.

Girls Gone Strong. https://www.girlsgonestrong.com/. Accessed on February 5, 2017.

> Girls Gone Strong is an organization that provides resources for women's health, wellness, nutrition, training, and lifestyle information. It fights against mainstream media notions and maintains that there is no "right" body type, encouraging women to embrace all types of bodies and possibilities.

Girls in the Game. https://www.girlsinthegame.org/. Accessed on February 5, 2017.

> Girls in the Game is a nonprofit organization in Chicago that aims to empower girls to live healthy and fit lifestyles. It encourages girls to get involved in any game so that

they can learn invaluable life skills while leading a happier, healthier life.

Girls on the Move Leadership Programme—Scotland. http://www.youthscotland.org.uk/projects/girls-on-the-move/the-leadership-programme.htm. Accessed on February 5, 2017.
Girls on the Move Leadership Programme is based in Scotland and aims at providing opportunities for young girls to gain leadership skills through its offering of various courses.

Global Sports Mentoring. https://globalsportsmentoring.org/. Accessed on February 5, 2017.
Global Sports Mentoring Program is an initiative that aims to empower women through sport or sport for community. It offers one-month mentorship experiences, which emphasize empowering emerging leaders to serve their local communities by increasing opportunities for participating in sport.

Kane, Mary Jo. "Sex Sells Sex, Not Women's Sports." *The Nation.* https://www.thenation.com/article/sex-sells-sex-not-womens-sports/. Accessed on February 5, 2017.
This article describes accounts of female athletes being portrayed in sexual ways by sports media and the problematic nature behind the notion that "sex sells" women's sports.

Ladies Professional Golf. http://www.lpga.com/ Accessed on February 5, 2017.
The LPGA is an American organization for female professional golfers founded in 1950.

"MAKERS: The Largest Video Collection of Women's Stories." http://www.makers.com/blog/tag/women-sports. Accessed on February 5, 2017.

MAKERS was launched in 2012 as a platform for providing videos on the trailblazing women of today and tomorrow. It currently has over 4,500 videos featuring well-known, groundbreaking women.

Malik, Margo. "A Content Analysis of Gender-Specific Media Cover of Sport: NCAA Athletic Department Home Webpages." Digital Scholarship at UNLV. http://digitalscholarship.unlv.edu/thesesdissertations/2703/. Accessed on February 5, 2017.

Media coverage of female athletes is oftentimes inadequate in relation to the amount of coverage and type of coverage they receive. This study aims to determine if NCAA athletic departments specifically cover their female athletes in a more equitable manner by using a content analysis method of athletic department websites. It was determined institutions within the NCAA represented their female athletes equitably in relation to the type of media coverage they produced, yet female athletes were still severely underrepresented in the amount of media coverage they received.

"Meet the 30 Most Powerful Women in Sports." *Ad Week*. http://www.adweek.com/brand-marketing/meet-30-most-powerful-women-sports-172202/. Accessed on February 5, 2017.

Adweek presents its inaugural list of the 30 most powerful women in sports for 2016, with detailed profiles of each woman selected.

National Association of Collegiate Women Athletic Administrators. https://www.nacwaa.org/. Accessed on February 5, 2017.

This is a leadership organization for women involved in collegiate athletics. It aims to empower women and help them advance into positions of power and influence.

"National Center for Lesbian Rights Asks Penn State to Stop Decades of Antigay Harassment by Women's Basketball Coach

Rene Portland." http://www.nclrights.org/wp-content/uploads/2013/04/Winter-2005-Newsletter.pdf. Accessed on February 5, 2017.

The National Center for Lesbian Rights represented Jennifer Harris after her termination from the Penn State women's basketball team due to her sexual orientation and race in 2005. Penn State has been allegedly been involved in antigay acts previously, and the NCLR hoped that this case would help challenge the discriminatory culture embedded in the program by the head coach, Rene Portland.

National Girls and Women in Sports Day. http://ngwsd.org/. Accessed on February 5, 2017.

National Girls and Women in Sports Day has been celebrated for the past 31 years in hopes of empowering girls to embrace physical activity and get moving. Hundreds of thousands of people participate in various events hosted throughout the country to promote this cause.

National Women's Hockey League. http://www.nwhl.zone/. Accessed on February 5, 2017.

The National Women's Hockey league was established in 2015 and serves as the first women's hockey league in U.S. history to pay its players. The league consists of four teams, located in the Northeastern part of the United States.

National Women's Soccer League. http://nwslsoccer.com/. Accessed on February 5, 2017.

The National Women's Soccer League was founded in 2013 and is the third attempt at a women's professional soccer league in the United States. Previous leagues folded due to financial instability, yet the NWSL thrives due to the involvement of the U.S. and Canadian soccer federations funding the national team players' salaries. The league has expanded from its original eight teams to ten teams for the 2017 season.

Outsports. http://www.outsports.com/. Accessed on February 5, 2017.

Outsports is a news website dedicated to LGBT issues in sports and serves as a voice for LGBT athletes.

Pia, Caroline. "Why I'm Fighting for Girls Who Want to Play Football." *Huffington Post.* http://www.huffingtonpost.com/caro line-pla/post_8990_b_6608062.html. Accessed on February 5, 2017.

This blog post written by 13-year-old Caroline Pia accounts her experiences playing youth football. When her CYO league announced that girls would no longer be allowed to participate in football, Pia started a petition and told her story on national news networks. She still continues to advocate for girls playing football.

Play It Forward Sport. http://www.playitforwardsport.org/. Accessed on February 5, 2017.

Play It Forward Sport was created to advance gender equity in sports. It hopes to increase opportunities for women to be professional athletes, managers, and leaders in sport by educating, training, and mentoring female athletes to be sport ambassadors in their communities.

Professional Softball. http://www.profastpitch.com/home/. Accessed on February 5, 2017.

The National Pro Fastpitch league was revived in 2004 and consists of six teams across the United States.

Reclaim Childhood. http://www.reclaimchildhood.org/. Accessed on February 5, 2017.

Reclaim Childhood is a nonprofit organization based in Amman, Jordan, that strives to empower refugee and local women through sport. It runs after-school sports leagues and summer camps for girls.

Sibson, Ruth. "I Was Banging My Head against a Brick Wall: Exclusionary Power and the Gendering of Sport Organizations." Edith Cowan University. http://ro.ecu.edu.au/cgi/viewcontent.cgi?article=7342&context=ecuworks. Accessed on February 5, 2017.
    This study illustrates how exclusionary power exercised by men limits participation, input, and influence of female members.

Sinha, Smriti. "3 Reasons Mo'ne Davis' 'Sports Illustrated' Cover Is an Even Bigger Deal Than You Realize." *Sports Mic.* https://mic.com/articles/96654/3-reasons-mo-ne-davis-sports-illustrated-cover-is-an-even-bigger-deal-than-you-realize#.7LsxxCzjM. Accessed on February 5, 2017.
    This article discusses the iconic nature of *Sports Illustrated*'s decision to include a Little League World Series female player, Mo'ne Davis, on its cover. This decision was iconic considering previous *Sports Illustrated* covers featuring women almost always included a white woman accompanied by a swimsuit or man, and the number of women included on covers has been trending downward in recent times.

The S.H.E. Network. https://www.womenssportsfoundation.org/she-network/. Accessed on February 5, 2017.
    The S.H.E. network is powered by the Women's Sports Foundation and focuses on keeping women informed on sports, health, and education, in hopes of inspiring and empowering female athletes.

United Women's Lacrosse League. http://unitedwlax.com/. Accessed on February 5, 2017.
    The United Women's Lacrosse League recently began operations in 2016 with four teams, and was launched by United Women's Sports, LLC, and the Play It Forward Sport Foundation. It hopes to provide a platform that

enables women to continue playing lacrosse by offering reasonable salaries.

Women Athletes Business Network. http://www.ey.com/br/ pt/about-us/our-sponsorships-and-programs/women-athletes-global-leadership-network-perspectives-on-sport-and-teams. Accessed on February 5, 2017.

Ernst and Young conducted an online survey of 821 senior managers and executives, of which 40 percent were women. It discovered correlations between women's sport participation and their success professionally, and maintains that sport can positively contribute to female executive's leadership development.

Women's Movement: Adventure for Women. http://www .womensmovement.com/. Accessed on February 5, 2017.

The Women's Movement provides a variety of information for women relating to adventure activities, in blog format.

Women's National Basketball Association. www.wnba.com. Accessed on February 5, 2017.

The WNBA was founded in 1996 at the female counterpart to the NBA, and currently consists of 12 teams featuring the best women's basketball players in the world.

Women's Sport Leadership Academy. http://www.chi.ac.uk/ research/sport/womens-sport-leadership-academy. Accessed on February 5, 2017.

The Women's Sport Leadership Academy is a weeklong academy at the University of Chichester that is dedicated to developing tomorrow's sport leaders.

Women's Tennis Association. http://www.wtatennis.com/. Accessed on February 5, 2017.

Historic women's tennis player Billy Jean King founded the Women's Tennis Association in 1973 to act as the principal organizing body of women's tennis throughout the world.

YWCA. http://www.ywca.org. Accessed on February 5, 2017.
The YWCA has worked toward women's empowerment and civil rights for more than 150 years. It aims to eliminate racism, empower women, and promote justice for all.

ZGirls. http://zgirls.org/. Accessed on February 5, 2017.
ZGirls is an organization that aims to empower girls to overcome barriers by utilizing sport. It promotes healthy body image, goal setting, resilience, and community support in its curriculum, which includes small-group sessions led by a female mentor.

The history of women in sports and physical activity is a story of humans in action. It is the story of desire, resistance, acknowledgment of problems, grappling with continuing controversies, and arriving at new levels of sport and physical activity for girls and women.

This chapter lists some of the most important events that have occurred throughout that history.

1866 Vassar College, an all-women's college, establishes two baseball teams.

1874 Motherhood is a woman's primary function. Physical activity should be limited. "Both muscular and brain labor must be reduced at the onset of menstruation" writes Dr. Edward Clarke. Sport represents a threat to women's societal role.

1880s Lawn tennis becomes the first real sport for American women.

1885 *New York World* publishes an article on 40 things a woman should do when riding a bicycle in order to maintain her "dignity and decorum." Sports become "gendered." Bicycles are not feminine.

1890–1930s Women's baseball is framed as a "novelty" as hundreds of female baseball teams travel the country playing

Itoya Juliet of Spain competes during the women's long jump event in the 2016 Olympic Games in Rio de Janeiro, Brazil. (Celso Pupo Rodrigues/ Dreamstime.com)

baseball against men's teams. They are called "Bloomer Girls" because that is what they originally wore in order to be able to move and play more easily.

1892   Senda Berenson introduces basketball to female students at Smith College. She modifies the rules because women at the time had little experience with team play.

1896   The first women's intercollegiate basketball championship is held between Stanford University and the University of California at Berkeley.

1900   The first time women are allowed to compete in the Olympic Games. Nineteen women from Great Britain, France, Switzerland, Bohemia, and the United States competed in golf and tennis.

1910   Two all-black female basketball teams play in the first official recorded game for the Black Fives Era (1910–1914), highlighting the five all-black female basketball teams competing against each other during this time period.

1923   The Women's Division of Intercollegiate Sports decides to be more proactive about controlling and guiding women's sports toward a participation emphasis and away from a competitive emphasis.

1924   Students at the all-female women's college, Wellesley, vote 237 to 33 in favor of competitive collegiate athletics.

1926   The first National Women's Basketball Championship is sponsored by the Amateur Athletic Union.

1930–1940s   Tuskegee and Tennessee State recruit and support black female students not only for women's basketball, but also for track and field. Female black athletes have opportunities few white women have at the collegiate level.

1931–1942   Japanese American softball league is established throughout the Los Angeles area. The girls' softball league was formed prior to a boys' baseball team. The league lost momentum in 1942 when Executive Order 1066 called for the relocation of all Americans deemed "sensitive" to the war effort.

Softball continued to be played in the Santa Anita internment camp in the Los Angeles area, and upon reinstatement of Japanese Americans, softball was one of the ways Japanese Americans reconnected postwar.

1932   Helene Madison becomes the first woman to swim the 100-yard freestyle in 60 seconds at the Olympics.

1934   Lastex is called the "miracle fiber." It is a yarn that has an elastic core wound around with cotton or silk or rayon threads. Swimsuits fit better than the traditional wool, cotton, linen, and silk construction. Movement is enhanced. It sheds water well.

1938   Babe Didrikson Zaharias is the first woman to qualify for and play in a men's PGA Tour event, the Los Angeles Open.

1943   During World War II, Chicago Cubs owner, Phillip Wrigley, founds the All-American Girls Baseball League. These working-class women are offered salaries and they play games all over the Midwest.

1950   Althea Gibson is the first black tennis player (female or male) allowed to compete at the U.S. Nationals. She later became the first African American woman to join the Ladies Professional Golf Association.

1952   Seventeen-year-old female pitcher, Jackie Mitchell, strikes out Babe Ruth and Lou Gehrig in an exhibition game. Her contract is canceled.

1957 and 1958   Althea Gibson becomes the first black tennis player to win Wimbledon and the U.S. Open, respectively.

1958   Maria-Teresa de Filippis of Italy is the first woman to compete in a European Grand Prix auto race.

1960   Wilma Rudolf wins three gold medals at the Summer Olympics, becoming the first American woman to do so. Her popularity and success not only brought attention to track and field, but also raised awareness of the civil rights movement.

1965   Eleanor Metheny develops the theory that there is a direct correlation between the sports women will take up and whether the sport seems "sex appropriate" for females. This classic theory positions sport as a gendered typology.

1967   Katherine Switzer becomes the first woman to officially finish the Boston Marathon (Bobbi Gibb was the first woman to run the entire Boston Marathon without officially entering the race in 1966). Kathrine Switzer registers under the name "K. V. Switzer" in order to conceal that she was a woman. Famously, a race official shouts, "Get the hell out of my race and give me those numbers" and tries to pull her off the course. Several men, including her boyfriend, keep the official from interfering, and she finishes the race.

1968   Gender testing was first introduced at the Olympic Winter Games in Grenoble.

1970s   The Six Nations women's sports teams have a strong winning reputation, especially in softball/fastball.

1970   Lycra is a synthetic fiber that revolutionizes many areas of the clothing industry. This "skirtless, second skin" is revealed at the world championship games in Belgrade. Speed records are smashed. This development of swimwear gives way to the idea that sportswear for women should be as functional as that for men.

1971   The Association for Intercollegiate Athletics for Women pushes for change in intercollegiate athletics, and competitive sport once again begins to make significant progress within schools and colleges.

Billie Jean King is the first woman to win more than $100,000 in professional sport.

1972   Title IX is enacted as part of the as part of the Education Amendments Act.

1973   Billie Jean King defeats Bobby Riggs in straight sets (6–4, 6–3, 6–3) in the "Battle of the Sexes" tennis match at the Houston Astrodome. Over 50 million people watch the match live. It symbolically represented the equal status that women across America were trying to achieve.

1974   The Women's Sports Foundation is founded by Billie Jean King. It is a nonprofit organization that serves girls and women in sport by advocating for participation, raising awareness of inequality, educating about the benefits of sports for girls and women, and sharing resources to work toward gender equality in sport.

1976   Nadia Comăneci scores the first perfect 10 in the history of the sport at the Summer Olympic Games in Montreal, Canada.

1977   The first varsity women's soccer program begins at Brown University.

Janet Guthrie becomes the first woman to start in both the Indianapolis 500 and Daytona 500.

1979   Ann Meyers Drysdale becomes the first woman to sign an National Basketball Association (NBA) contract. She signs with the Indiana Pacers, but is cut from the team shortly thereafter. Despite being cut from the team, Bill Russell of the Boston Celtics regards her as an exceptional player. Upon being released, Meyers Drysdale becomes the first woman to broadcast an NBA game.

1981   Martina Navratilova becomes the first high-profile athlete to come out publicly willingly. She was also at the height of her tennis career at the time. She loses over $10 million in endorsements.

1984   Nawal El Moutawakel of Morocco is the first woman from an Islamic nation to win an Olympic medal for the 400-meter hurdles at the Olympics.

1987   The Association for Women in Sports Media is founded as a support network and advocacy group for women who work in sports writing, editing, broadcast and production, and public and media relations. The Mary Garber Pioneer Award is given in tribute to those who pave the way for women in sports media.

1991   The first Federation International Football Association World Cup for women's soccer takes place in China. The United States wins the championship, which starts a national interest among both players and fans.

Goldman, Heath, and Smith coin the term *commodity femi-nism* to describe the "commercial marriage of feminism and femininity" to co-opt individual freedom and power into mere powerless appearance. In their article, they point out how cor-porate support of "feminism" is really just a corporate means to sell.

1992   Manon Rheaume is the first female to play on one of the four major men's North American professional sports teams (NFL, NBA, MLB, and NHL) when she signed as a free agent with the Tampa Bay Lightning and played goalie during an exhibition game against the St. Louis Blues. She made seven saves on nine shot attempts.

1993   Lynn Hill becomes the first person (female or male) to free solo climb The Nose, a famous route on El Capitan in Yosemite National Park. Free climbing solo means rock climb-ing all by oneself with no ropes or protection if one should fall. It would be 12 years until a man would complete a free solo climb of the same route.

1994   Tegla Loroupe of Kenya is the first African woman to win a major marathon, the New York City Marathon.

The International Olympic Committee amends the Olym-pic Charter to explicitly articulate the need for global action to improve sport for girls and women.

The Brighton Declaration on Women and Sport is drafted and approved by International Working Group on Women and Sport.

1996   Four-time Hawaii Ironman triathlete, Molly Barker, founds Girls on the Run®, a nonprofit organization that pur-posefully helps young girls develop strengths, voice, and resil-iency skills through a running program. The programs begins with 13 students in Charlotte, North Carolina.

1997   The current Women's National Basketball Association (WNBA) League begins its first seasons with many players from the 1996 Women's National Olympic Team playing on different teams across the United States. The league begins with eight teams: The Charlotte Sting, Cleveland Rockers, Houston Comets, New York Liberty, Los Angeles Sparks, Phoenix Mercury, Sacramento Monarchs, and the Utah Starzz.

Lisa Leslie becomes the first woman to dunk in a professional WNBA game.

1999   Women's National Soccer Team wins the World Cup Championship hosted by the United States. Over 90,000 fans attend the game, breaking all records for attendance at a women's sports event. In addition, it is the most watched soccer game in U.S. television history with a slightly higher rating than the average NBA finals in the same year.

2002   Skintight ski racing suits are worn by both sexes in the Winter Olympics in Salt Lake.

2004   Michelle Wie posts the lowest score, 68, by a female golfer in a Professional Golf Association (PGA) Tour, the Open in Hawaii. Her total tournament score was on par at 140.

Kelli Masters becomes one of a handful of female sports agents when she establishes her own firm, Kelli Masters Management.

2006   Leigh-Ann Naidoo, an openly lesbian beach volleyball player from South Africa, is the first African ambassador to the Gay Games. Her LGBT advocacy is important for a continent that is not known for being gay friendly.

2007   McDonaugh and Pappano's *Playing with the Boys: Why Separate Is Not Equal in Sports* is published by Oxford University Press. The authors make six rational arguments about how current sex-segregated ways actually continually *construct* differences.

2008–2010   University of Connecticut women's basketball team compiles a 90-game winning streak, surpassing the prior record held by the University of Southern California Los Angeles men's basketball team's 88-game winning streak established during the 1970s with coach John Wooden.

2008   Danica Patrick wins the Indy Japan 300. She becomes the first woman to win an Indy race sanctioned by the U.S. open-wheel category. Patrick finishes the year in sixth place overall.

Jolene Van Vugt becomes an official *Guinness Book of World Records* holder as the first woman to backflip a dirt bike as well as complete the longest backflip at the Nitro Circus demo.

2009   Lesa France Kennedy is ranked No. 1 on the list of "The Most Powerful Women in Sports" by *Forbes*. Because of her roles as the chief executive officer of International Speedway Corporation, vice chairperson of NASCAR (National Association for Stock Car Auto Racing) and a member of NASCAR's board of directors, she is honored for her consistent and important contributions to the sport.

2010   Laura Gentile, a vice president at ESPN, founds EspnW, a network dedicated solely to female athletes and fans. Her vision is to create a platform in which women's sports are not "dumbed down," trivialized, or subject to "pinking" (the tendency to change branding and marketing colors to "girl" colors).

2011   Li Na becomes the first Asian-born tennis player to win a Grand Slam singles tournament. She wins the French Open while 116 million fans watch. Her success triggers the explosion of tennis in China.

Kaya Turski becomes the first female skier to complete a switch 1080 in competition. The maneuver requires taking off a jump backward, completing three full spins, and landing backward.

2012   The London Olympic Games becomes known as the women's games because of the following "firsts" for female athletes: (1) first Olympic Games in which all participating countries had at least one female athlete, (2) Habiba Ghribi is Tunisia's first female athlete to win a medal in the games, and (3) the United States fields an Olympic team with more female athletes (269) than male athletes (261) for the first time in Olympic history.

Rhonda Rousey is the first female to sign with the Ultimate Fighting Championship (UFC) and to headline a UFC event in the same year.

Debbie Jevans, previous director for the London Organizing Committee of the Olympics, is appointed the chief executive of England Rugby 2015 and becomes the first woman to organize a Rugby World Cup.

Nikki Kimball, accomplished ultrarunner, sets new women's record for a supported point-to-point run on the Long Trail in Vermont. She completed the 273 miles in 5 days 7 hours 42 minutes, which lasted from August 13 to 18.

Pat Summitt receives the Billie Jean King Legacy Award for her lifetime accomplishments and contributions to women's basketball for her 38-year tenure at Tennessee. Her record of 1,098 wins and 208 losses included 8 National Collegiate Athletic Association (NCAA) titles as well as a combined 32 Southeastern Conference tournament and regular season championships. Summitt led the Tennessee "Lady" Vols to 31 consecutive appearances in the NCAA Tournament and 14 athletes she coached were Olympians while 34 of them became WNBA players.

2013   Diana Nyad becomes the first person to swim from Cuba to Florida without a shark cage. At the age of 63, Nyad completes this historic swim on her fifth attempt, swimming 110 miles from Havana to Key West.

Serena Williams is named "Female Athlete of the Year" by the *Associated Press* for her unsurpassed tennis success. By this year, Williams had won 13 single Grand Slams, 8 doubles Grand Slams, and 3 Olympic gold medals.

Gay WNBA star, Brittney Griner, lands Nike endorsement deal. "It's big-time, let's just say that," Griner says of the deal.

2014   Kelly Clark wins the SuperPipe at X Games, which brings her total X Games medal tally up to 12 (7 of which are gold) and marks her as the most decorated female athlete in

X Games history. She earns recognition as one of the top 50 female athletes in action sports.

Mo'ne Davis is the first female pitcher (girls or boys) to pitch a shutout in Little League History. Her precision is more significant than her strength.

Becky Hammon becomes the first full-time female assistant coach in the NBA, making her the first female to hold such a position in the four major men's professional sports (NFL, NBA, MLB, and MLS) in the United States.

Victoria, "Vicky," Chun becomes the only Asian American female athletic director of a NCAA Division I school. Chun's commitment to student-athlete well-being, successful hiring of coaches who align with that vision as well as create winning teams, and fund-raising skills that help improve facilities stand out among all athletic directors. Street & Smith's *Sports Business Journal* recognizes Chun as a "Game Changer" in 2014 due to her hard work, accomplishments, and ability to inspire change.

2015 Women's World Cup soccer final is the most-watched soccer game in the history of television in the United States. More viewers in the United States watch this women's World Cup final on Fox than men's World Cup final on ESPN the prior year.

Katie Nolan, a 28-year-old sports journalist, hosts a Fox Sports 1 weekly show. Called *Garbage Time*, it is considered the future of Sports TV.

2016 Alexis Sablone is named one of the X Games's top 50 female athletes in action sports. Sablone's dual passion for architecture and skateboarding has led to two X Game medals in Women's Skateboard Street and earned her admission to the Massachusetts Institute of Technology (MIT) graduate program in architecture. She says, "Skateboarding has definitely helped me see my environment in unique and creative ways. . . . I am more attuned to different angles, textures and surfaces thanks to skateboarding."

Ibtihaj Muhammad, a sabre fencer, becomes the first Muslim American female athlete to earn a medal at the Olympics, winning a bronze medal.

The International Olympic Committee changes its transgender policy. All trans-athletes from female to male gender are free to compete. Trans-athletes aiming to compete in female events are not required to undergo reassignment surgery. However, they must demonstrate a total testosterone level below 10 nmol/L for at least 12 months prior to their first competition.

Jax Mariash Koudele is the first woman and one of only four individuals to complete the ultrarunning (mostly) desert series known as the Grand Slam Plus within the same calendar year. Five races comprise the series and feature unique weather challenges. The races are the Roving Race in Sri Lanka, followed by four races in the world's most famous deserts, the hottest (Namibia), windiest (Gobi March), driest (Atacama Crossing), and coldest (Antarctica). Each race consists of seven days out in the desert, and support staff move the camps each day for the runners. The first four days consist of 22–28 miles, then a 50-mile day, followed by a 6.2-mile day. The total distance covered in seven days is 155 miles (250 kilometers).

U.S. Women's National Soccer Team files an official complaint with the Equal Employment Opportunity Commission (EEOC). They point out that being paid on average four times less than their male counterparts in the 2015 World Cup violates EEOC legislation.

2017   The U.S. women's national hockey team successfully negotiates fair compensation, better marketing, and support for women's hockey, as well as development for youth teams with USA Hockey. Meghan Duggan, the team's captain, publicly announces that the deal is a major step forward for women's sports.

Glossary

Gender is one of society's most pervasive social constructions that give rise to prevailing ideas about male and female, men and women. The terms in this chapter provide the most common expressions and concepts used in gender equality efforts and understandings. While these terms are not restricted to sport, they are terms and concepts used by sport scholars who study cultural aspects of sport as well as those individuals doing specific advocacy and workshops within sport. The terms give readers a solid working vocabulary for making sense of and engaging in the many issues surrounding women's participation and leadership in sport.

ally   A cisgender, heterosexual individual who advocates for social change and social justice in order to make sport safe for all genders, sexual orientations, and the LGBT community.

benevolent sexism   Attitudes about women and men based on stereotypes in which compliments or strengths mentioned or highlighted are based on those stereotypes.

bias blind spot   The condition when a person recognizes and understands how bias among others affects individuals and groups but does not see how it impacts her or his own judgment.

bicycle face   A medical condition identified in the 1800s by physicians who believed that the strain of riding a bicycle would cause health issues and permanent physical damage to women.

bloomers   Baggy trousers or pants that were associated with the women's rights movement of the 1850s as well as worn by women participating in sport. Although practical, bloomers were controversial because of the deeply held belief that men should be the ones to "wear trousers."

cisgender   An individual whose gender identity aligns with the sex designated at birth.

commodity feminism   When feminist ideas and feminism are used by companies or organizations for commercial gain rather than to promote real social change.

double bind   The experience for women in leadership in which they feel that if they are too nice, they will be seen as incompetent. If they are too assertive, they will be viewed as too cold.

ethnicity   A person's cultural identity, typically based on a sense of shared history, values, and accepted behaviors.

extreme sports   Physical activities and sports involving high risk due to height, speed, technical difficulty, or objective environmental risk.

female athlete triad   Medical condition of female athletes in which three conditions are present: eating disorders (starving, binging, or purging), amenorrhea (irregular appearance or disappearance of a woman's menstrual cycle), and osteoporosis (loss of bone mass that weakens bones).

feminism   Advocacy for women's equality in terms of treatment and rights.

feminist   The perspective that gender is a powerful organizing principle in society, and any person who examines society through this lens to create social change.

flappers   Women during the 1920s from the Western world, who behaved in ways counter to traditional views of how women should act. Flappers were viewed as flamboyant because of frequent drinking, smoking, wearing short skirts, and displaying a casual attitude toward sex.

gender expression   How a person expresses gender through clothing, style, behavior, and verbal expressions.

gender identity   A person's internal deep sense of identification as female, male, or a nonbinary understanding of gender determined by an individual.

gender nonconforming   Displaying a gender identity or expression that differs from that typically associated with one's birth sex and differs from expectations about how females and males are "supposed to" look or act. Such behavior occurs along a continuum, and does not indicate an individual is transgender.

gender   A social construction around the signifiers "male" and "female."

hegemonic masculinity   The collective beliefs and practices associated with the socially dominant version of masculinity that subordinates women and other masculinities.

heteronormativity   The assumption that heterosexuality is the default, correct form of sexuality reinforced through practices that reinforce the partnership of a male and a female.

homohysteria   The fear that any behavior deemed atypical for one's identified gender will make others believe that one is homosexual.

homologous reproduction   The practice of hiring or bringing individuals that are similar to oneself into a group.

homophobia   Dislike for homosexuals that manifest in multiple negative beliefs about homosexuals such as contempt and prejudice that lead to discrimination.

inclusivity   Intentional behaviors and attitudes to include individuals in historically marginalized groups, especially along the lines of race, ethnicity, gender, and sexual orientation.

intersectionality The multiple ways in which individuals experience social categorizations such as race, class, gender, and sexuality that are layered and provide unique ways in which individuals are marginalized.

LGBTQ An acronym that stands for "lesbian, gay, bisexual, transgender, and queer/questioning," the latter including individuals who are uncertain or fluid with their sexuality and/or gender identification and expressions.

lifestyle sports Sports such as surfing, skateboarding, skiing, and snowboarding that are characterized by three features: (1) alternative in that they are practiced in different ways than mainstream sport, (2) individuals participate with multiple meanings well beyond but not exclusive of competition, and (3) often associated with "extreme" in that there is considerable risk or perceived risk. Notably, participants refer to their sport participation as a "way of life," thus blurring the lines between sport and lifestyle.

male gaze A term coined by feminist film critic, Laura Mulvey, in 1975 in order to describe the ways media depicts women from the male point of view as objects of desire.

marginalization The treatment of a group or individual as insignificant, unnoticed, and/or unimportant.

pedestrienne A woman who competed in the ultra endurance competitive walking events during the late 19th century.

polygender Gender identity in which a person experiences multiple gender identities fluidly.

privilege Special advantage ascribed to a group of people who belong to a group that symbolizes attributes desired and valued by society. For example, male and masculinity are privileged in most societies and especially in sport.

role congruity When an individual or group fulfill roles that are in accordance with the traits associated with that group. For instance, role congruity occurs when a male is a head coach.

sex Biological and physical features that designate a person as male, female, intersex, or other designations.

sexual orientation/sexuality   An individual's emotional and sexual attractions, consisting of the categories (Western world) heterosexual, lesbian or gay, or bisexual.

social construction   A theory suggesting that understandings of the world are jointly constructed as truths about the world, forming the foundation for shared assumptions.

stereotype   An assumption or generalization held by a wide group of individuals about other individuals or group based on gender, sexual orientation, race, social class, and/or other identity markers.

third-wave feminism   A movement at the beginning of the 1990s that celebrates multiple ways of being female and feminine. In sport, female athletes who choose to pose in sexualized ways in sport media in order for personal financial gain are third-wave feminists.

transgender   A person whose gender identity differs from the gender assigned at birth, and who desires to live permanently as a gender different from birth-assigned gender.

About the Author

Maylon Hanold is director of the Master in Sport Administration and Leadership program at Seattle University. She has taught courses in research methods for sport, sport sociology, sport leadership, and organizational effectiveness. She holds a BA in French from the University of Washington, an EdM in learning and teaching from Harvard University, and an EdD in leadership with a cognate in sport from Seattle University. Her research interests lie at the intersections of sport sociology, gender, and leadership. She has written about ultrarunning subcultures and lived experiences. She also coauthored a book chapter on transgender athletes and running in *Transgender Athletes in Competitive Sport* (2017). In addition, her leadership research focuses on the physicality of leadership as related to embodied biases, empathy as a leadership skill, and leadership development. She has published in several journals on these topics, including *Advancing Women in Leadership, Global Sport Business Journal*, and *Advances in Developing Human Resources*. She has also written book chapters in *Sport Leadership for the 21st Century, The Embodiment of Leadership*, and *Theorizing Women and Leadership: New Insights and Contributions from Multiple Perspectives*. She has published *World Sports: A Reference Handbook* (2012) with ABC-CLIO. She has been an invited speaker on many topics including Generation iY; inclusive leadership; intersections between gender, media, sport, and leadership; sports psychology; and embodiment and leadership. She was a member of the 1992 Olympic team in whitewater kayak slalom. These days, she enjoys trail running with her dog, mountain biking, snowboarding, and sea kayaking.